LINGUISTIC SURVEYS OF AFRICA

Volume 7

LINGUISTIC SURVEY OF THE NORTHERN BANTU BORDERLAND

LINGUISTIC SURVEY OF THE NORTHERN BANTU BORDERLAND
Volume One

MALCOLM GUTHRIE AND A. N. TUCKER

LONDON AND NEW YORK

First published in 1956 by Oxford University Press

This edition first published in 2018
by Routledge
2 Park Square, Milton Park, Abingdon, Oxon OX14 4RN

and by Routledge
711 Third Avenue, New York, NY 10017

Routledge is an imprint of the Taylor & Francis Group, an informa business

© 1956 International African Institute

All rights reserved. No part of this book may be reprinted or reproduced or utilised in any form or by any electronic, mechanical, or other means, now known or hereafter invented, including photocopying and recording, or in any information storage or retrieval system, without permission in writing from the publishers.

Trademark notice: Product or corporate names may be trademarks or registered trademarks, and are used only for identification and explanation without intent to infringe.

British Library Cataloguing in Publication Data
A catalogue record for this book is available from the British Library

ISBN: 978-1-138-08975-4 (Set)
ISBN: 978-1-315-10381-5 (Set) (ebk)
ISBN: 978-1-138-09359-1 (Volume 7) (hbk)
ISBN: 978-1-138-09429-1 (Volume 7) (pbk)
ISBN: 978-1-315-10617-5 (Volume 7) (ebk)

Publisher's Note
The publisher has gone to great lengths to ensure the quality of this reprint but points out that some imperfections in the original copies may be apparent.

Disclaimer
The publisher has made every effort to trace copyright holders and would welcome correspondence from those they have been unable to trace.

Due to modern production methods, it has not been possible to reproduce the fold-out maps within the book. Please visit www.routledge.com to view them.

LINGUISTIC SURVEY
OF THE
NORTHERN BANTU
BORDERLAND

VOLUME ONE

Published for the
INTERNATIONAL AFRICAN INSTITUTE
by the
OXFORD UNIVERSITY PRESS
LONDON NEW YORK TORONTO
1956

Oxford University Press, Amen House, London E.C.4
GLASGOW NEW YORK TORONTO MELBOURNE WELLINGTON
BOMBAY CALCUTTA MADRAS KARACHI CAPE TOWN IBADAN
Geoffrey Cumberlege, Publisher to the University

*This volume has been published
with the aid of a grant from
the British Colonial Development
and Welfare Funds*

PRINTED IN GREAT BRITAIN
AT THE UNIVERSITY PRESS, OXFORD
BY CHARLES BATEY, PRINTER TO THE UNIVERSITY

FOREWORD

THE proposal that the International African Institute should organize a field survey of the border area, extending over most of the breadth of Africa, where Bantu and non-Bantu languages come in contact, was first discussed by the Linguistic Advisory Committee of the Institute in 1946. The linguistic situation in this area was known to be very complex, and existing information on most of the languages was inadequate. Reliable data, on which a classification of these languages could be based, were meagre where not entirely lacking. It became clear that systematic and reliable information on these languages would be of value, not only to linguistic specialists and students but to those concerned with administration, education, and the publication of vernacular textbooks and literature.

A plan for carrying out a linguistic investigation of the area was prepared, in which it was recommended that a team of four linguistic research workers should, after a period of study together in London, spend 12–15 months in the field, surveying the area from the Atlantic Coast to the Great Lakes. It was proposed that the team should include Belgian and French as well as British investigators, two members to be specialists in Bantu and two in non-Bantu languages.

The scheme, as approved by the Officers of the Institute, was circulated to a number of British, French, and Belgian experts and finally submitted to the British, French, and Belgian Ministries of Colonies in 1948.

After much consultation and discussion, support for the scheme was approved by the three governments concerned. The British, French, and Belgian governments each offered financial contributions; the Government of the Anglo-Egyptian Sudan and the Government of Nigeria offered transport and other facilities; the School of Oriental and African Studies, University of London, offered the services of Professor Malcolm Guthrie and Professor A. N. Tucker for the initial training of the team and to supervise work in the field. The International African Institute undertook the organization of the project and the publication of the findings of the Survey.

The field investigation occupied in all eighteen months, from June 1949 to December 1950. The wealth of material obtained, and the fact that all the members of the team had to take up other work shortly after their return from the field, caused some unavoidable delay in the publication of their results. Reports prepared by them were finally presented to the Institute in 1952, but various problems of arrangement, translation, and means of publication which then arose caused further delay. Following discussions by the Linguistic Advisory Committee and the Executive Council of the Institute, it was agreed that the material prepared by the research teams should be presented in four volumes as follows:

I. A summary report of the field study carried out by the research team, with demographic and geographical data, classification, and maps.
II. Linguistic analyses of languages of the Western Area.
III. Linguistic analyses of the Central (Belgian Congo) Area.
IV. Linguistic analyses of the languages of the Far Eastern Section.

FOREWORD

The present volume (Volume I of the whole) contains an account of the Survey as carried out by the two research teams, together with additional material supplied by Professor Tucker and Miss M. A. Bryan which extends the area of investigation from the Great Lakes to the Indian Ocean. Publication of the other volumes will be proceeded with as rapidly as possible.

The International African Institute desires to express its sincere thanks to the governments of Great Britain, France, and Belgium, of the Anglo-Egyptian Sudan, Nigeria, and Cameroun Français, to the Institut Français d'Afrique Noire, the Institut pour la Recherche Scientifique en Afrique Centrale, the Commission de Linguistique of the Belgian Ministry of Colonies, the School of Oriental and African Studies, the British Colonial Social Science Research Council, for the generous provision of financial assistance, transport, and other facilities; to numerous missionary bodies for assistance and hospitality in the field, and to those individuals who, by their cordial interest in the scheme and their untiring exertions on its behalf, have made it possible for this international research project to be brought to a successful conclusion. Particular mention should be made of the Rev. Dr. E. W. Smith and the late Professor Ida Ward, who first proposed the scheme; the late Professor E. de Jonghe, through whose good offices the co-operation of the Belgian government was secured, and M. Albert Charton, for his approaches to the French government.

DARYLL FORDE
Director, International African Institute

INTRODUCTORY NOTE

THE northern limit of the Bantu languages is one of the important linguistic boundaries of Africa, and it has long been felt that an investigation directed towards delimiting the frontier would be most valuable. The International African Institute was able in 1948 to secure the co-operation of the British, French, and Belgian governments in putting into operation the plans for such an investigation which had been discussed with its Linguistic Advisory Committee. Briefly the scheme involved field research by a team of four investigators, two to work between the Atlantic coast and the River Oubangui and the others between the River Oubangui and the Great Lakes. The personnel of the teams was made up of two British workers, Mr. P. H. Hackett and Mr. I. Richardson, with the Rev. Professor G. Van Bulck from Belgium and M. André Jacquot from France. The training of the teams and the supervision of the whole project were jointly undertaken by Professor Malcolm Guthrie and Professor A. N. Tucker, of the School of Oriental and African Studies, University of London, the former being directly concerned with the western half and the latter with the eastern half of the scheme.

After a preliminary course of training in London at the School of Oriental and African Studies, the teams set out in the summer of 1949, M. Jacquot and Mr. Richardson going to Douala for work in the western area and Professor Van Bulck and Mr. Hackett to Juba for the eastern area. Arrangements were made for a limited amount of direct supervision in the field, and Professor Guthrie was able to visit the French Cameroons to meet and consult with the workers in his area, while Professor Tucker spent two periods in the field when he accompanied the two members of the team investigating the eastern section. Apart from these direct contacts with their supervisors, the two halves of the team had to work independently, and indeed the difference in the two areas, from the point of view both of the general situation and of the linguistic problems encountered, made inevitable a considerable difference in emphasis in the investigations.

During the period of field study the members of each team worked closely together, correlating their results at each stage. At the conclusion of the field-work, M. Jacquot had to return to France while Mr. Hackett, after a short interval, went to Africa to carry out a separate investigation.

A report containing a summary of the most important demographic and linguistic results of the investigation was prepared at the end of the period of field research. The outline for the first section was planned jointly by M. Jacquot and Mr. Richardson, but the onus of the final preparation fell entirely on Mr. Richardson. Similarly the task of preparing the section dealing with the work of the eastern team fell to Professor Van Bulck, who wrote in French. Since it was proposed that the whole report should be published in the first instance in English, Mr. Richardson was asked to undertake the translation of the manuscript of the second section, which was then finally prepared for publication by Professor Van Bulck.

In order to give as complete a picture as possible of the northern frontier of the Bantu languages, a third section dealing with the area from the Great Lakes to the

INTRODUCTORY NOTE

Indian Ocean was included, although not strictly a part of the report of the main project. This section was prepared by Professor Tucker and Miss M. A. Bryan from various documentary sources, including manuscript notes of their own field researches into the languages of this area.

The maps, which constitute a most valuable adjunct to the report, were prepared by Professor Van Bulck, Mr. Richardson, Professor Tucker, and Miss Bryan.

Since a number of the languages investigated in the course of this research had not hitherto been recorded, while with regard to many others the published information was extremely inadequate and confused, this project may justly be described as a pioneer study, and it is hoped that the Report of the Survey will provide a basis for further much needed research.

When the Report was ready for press, however, it was found that the cost of publishing a single volume containing such a large amount of linguistic material would exceed the funds immediately available. Consequently the Institute's Executive Council decided to publish, in the first instance, an abridged version of the Report, leaving the detailed linguistic evidence to be published later. The present volume therefore consists of demographic information together with the three maps and general indications of the affinities of the languages tabulated. A large part of the valuable material collected during the survey remains to be published, but in the mean time it has proved to be of great value for the *Handbook of African Languages* which is in course of publication by the Institute.

MALCOLM GUTHRIE
A. N. TUCKER

November 1954

CONTENTS

FOREWORD BY THE DIRECTOR, INTERNATIONAL AFRICAN
    INSTITUTE   3

INTRODUCTORY NOTE BY THE SUPERVISORS   5

PART I. REPORT OF THE WESTERN TEAM   9
    ATLANTIC COAST TO OUBANGUI
    A. JACQUOT *and* I. RICHARDSON

PART II. REPORT OF THE EASTERN TEAM   63
    OUBANGUI TO GREAT LAKES
    R.P. G. VAN BULCK S.J. *and* PETER HACKETT

PART III. FAR EASTERN SECTION   123
    GREAT LAKES TO INDIAN OCEAN
    A. N. TUCKER *and* M. A. BRYAN

MAPS   *At end*

Part I
REPORT OF THE WESTERN TEAM
ATLANTIC COAST TO OUBANGUI

CONTENTS

Introduction   11
Abbreviations   18

SECTION A: BANTU LANGUAGES

1. The Lundu Group.   19
   Lundu (1.1), Ŋgoro (1.7), Bakundu (1.6), Bataŋga (1.4), Bima (1.5a, b), Mbɔŋgɛ (1.3), Ekumbɛ (1.2), Barue (1.8).
2. The Duala Group.   21
   Mokpe (1.10), Ḅomboko (1.11), Su (1.12), Oli (1.13), Poŋgo (1.14), Muŋgo (1.15), Bodiman (1.16).
3. The Mbo Cluster.   22
   General Remarks, Mwahɛt (1.20g), Akɔɔsə (Muamenam) (1.20h), Mbo (Bareko) (1.20d), Baneka (1.20e), Baləndə (1.18), Babɔŋg (1.19);
   Bafɔ (1.17), Akɔɔsə (1.20i), Nswəsə (1.20j), Elöŋ (1.20k), Nnenŭ (1.20l), Kaa (1.20f), Mbo (1.20a, b, c).
4. The North Mbɛnɛ Group (Basa).   26
   Baluŋ (1.21a), Bəŋkɛŋ (1.21b), Bakoko (1.21c), Baŋkon (Abo) (1.21d), Ləmbi (1.21e), Yabasi (1.21g), Mbaŋg (1.21m), Dibum (1.21n).
5. The Banɛn Group.   28
   Bənɛk (1.22b), Nyɔ̆'ɔ̆ (1.22d).
6. The Bafia Group.   29
   General Remarks, Fa' (Balom) (1.23), Kpa (Bafia) (1.24), Ŋgayaba (Djanti) (1.26), Ŋgərə (1.27a), Ciŋga (1.28).
7. Some Languages of the Ewondo–Bulu Group.   31
   General Remarks, Yɛzum (Mvĕlĕ́) (1.31), Avək (1.32), Yaŋgafuk (1.33), Gbĭgbĭl (1.34), Eki (1.36).
8. Mäkaa and East Cameroons Group.   33
   Mäkaa (1.38), Baayəto (1.40b), Mɛdjime (1.40a), Mpiɛmə (1.41).
9. Kakə (1.45) and Pol (1.46).   35
10. The Pande–Mbomotaba Group.   36
    Ŋgondi (1.49b), Pande (1.49a).
11. The Ŋgando–Kota Group.   37
    Ŋgando (1.50a), Kota (1.50b), Mbati (Issongo) (1.51).

SECTION B: BANTOID LANGUAGES

1. Bandem (2.1), Nyaŋg (2.2), Kitw̃ii (2.3), Kiŋkwa (2.8), Tiḳar (2.9); Keaqə: Edjagam (2.10), Ekɔi (2.11), Ɔbaŋg (2.12); Kərəp (2.13).   39
2. The Ɖkom Group.   42
   Ɖkəm (2.14), Iyirikum (2.15), Ŋgamambo (Məgamo) (2.16), Oso (Fuŋgəm) (2.22), Lamsə' (2.23), Okii (2.24); General linguistic information on N.A. areas in Bamenda Division:—Biba-Befang, Esimbi, Fungom, Bum, Misaje, Nsungli, Nfumte, Mbem, Mbaw, Ndop, Bafut.
3. The Bamileke Group (2.27).   43
   General remarks; Dschang–Bangwa (2.27a), Babadjou (2.27b), Bagam (2.27c), Bamougoum–Bamendjou (2.27d), Bafoussam (2.27e), Bandjoun–Baham (2.27f), Babouantou (2.27g), Bafang (2.27h), Bangou–Batchingou–Bamana (2.27i), Bangoua–Batoufam (2.27j), Bangangté (2.27k), Batongtou (2.27l), (2.27m), Bamum (2.28), Ŋgaaka (Bali of Bali Town) (2.26).

SECTION C: NON-BANTU LANGUAGES

1. Miscellaneous Languages: Silqadɛt (3.1), Ndagam (3.2), Nŏale (3.3), Wute (3.4), Kɛpɛrɛ (3.5).   54
2. The Gɓaya–Ɖgɓaka–Mandjia Group (3.6).   56
   General remarks on Gɓaya; Gɓofi (3.6n), Yaŋgɛlɛ (3.6j), Ali (3.6p).
3. The Banda Group.   58
   Yaŋgere (3.7).
4. The Ŋgɓaka–Maɓo Group.   59
   Ŋgɓaka Maɓo (3.8), Məndjombo (3.9).

   Key to Linguistic Map of the Western section and Index.   61

INTRODUCTION

Aim. The aim of this survey was to provide as complete a picture as possible of the northern Bantu linguistic border by collecting sufficient first-hand information to enable us to classify the languages of the area into Bantu, Non-Bantu, &c., the field of operations having been roughly delimited by the zone of discrepancy between previous writers on this subject, notably Johnston, Doke, Guthrie, and Van Bulck.

Scope. Our terms of reference demanded that we ascertain the location of the northern Bantu linguistic border between the Atlantic Coast and the Oubangui. Subsequent events, however, modified the extent of the area to be investigated. Enormous distances, shortage of time, difficulty of access, and non-availability of suitable informants all played an important role in limiting the scope of our inquiry to that part of Africa bounded by 8° to 19° E. and 2° to 7° N. Even within this area the obtaining of first-hand information had to be confined to speeches closely adjoining the linguistic borderline. Less accessible localities had to be dealt with by means of second-hand information, generally gathered in the field, however, and cross-checked as far as practicable. Johnston has said that the languages of south-east Nigeria all have something Bantu in their vocabularies and prefixes, and that this influence extends even to the Gambia. It was, of course, impossible to undertake the examination of this vast area, and no work was done on Nigerian languages except in so far as they extend into British Cameroons. Similarly Fernando Po, Rio Muni, Gabon, Moyen Congo, and Congo Belge had to be excluded from investigations conducted *in situ*. A further limit was imposed on our activities by the exclusion of pygmy speeches from the field to be examined. This step was taken to prevent digression from the main purpose. Pygmy speech is a subject in itself which cannot be treated hurriedly in view of such special problems as ensuring that the mother tongue and not the language of the hosts is recorded.

Itinerary and time-table. Circumstances beyond our control reduced the original fifteen months research period to one of thirteen months from which must again be deducted at least two months for time lost through mechanical trouble, difficulties of travel, and other unpredictable delays. During August and September 1949 we undertook the opening stage of our researches, taking in part of western Cameroun, i.e. the vicinity of Douala, Nkongsamba, Bafang, Bangangté, Ndikiniméki, Bafia, and Nanga Eboko. This was succeeded by work in British Cameroons at Buea, Kumba, Mamfe, and Bamenda (October, November, and December 1949). The first six weeks of 1950 were taken up by investigations in the Bamileke and Bamum regions, followed by a period of immobilization through mechanical defects at Nkongsamba, which was utilized as far as possible for filling in gaps in our information on western Cameroun. From mid-April to mid-May after a visit to Yoko we dealt with the parts of eastern Cameroun through which the Bantu borderline passes, using Bertoua and Batouri as centres of operation. Between mid-May and early July the languages of southern Oubangui Chari were examined at Berbérati, Banga, Bania, Carnot, and Mbaïki. The time remaining before our departure from Douala in mid-August 1950 was spent in travel, consolidation of material, and the winding up of the affairs of the survey in Africa.

Difficulties. To leave unmentioned the many difficulties both practical and linguistic which assailed us would be to present an entirely false account of the western section of the survey. Professional problems are dealt with in the main body of the report, so that perhaps it will be sufficient here to point out that where languages were the most problematic *per se* they were also the most localized and numerous, thus having to be dealt with most summarily. In Bamenda Province it is felt that these factors have rendered our investigation somewhat unsatisfactory. The necessity of making up the lost months and of keeping to a time-table caused investigations in some areas to be conducted at a speed which was incompatible with the procuring of accurate material.

Frequent mechanical and transport troubles were responsible for prolonged delays and prevented us from obtaining informants for some areas when we had adequate time to deal with them. The vacations of schools and teachers' training centres also on occasion prevented our working with informants who had a reasonable command of English or French. Road and postal communications often left much to be desired in view of our constant displacements. For months at a time we were out of touch with our supervisor owing to mail being wrongly redirected. As our stay in Africa included two rainy seasons (the second of which being a record one) we experienced most of the vicissitudes which fall to the lot of the traveller in modern Africa—impassable roads, broken bridges, flooded causeways, and sunken ferries. It was a combination of these circumstances which caused us to return to Douala sooner than was anticipated rather than be isolated in the interior.

Method of operation. Throughout the Survey the western team worked as one unit, only rarely splitting up, as for example when pressure of time demanded that we examine two different languages simultaneously, or when one of us was prevented by *force majeure* from attending an investigation. On our return to the United Kingdom we shared the task of comparing and collating material until, in early April, 1951, M. Jacquot had to return to France. The final preparation of this section was therefore undertaken by Mr. Richardson who would like to take this opportunity of putting on record the sterling services of his friend and colleague, not only as a research worker but also in the highly important office of driver and mechanic to the expedition. It is largely due to M. Jacquot that, despite the frequently demonstrated mechanical inadequacy of our vehicle, and the terrible conditions of some roads, our section of the survey was ever completed.

We sought informants whose mother tongue was the language to be investigated, and whose knowledge of English or French was sufficient to eliminate misunderstanding of our requirements. Rarely did we have to resort to the employment of interpreters. Viva voce linguistic items elicited from our informants were recorded by both of us in International Phonetic Association script. Professor Guthrie devised a short questionnaire for Bantu languages (used also for Sub-Bantu and Bantoid) which comprised a vocabulary of about 120 words (nominals in singular and plural form, verbals, and numerals) and short sentences designed to give the maximum information on main points of grammar in the minimum time. Other languages were dealt with by means of an abridged form of the Non-Bantu questionnaire drawn up by Professor Tucker.

Demographic material was obtained from various publications, and also from statements official and otherwise made by Europeans and Africans. Numerous maps were copied from those so kindly lent by administrators and missionaries. Perhaps it would not be inopportune to comment at this point on the nature of our linguistic map. It is a consolidation and integration of all relevant ethnic and linguistic maps discovered by us to date. Ethnic boundaries were checked as far as practicable with natives of the area to ascertain whether in fact they coincided with linguistic differences, and whether they enclosed more than one form of speech. In the absence of tribal maps, a large-scale map was taken and a boundary drawn round villages said by our informants to speak the same language. The gravest defect of this method is that regions thus demarcated may contain vast expanses of sparsely inhabited or even deserted country. As detailed statistics for such districts are unavailable, it is hard to know what is the best method of indicating graphically the fluctuating density of population.

Criteria. It cannot be too strongly emphasized that in our report the classification of languages into Bantu, Bantoid, and Non-Bantu is based entirely on linguistic principles. No other factors have been allowed to prejudice linguistic evidence—not even the size and shape of the informant's head. If the mother tongue of the inhabitants of an area is Bantu by linguistic considerations, then it is classified as Bantu regardless of the ancestry of its speakers.

The criteria used to determine whether or not a language is *Bantu* are the principal ones formulated by Professor Guthrie.[1]

1. A system of grammatical genders, usually at least five with these features:
   (a) The sign of gender is a prefix, by means of which words may be assorted into a number of classes varying roughly from ten to twenty.
   (b) There is a regular association of pairs of classes to indicate the singular and plural of the genders. In addition to these two-class genders, there are also one-class genders where the prefix is sometimes similar to one of the singular prefixes occurring in a two-class gender, and sometimes similar to one of the plural prefixes.
   (c) When a word has an independent prefix as the sign of its class, any other word which is subordinate to it has to agree with it as to class by means of a dependent prefix.
   (d) There is no correlation of the genders with sex reference or with any other clearly defined idea.

2. A vocabulary, part of which can be related by fixed rules to a set of hypothetical common roots.

The widespread term 'Semi-Bantu' has been discarded. It is vague and unscientific, since a language may be incompletely Bantu in more ways than one. We have followed Professor Guthrie's example in calling *Sub-Bantu* those languages to which criterion No. 2 may be successfully applied but whose class and agreement systems are merely fragmentary. Like him we have included them in the section dealing with Bantu.

[1] *The Classification of the Bantu Languages*, O.U.P., 1948, p. 11. To the first criterion should be added the proviso that these classes and genders should be regularly associable with those found in other Bantu languages.

The term *Bantoid* is applied to languages in which the second criterion does not hold good, and which have an elaborate system of class prefixes and agreements showing no regular relationship to the Bantu classes. Such languages often have a complicated vowel system.

Non-Bantu. Though perhaps the only operable term in our area, this is an unsatisfactory label. It is a negative description uniting languages whose only similarity may well be their dissimilarity to Bantu, Sub-Bantu, and Bantoid.

The words 'language', 'dialect', and 'speech' are often employed as though synonymous. There can be no justification for dividing 'speech' into 'languages', and 'languages' into 'dialects', where one is incapable of defining these terms in relation to each other. How different in fact does a 'dialect' have to be from another 'dialect' before it can claim to be a different language? The terms *dialect* and *dialectal variant*, have sometimes been used to describe speech forms which are different from though particularly closely related to each other, since this is the generally accepted non-professional meaning of these words.

The presentation and interpretation of the material. Throughout the text, the name by which a language is known occurs in roman capitals. This is almost invariably the name as given by the informant for his own language. If necessary a phonetic transcription follows this name when it is used as a heading, also any other names applied to the language. The language areas demarcated on the map have been numbered generally from west to east *within each classificatory group*. Each group has a code sign which precedes the language number, e.g. Bantu 1, Bantoid 2, Non-Bantu 3, Unclassified 4. The first languages in these groups are respectively LUNDU, BANDƐM, SILQADƐT, and the language of Bebe Jatto, which would therefore have the following references: 1.1, 2.1, 3.1, 4.1. These numbers are listed separately (p. 62) and also occur in brackets after the language heading (or the first mention of the language if it does not appear as a heading). Some languages beyond the scope of the survey are shown on the map (in roman capitals) to give some idea of the linguistic context of the area. Regions left blank denote territory which had to be left untouched, except in the case of BAMILEKE (27). In mapping this complicated area various intercomprehension zones were marked off and numbered. The remainder of the district which was left blank includes uninhabited mountain tops, isolated villages, and main motor roads. When any language at all is spoken in this area it will, therefore, most probably be Pidgin English, the universal medium of intercourse in this highly localized region. To the few enclaves marked as 'Mixed' should, of course, be added all the main localities indicated on the map.

It is with some misgivings that reference is made to a peculiar procedure followed in the marking of *Bantu* (21) and (22*a*), and *Non-Bantu* (6). Some of the information shown here comes from non-linguistic data; linguistic and ethnic (i.e. sub-tribal or clan) differences may or may not coincide in these cases. Our only reason for including it is to indicate that certain ethnic names (and presumably groups) occur in linguistic areas the main content of which is known, and where we have reason to suspect that subsidiary language differences exist. The converse of this should be noted, e.g. in the case of MVĖLĖ, where many small ethnic groups speak the same language.

The use made of existing material. Although published material has been used to a certain extent in checking, identifying, and occasionally amplifying our own records, it is realized how strikingly ineffective such comparisons may prove to be from time to time. While we for our part have some idea of the relative reliability of *our* material, the other member of the comparison is often an unknown quantity as regards its authenticity. Consequently discrepancies may be ascribed either to dialectal variation, inaccuracy of perception, or linguistic change since the first investigation took place. This situation is often aggravated by the absence of clear-cut linguistic boundaries and the employment of idiosyncratic nomenclature.

Bibliography. As the primary object of the survey was to examine languages at first hand rather than to base our findings on the material of others, no bibliography as such will be included in this section of the report. Works dealing with this field of African languages are rare and, when used, have been mentioned either in the main body of the text or in footnotes. It is doubtful whether in view of the extreme pressure of space a repetition of these entries would be justifiable.

Vehicular languages. As this is one of the more complicated and localized linguistic areas of the world it is not to be wondered at that numerous forms of linguae francae have sprung up in it, sometimes even being superimposed. Although in due course these may well be ousted by English and French, at present European languages are used by Africans only when they possess an exceptional proficiency in them, or when a special technical or social context demands it. Some of the more important vehicular languages are PIDGIN, DUALA, BANƐN, EWONDO ('populaire'), BULU, NDJEM, HAUSA, FULANI, MAƉGALA, and SAƉGO. Others, not so widely used, are JUKUN, FUƉGƆM, ƉGAAKA, and BAMUM; these are mentioned in the text of the report. A discussion of the nature, use, and location of these media of intercourse would form a study in itself and is beyond the scope of the survey. For purely practical purposes, however, we indicate roughly the distribution of the principal ones:

PIDGIN (Br.C., F.C.). By far the most widespread language of the west coast, it is spoken in most of the territories by African and European alike. It assumes many forms and extends throughout British Cameroons. It is used in the west of Cameroun and stretches eastwards along the main communications fading out about a hundred miles from the Oubangui Chari border. Pidgin is the language of transport personnel and of immigrants from the west in this area.

DUALA (Br.C., F.C.). Africans of southern British Cameroons and western Cameroun whose language is closely related to DUALA use the latter as a lingua franca, often to the detriment of their mother tongue. Although it is employed by some missions and is on the official list of languages in which British administrators may be examined, very few Europeans speak it.

BANƐN (F.C.). The administration and missions of S.D. Ndikiniméki have established this language as the medium of intercourse in an area where most speeches appear to be closely related to it.

EWONDO ('populaire') (F.C.). This would seem to be an 'up-country' version spoken outside the area of EWONDO proper. It is to be found throughout the centre of Cameroun extending as far north as Yoko. In addition to Africans whose mother tongue is related to EWONDO, missionaries and administrative clerks find this medium to be of great service.

BULU (F.C.). Apart from the regions of southern Cameroun where it is the mother tongue, BULU may be encountered in parts of eastern Cameroun as far north as Batouri. It is much favoured by the American Presbyterian Mission and some administrators.

NDJEM (F.C., O.C.). This is employed by Africans of east Cameroun and west Oubangui Chari who speak languages closely related to it.

HAUSA and FULANI. Although the great importance of these languages is not particularly apparent in our field of operations HAUSA was frequently encountered in native commerce in all the larger centres. FULANI is probably used as a lingua franca in the extreme north of our area in Cameroun, but we have no concrete evidence as to this. It is also useful in the north-west of Bamenda Province.

MADGALA (O.C., C.B.). We never met this language but understand from Professor Guthrie that it is in common use in Moyen Congo and that Mbomotaba from different villages are forced by the extreme localization of their dialects to speak together in MADGALA.

SADGO (O.C.). This is the lingua franca form of SADGO proper. It is as omnipresent in the parts of Oubangui Chari we visited as is PIDGIN on the coast, and has as many manifestations as 'up-country' SWAHILI in East Africa. It is spoken by Europeans and Africans, administrators and missionaries.

Achievements. No claim is made for outstanding achievements in this field of linguistic research. The project, in so far as the western team is concerned, may be considered valuable as a pilot survey which has shown how great is the confusion and how profuse and involved the problems of this part of the northern Bantu border. Our report is presented therefore not with the arrogance of experts making incontrovertible statements but humbly and with the hope that it may prove to be not too imperfect an interpretation of the linguistic content of the area examined by us. Any corrections of a factual nature, or amplification of incomplete evidence will therefore be welcomed by the writers.

Acknowledgements. The report would be incomplete without some mention, inadequate though it may be, of the part played by the supervisors of the scheme, Professors Guthrie and Tucker. They, together with the late Professor Ida Ward, were responsible for training the teams for research work and guided us in the preparation of the report in its final form, Professor Guthrie superintending the Bantu and Bantoid sections of the western half and Professor Tucker the portion dealing with Non-Bantu languages. We are particularly indebted to Professor Guthrie for putting at our disposal his wide experience of western Bantu languages, and for his great helpfulness in linking our survey with his personal researches immediately to the south of the Bantu border in this part of Africa. Without his help this report would have been a much less accurate statement of fact than it is.

INTRODUCTION

To the members of the eastern team we are indebted for help in the area where the two fields of research adjoined and also for the time they spent in comparing material with us. We wish to thank Miss M. A. Bryan for the demographic information she passed on to us, and especially for population figures for British Cameroons. In compiling this work we have made frequent and extensive use of Mme Dugast's excellent ethnic survey which was particularly appreciated for its statistics and detailed ethnographic maps. We also owe much to Tessmann for his remarkable linguistic map of German Kameruns.

For non-academic assistance we would like to acknowledge the kind co-operation of the British Colonial Office and of the Office de la Recherche Scientifique Outre Mer. To M. le Gouverneur Deschamps of the latter institution we express our thanks for reducing our period of immobility at Douala to the minimum and arranging questions of transport. Senior colonial administrators were very co-operative and we thank them for the official standing given to us throughout our survey. To all those British and French officials, and to the missionaries of all nationalities with whom we came into contact we would offer an omnibus expression of gratitude which we hope will be taken as a personal acknowledgement by all who read this. The charming treatment received from these most generous people turned our expedition into a practical proposition. Without their help we should have had no accommodation worthy of the name, no fuel for our vehicle (and often no repair facilities), no informants (other than by hire), no local demographic information, no water, and sometimes no food. Apart from assistance in procuring for us the necessities for maintaining a reasonable existence and conducting our investigations, they also extended to us the greatest hospitality, even supplying us with transport when our own failed.

Last but not least amongst our helpers in Africa is M. J. P. Nicolas of the Institut Français d'Afrique Noire at Douala. He threw open to us his centre as a place of reference, and during his absence in Europe allowed us to use his quarters as a base where we could be sure of accommodation when we had to spend time in Douala. Furthermore it is largely to 'Centrifan' Douala (which we used as a clearing address) that we owe the arrival of our mail in various forgotten parts of Africa.

The staff of the International African Institute was hard put to it to keep in constant touch with us in all our peregrinations; the administering of the Survey must have been an onerous task. It fell largely on the shoulders of Mrs. Wyatt, who, in the face of almost insuperable obstacles acquitted herself well and is deserving of special acknowledgement.

ABBREVIATIONS

Demographic

A.E.F.	Afrique Équatoriale Française	D.	District (French territory), Division (British territory)
Br.C.	British Cameroons		
F.C.	Cameroun (French Cameroons)	N.A.	Native Authority
M.C.	Moyen Congo	Prov.	Province
N.	Nigeria	Rég.	Région
O.C.	Oubangui Chari	S.D.	Sub-division
T.P.	Taxpayers only	M.A.B.	Information from Miss M. A. Bryan

Publications

B.S.O.S.	*Bulletin of the School of Oriental and African Studies*, London.
Bufe	'Die Dualasprache in ihrem Verhältnis zu den Dialecten des Nordgebiets der Station Bombe', *Z.f.K.* i, 1910, pp. 25–36.
C.E.C.	*Carte Ethnique du Cameroun*, Institut Français d'Afrique Noire, Centre du Cameroun (Dépôt légal No. 49 — le trimestre 1949).
I.E.S.C.	*Inventaire Ethnique du Sud Cameroun*, Mme I. Dugast, printed by A. Coueslant at Cahors (Lot), 1949.
M.C.	*Memento, Cameroun*, Service de Presse et d'Information du Cameroun, Yaoundé, 1949.
M.S.O.S.	*Mitteilungen des Seminars für Orientalische Sprachen.*
Talbot	*The Peoples of Southern Nigeria*, vol. iv, by P. Amaury Talbot, Oxford University Press, 1926.
Z.f.E.S. \}	*Zeitschrift für Eingeborenen-Sprachen.*
Z.f.K.	*Zeitschrift für Kolonial-Sprachen* (later *Z.f.E.S.*).

SECTION A

BANTU LANGUAGES

1. THE LUNDU GROUP

LUNDU[1] (1.1) (Balundu)

Locality. (Br.C.) D. Kumba. Almost the entire western portion of the division. This language has the distinction of being the most westerly of true Bantu languages.

Population. 6,234 Talbot.[2]

Relationships. LUNDU[3] forms a very compact group with other languages immediately to the north-west. EKUMBƐ and MBƆŊGƐ are particularly closely related. BATAŊGA, BIMA, BAKUNDU, ŊGORO, BARUE complete the group. Throughout these languages the vocabulary is of Bantu origin with regular correspondences.

ŊGORO (1.7) (Ngolo)

Locality. (Br.C.) D. Kumba. The heights and western slopes of the Rumpi hills.

Population. 5,837 Talbot.[4]

Relationships. Especially closely related to BAKUNDU, MBƆŊGƐ, BATAŊGA, and BIMA.

BAKUNDU (1.6) (Lokundu,[5] Kundu)

Locality. (Br.C.) D. Kumba. Two areas, one on the north-east slopes of the Rumpi hills along the fifth meridian north, and the other an irregularly shaped patch to the south-west and south of Kumba township.

Population. 5,010 Talbot. 30,000 Bufe[6] (1910).

Relationships. Bufe states that this language had suffered less under foreign influence than its neighbours. There are considerable differences of vocabulary between our material and Bufe's, due perhaps to foreign influence in later years, or perhaps to the fact that his Lokundu and our BAKUNDU are two different dialects. Vocabulary relates this language more closely to MBƆŊGƐ and ŊGORO than any other members of the group.

---

[1] This is Bruens's version and is probably correct. We ourselves recorded the name as 'Balundu', but this was probably due to 'europeanization' by the informant.

[2] This figure is probably very unreliable as Talbot's map shows as 'Balundu' an area which takes in not only the Bima and Balundu–Badiko (both BIMA-speaking according to our African informant), but also the Isangele (SILQADƐT) and Korup.

[3] A grammar of Lundu by Fr. A. Bruens, pp. 51, reproduced from typescript, is held by the School of Oriental and African Studies, London.

[4] We cannot say whether these figures are in respect of BATAŊGA or of ŊGORO including BATAŊGA.

[5] This is as recorded by E. Bufe ('Die Dualasprache', &c.). Our informant was most insistent, however, that BAKUNDU was the name of the language and also of the tribe.

[6] This figure (estimated on 125 villages) is either totally optimistic or includes the whole LUNDU group.

BATADGA (1.4)

(The informant for this language was considered unreliable but was the only one available.)

Locality. (Br.C.) D. Kumba, on the northern slopes of the Rumpi hills, bounded by the divisional frontier in the north.

Population. 5,837 Talbot.[1]

Relationships. Closely related to DGORO. BATADGA and BIMA are merely dialectal variants of one language, although the vocabulary content of all the languages of the group is strikingly similar.

BIMA (1.5a)

Locality. (Br.C.) D. Kumba. The west and north-west slopes of the Rumpi hills, bounded in the north by the divisional boundary; also the Balundu–Badiku area (1.5b) stretching west from Ndian to Nigeria.

Population. 6,234 Talbot.[2] They call themselves Baima and were formerly Bauma.

Relationships. See BATADGA.

MBƆDGƐ (1.3)

Locality. (Br.C.) D. Kumba. The south-east slopes of the Rumpi hills, extending north-west almost to 9° E. by 4° 30′ N.

Population. 6,107 Talbot.

Relationships. Only dialectal differences from EKUMBƐ.

EKUMBƐ (1.2)

Locality. (Br.C.) D. Kumba. Two areas, one to the south of Kumba on both sides of the Kumba–Victoria road stretching east to the international frontier, the other at about 9° 10′ E. bounded north and south by 4° 30′ N. and the divisional limit.

Population. 894 Talbot.

Relationships. Only dialectal differences from MBƆDGƐ. Also closely related to BALUNDU and BATADGA. Less closely related to BAKUNDU.

BARUE (1.8) **barue** (Lue)

Locality. (Br.C.) D. Kumba. On the southern slopes of the Rumpi hills around the headwaters of the Rivers Makunge and Meme.

Population. 4,733 Talbot.

Relationships. The LUNDU group in general.

---

[1] Talbot's figure probably includes DGORO.

[2] This presumably also includes the Balundu, Korup, and Isaŋgelɛ, since Talbot's tribal map groups these together in his Balundu area which more than occupies the district inhabited by the Bima, of whom he makes no mention. A most unreliable figure.

2. THE DUALA GROUP

MOKPE or ḄAAKPE (1.10) (Bakwiri, Kwire, Kwili)

Locality. (Br.C.) On and around Mount Cameroon, descending to the Atlantic coast.

Population. 17,878 Talbot.

Relationships. MOKPE, ḄOMBOKO, and SU form a definite linguistic unit within the DUALA group. Although showing a strong vocabulary relationship to DUALA (1.9), OLI, POƊGO, and MUƊGO, in several grammatical points there is a distinct cleavage. The vocabulary has many DUALA and PIDGIN loan words.

ḄOMBOKO (1.11) (Bumbuko)

Locality. (Br.C.) To the north and north-west of Mount Cameroon descending to the Atlantic.

Population. 1,093 Talbot.

Relationships. See MOKPE.

SU (1.12) (i)su (Isubu, Bimbia)

Locality. (Br.C.) Two small enclaves on the Atlantic coast, east and west of Victoria in Bakwiri Territory. Bimbia, Likolo, Wunaŋgombe and Wunabile are three of the localities concerned.

Population. 652 Talbot.[1]

Relationships. Very closely related to MOKPE and ḄOMBOKO while showing evidence of marked contamination from DUALA. Because of this, much of our material is of doubtful value. The male speakers of the language are mostly fishermen who are in close touch with DUALA-speaking peoples. There is a strong blood relationship between the people of Bimbia and those of Douala.

OLI (1.13) (Wouri)

Locality. (F.C.) Rég. Moungo, S.D. Yabassi. Both banks of the River Wouri just above the estuary.

Population. 3,621 *I.E.S.C.*

Relationships. Especially closely related to POƊGO and BODIMAN. There are two branches of this tribe, the Wuri Bɔswa and the Wuri Bwili, which are said by native informants to speak the same language.

POƊGO (1.14)

Locality. (F.C.) Rég. Moungo, S.D. Mbanga. In the southern part of the

---

[1] This was of course in 1921. Since then a high death-rate and emigration to Victoria have greatly reduced this community. An elder of the tribe estimated their numbers in October 1949 at less than 500 although he admitted that accurate figures would be hard to come by owing to the exodus to Victoria.

Sub-division on both sides of the main road to Bonaberi, stretching west to the international frontier.

Population. 6,584 *I.E.S.C.*

Relationships. Closely resembles MUDGO (as spoken on the French side of the river of the same name). The informant claimed that in spite of vocabulary differences DUALA and PODGO are intercomprehensible. It is worthy of note that while the older people prefer to speak PODGO, the rising generation in the tribe speak DUALA.

MUDGO (1.15)

Locality. (Br.C., F.C.) D. Victoria, and Rég. Moungo, S.D. Mbanga. Scattered villages on both banks of the Mungo around Tiko and down to the coast.

Population. (Br.C.) Probably no more than 1,000;[1] (F.C.) about 300 *I.E.S.C.*

Relationships. MUDGO and PODGO are especially closely related. Slight dialectal differences occur between the varieties of this language spoken on British and French banks of the Mungo.

BODIMAN (1.16)

Locality. (F.C.) On both banks of the Wouri south of Yabassi.

Population. 2,006 *I.E.S.C.*

Relationship. A dialect of DUALA, closely related to PODGO and OLI. This language was not the subject of an investigation.

3. THE MBO CLUSTER

This name has been bestowed on an agglomeration of languages and dialects of disputed inter-intelligibility for various reasons and also on the evidence of Africans who lived nearby and did not speak any of these languages as their mother tongue. They referred to them as 'Mbo'. 'I speak Duala, Bakwiri, and Balundu', they would say, 'but I find Mbo (meaning *any* Mbo language) very hard to understand.'

Viewed in the light of MOKPE, LUNDU, and DUALA it is indeed a strange cluster, and at first glance not remarkable for an obvious affinity to the Bantu family. Its 'Bantu-ness', however, becomes more apparent if the cluster is considered in relationship to EWONDO, BULU, MPODGWE, and N. MBƐNƐ. Class prefixes which seem totally eccentric with regard to the Bantu system when viewed from the standpoint of DUALA, &c., appear much less abnormal when one attempts to relate them to EWONDO, &c. MBO languages show vocabulary affinities with EWONDO, BULU, N. MBƐNƐ, and DUALA; phonetically their relationship tends towards BAMILEKE; grammatically they seem to be linked especially to EWONDO, BULU, and N. MBƐNƐ—particularly by the nature of their prefix system, although some of the latter traits are common to DUALA. Word shape clearly indicates a close similarity to EWONDO, &c., closed syllables (with very diverse final consonants) being common. Word order too links this cluster to EWONDO, &c.

[1] Estimated.

However, despite the rival claims of various Bantu groups in W. Cameroons, the cluster exhibits such unity in most aspects that for purposes of classification it can be usefully considered a separate entity, with a particular relationship to EWONDO, N. MBƐNƐ, and BULU.

It should be noted that, since we are speaking of languages *as they are today*, classification is, as far as possible, by means of our own material. Johnston's vocabularies have been used to a small extent, but were found to be unreliable in this area on several occasions, in so far as some linguistic material has been wrongly labelled; e.g. he calls material strongly reminiscent of the N. MBƐNƐ cluster, 'Bangangte', the latter being the name of a BAMILEKE (Bantoid) language close by. Furthermore, he mixes in one column of vocabulary, languages which may be classified into different clusters; vocabularies appear to be contaminated with unacknowledged loan words from neighbouring languages; discrepancies in independent prefixes often occur between his material and ours. The latter may be due either to a change of linguistic habits in the last few decades—a factor which must not be lightly passed over in this melting-pot of Bantu languages—or else to dialectal differences in the languages recorded by Johnston and by the Bantu Borderline Survey. Where so many small languages are spoken it is inevitable that on the fringe of linguistic areas considerable 'shading-off' may take place even in matters of grammar.

Some languages included in this cluster show characteristics which tend to situate them on the fringe of the MBO area. This is generally true geographically as well as linguistically, e.g. BAFƆ (1.17), BALONDO (1.18), BABOꝹG (1.19). Information regarding the two last named is fragmentary, but the first would seem to be a transition language between S. Cameroons Bantu and MBO, popular opinion placing it in the MBO sphere of influence rather than elsewhere.

The supreme chief of the Mbo proper, whom we visited at Mbouroukou (Rég. Moungo, S.D. Nkongsamba), said that the varieties of MBO spoken at Mbouroukou, in S.D. Dschang, and in Br.C. are easily mutually intelligible. Other Mbo informants made reservations on this point. Despite repeated *ethnic* classification with the Bakundu, *linguistically* the Mbo have little in common with them beyond general family characteristics of a Bantu nature. MBO is particularly closely related to AKƆƆSƏ,[1] NSWƆSƏ,[2] ELƆꝹ,[3] NNENÛ,[4] MWAHƐT,[5] AKƆƆSƏ,[6] MBO,[7] 'BANEKA',[8] and KAA[9]; and also 'similar' to BALONDO and BABOꝹG according to reports by various informants. We have no linguistic evidence for the two latter and only a very confused statement as evidence for including BALONDO in the MBO cluster. As for BABOꝹG, R. P. Héberlé, who has spent several years in the area, is quoted by Mme Dugast[10] as saying that they and the Mbo are probably *ethnically* related.

MWAHƐT (1.20g) (Manehas—called Bakaka by the informants for MBO proper).

Locality. (F.C.) S.D. Nkongsamba. To the east of Mount Koupé stretching to the Nkongsamba–Bonaberi motor road.

Population. 2,413 I.E.S.C. (including some 'related foreigners').

[1] Bakosi. [2] Basosi. [3] Elong. [4] Ninong. [5] Manehas. [6] Muamenam.
[7] Bareko. [8] Speech name unknown. [9] Bakaka of S.D. Nkongsamba. [10] I.E.S.C., p. 30.

Relationships. It would appear to be more closely related to AKƆƆSƏ (Bakosi) and NNENŨ than to ELƆD. Our informant stated that his people understood all these languages, but with difficulty.

AKƆƆSƏ (1.20*h*) (Muamenam—called Mbo by informants for MBO proper)

Locality. (F.C.) S.D. Nkongsamba. To the west of Nkongsamba on the international frontier, to the south of Mount Manengouba.

Population. 1,844 *I.E.S.C.*

Relationships. Probably a dialectal variant of AKƆƆSƏ (Bakosi). Closely related to ELƆD and NNENŨ, the latter being the more easily understood of the two. It should be noted of this informant that, though he stated that MWAHƐT and AKƆƆSƏ (Muamenam) were inter-intelligible, he had considerable difficulty in understanding the MWAHƐT-French interpreter.

MBO (1.20*d*) (Bareko)

Locality. (F.C.) S.D. Nkongsamba. To the north-east of Nkongsamba stretching to the River Nkam where it forms the limits of Rég. Bamiléké.

Population. 2,752 *I.E.S.C.*

Relationships. The informant claimed that his language was identical with that of the Baneka—but not of the neighbouring Balondo. It was inter-intelligible with MBO (of Mbouroukou), MWAHƐT, KAA, and BABODG, he said, but with the nearby Bakem, Mbang, Boŋkeŋ, and others he used Pidgin.

BANEKA[1] (1.20*e*)

Locality. (F.C.) The Nkongsamba area.

Population. 2,961 *I.E.S.C.*

Relationships. See MBO (Bareko).

BALONDO[1] (1.18)

Locality. (F.C.) S.D. Nkongsamba. To the south of Mount Nlonako.

Population. 263 *I.E.S.C.*

Relationships. It appears to form a subsidiary 'mutual intelligibility' unit with KAA and BABODG. It is understood with difficulty by the Mbo.[2]

BABƆDG[1] (1.19)

Locality. (F.C.) S.D. Nkongsamba. Between 9° 55' to 10° E. and 4° 40' to 4° 45' N.

Population. 1,217 *I.E.S.C.*

Relationships. This is understood by the Mbo, but is more readily comprehensible to the Bakaka and Balondo.

---

[1] This is the administrative name.
[2] This last sentence is extracted from a fairly confused statement by a Mbo informant.

BAFƆ (1.17) (Bafaw)

Locality. (Br.C.) D. Kumba. Two areas, the larger one along the main road stretching from Kumba northwards almost to the divisional limit, the other at about 9° 10′ E. by 4° 30′ N.

Population. 2,397 Talbot. Bufe[1] has 6,000 (calculated on 15 villages)—a totally optimistic figure.

Relationships. A transition language between southern Br.C. Bantu and MBO. Some close alternances of vocabulary with MBO were noted but many discrepancies in type of radical occur.

AKƆƆSƏ (1.20*i*) (Bakosi, Nkosi)

Locality. (Br.C.) D. Kumba. The heights and southern slopes of the Manenguba mountains, stretching to the French frontier—and even beyond, according to one informant.

Population. 13,547 Talbot.

NSWƆSƏ (1.20*j*) ǹswásə̀ (Basosi)

Locality. (Br.C.) D. Kumba. To the east of the Kumba–Mamfe road on the northwest slopes of the Manenguba mountains. Bounded in the north by the divisional limit.

ELƆ̃Ŋ (1.20*k*) llʌŋ (Elong)

Locality. (Br.C., F.C.) D. Kumba and S.D. Nkongsamba on both sides of the international boundary approximately between 5° and 5° 15′ N.

Population. 3,803 Talbot.

NNENŨ (1.20*l*) (Ninong)

Locality. (Br.C., F.C.) D. Kumba, S.D. Nkongsamba, on both sides of the international boundary around 5° N.

Population. 2,624 Talbot.

KAA (1.20*f*) (Bakaka)[2]

Locality. (F.C.) S.D. Nkongsamba, between 9° 42′–9° 58′ E. and 4° 35′–4° 50′ N.

Population. 5,327 I.E.S.C.

MBO

(1.20*a*) (i) **mbo** (British Cameroons Mbo). Ŋgɛn is a general name for languages of this type in Br.C.

(1.20*b*) (ii) **mbò** (of Mbouroukou).

(1.20*c*) (iii) **m̀bòó** (MBO of Dschang).

Locality. (Br.C., F.C.) The south-east of Mamfe Division; also Rég. Moungo, S.D. Nkongsamba. The north of the Sub-division reaching almost to Nkongsamba

[1] 'Die Dualasprache in ihrem Verhältnis zu den Dialekten des Nordgebiets der Station Bombe', Z.f.K. i, 1910, pp. 25–36. There are several discrepancies between Bufe's vocabulary and my own.

[2] Material for this language was recorded by M. Jacquot.

but not quite to the international frontier in the west. In the north-west and extreme north the area extends into Br.C. and Rég. Bamiléké.

Population. (Br.C.) 3,037 Talbot.
(F.C.) 7,816 *I.E.S.C.*

Relationships. (i) and (ii) are sufficiently close together to be called dialects of the same language. (iii) has more striking divergences and some informants state that it is understood by other MBO speakers with difficulty.

4. THE N. MBƐNƐ GROUP (BASA)

This group stretches from approximately 4° 30′ to 3° 30′ N. and from 10° to 11° 30′ E., also covering in the north a large part of S.D. Yabassi and encroaching on S.D. Nkongsamba and S.D. Bafang. To the north-east, in S.D. Yabassi and S.D. Ndikiniméki, its boundaries merge with those of BANƐN to such an extent that it is hard to say which dialects should be attributed to MBƐNƐ and which to BANƐN.

Population. 157,435 (excluding Bakoko) *I.E.S.C.* It should be noted that while this is the *total* Basa population figure, the area examined by us was the merest fringe of Basa country. No attempt, therefore, should be made to relate this figure to the number of speakers of the MBƐNƐ dialects mentioned.

Strictly speaking BALUŊ and BƆŊKEŊ do not belong to MBƐNƐ, but show a mixture of features of surrounding language groups with a predominance of MBƐNƐ characteristics.

BALUŊ (1.21*a*) **ɓaluŋ** (S. Balong)

Locality. (Br.C., F.C.) D. Kumba and D. Victoria; Rég. Moungo, S.D. Mbanga. In British territory a crescent-shaped area round the lower north-east slopes of Mount Cameroon stretching to the Mungo; in F.C. the left bank of this river extending east beyond Mbanga.

Population. Br.C. 2,033 Talbot ⎫ Bufe[1] gave 6,000 based on the existence of
F.C. 2,406 *I.E.S.C.* ⎭ 15 villages.

Relationships. There is very little difference between the language as spoken in British and French territory, although it should not be confused with N. Balong (KITW̄II). As stated above it shares some features with DUALA, MBO, and MBƐNƐ especially in the matter of the shape of independent prefixes. It is noteworthy that our material and Bufe's show considerable discrepancies of vocabulary.

BƆŊKEŊ (1.21*b*) **ɓɔŋkeŋ** (Bonkeng, Bonken Pendia)

Locality. (F.C.) Rég. Moungo, S.D. Mbanga. To the north-west of the Subdivision on both sides of the main road between Loum and Nyombe.[2]

Population. 1,690 *I.E.S.C.*

[1] Op. cit.
[2] Mme Dugast marks two further (and smaller) areas, one east of the Mbanga–Yabassi S.D. border, to the north of Yabassi, and the other at Boneko on the Wouri. Little seems to be known of these enclaves, however. They are not indicated on the administrative map in our possession. We have no linguistic information on this point, and Mme Dugast gives no population figures for these enclaves.

Relationships. There seems to be little doubt that this is a language containing elements of many of the surrounding groups, a situation probably brought about by the geographical location of the tribe on the main line of communication of the area. It shows vocabulary similarity with LƆMBI (MBƐNƐ group), KAA (MBO group); it has many features of the MBƐNƐ class system and some of MBO. Its word shape, however, would point to a DUALA or LUNDU origin.

BAKOKO (1.21c) Bakoko

Locality. (F.C.) Rég. Moungo, S.D. Mbanga. The extreme south-east corner bounded south and east by the Rivers Bonono and Wouri. To the north of Bonaberi.

Population. 20,215[1] *I.E.S.C.*

Relationships. Ethnically the classification of the Bakoko presents a problem of long standing. Are they of common stock with the Basa or not? Whatever the ethnic situation, the following linguistic facts have emerged from a very cursory examination of the most northerly BAKOKO and subsequent comparison with Johnston's S. BAKOKO vocabulary: (*a*) there are at least two different languages which have so far been loosely called by the same name; (*b*) to judge by Johnston's material, S. BAKOKO is far removed from MBƐNƐ and more closely related to DUALA;[2] (*c*) the N. BAKOKO speak a language which, while its vocabulary relates it closely to N. MBƐNƐ, shows unmistakable signs of being grammatically a mixture of DUALA and BULU type languages.

BAƊKON (1.21d) ɓaŋkun (Abo)

Locality. (F.C.) Rég. Moungo, S.D. Mbanga, the south of the area stretching from the Moungo to the Sub-division eastern border, i.e. almost to the Wouri between 4° 10′ and 4° 30′ N.

Population. 10,232 *I.E.S.C.*

Relationships. Closely related to MBƐNƐ and also to BANƐN with only dialectal differences from LƆMBI. There are theories amongst French ethnologists that two different peoples inhabit this area—the Abo and the Bankon—probably speaking two different languages. The Administration has divided the area concerned into two parts 'Abo Nord' and 'Abo Sud'. We interrogated informants from both districts in each other's presence and they said that there was only one Abo language, its name being as indicated above.

LƆMBI (1.21e) (Barombi)

Locality. (Br.C.) D. Kumba. Three enclaves, two of which are situated round crater lakes named Barombi; the other lies to the west of Kumba on both banks of the upper Makunge.[3]

Population. 1,406 Talbot.

---

[1] This definitely includes the Bakoko of the Edéa area who are far more numerous than those of S.D. Mbanga. The latter would appear to have only three villages.

[2] Professor Guthrie has some S. BAKOKO (Bakoyo) material and he agrees with me on this point.

[3] The map in the report to the United Nations Organization (1948) shows a fourth enclave near the Atlantic coast between Bamusso and Munyange. We have no information on this area.

Relationships. Tradition has it that the Barombi originate from the Baŋkon (whom they left less than 200 years ago, said our informant). The language supports this claim by its closeness to BADKON in particular and MBƐNƐ in general. Our LƆMBI material tallies well with Spellenburg's BADKON.

N. MBƐNE (Basa)

There are many small dialects of this language, most of which were located only at second-hand via informants speaking other languages, or by using an administrative map marked with tribal or clan areas. Those nearest the Bantu border line were: YABASI (1.21g), NDOKPENDA (1.21h), NDOKBELE (1.21f), NYAMTAM or Nyamtan (1.21i), DIBENG (1.21j), NDOKAMA (1.21k), BAKEM (1.21l), MBADG (1.21m), DIBUM (1.21n). It will be appreciated that the foregoing are not submitted as the authentic names of the dialects. Since most of them were not given by natives of the particular area concerned, it is reasonable to expect that they refer to the clan or locality rather than to the dialect. However, the names are useful in that they help to group together the 'Basa' speeches of an area.

YABASI (1.21g)

Locality. (F.C.) Rég. Moungo, S.D. Yabassi. The north of the Yabassi area stretching east and west.

Relationships. Closely related to MBADG and DIBUM. Vocabulary related to BAKOKO.

MBADG (1.21m)

Locality. (F.C.) Rég. Moungo; the north and north-west of S.D. Yabassi.

Relationships. Almost identical with DIBUM.

DIBUM (1.21n) dibum

Locality. (F.C.) Rég. Bamiléké and Rég. Moungo. In the south of S.D. Bafang and in the north of S.D. Yabassi on either side of the administrative border.

Population. 6,000 C.E.C.

Relationships. Inter-intelligible with MBADG. Close vocabulary relationship to BAKOKO. Although the Dibum state that their language is a dialect of 'Basa', they prefer to use Pidgin English with their southern neighbours as inter-intelligibility would otherwise be imperfect.

5. THE BANƐN GROUP (1.22a)

Locality. (F.C.) BANƐN proper stretches approximately from just east of Yabassi to east of Ndikiniméki in a narrow belt. This area includes NDOKBIAKAT (1.22a (i)), NDOKTUNA (1.22a (ii)), NDOGBANG (1.22a (iii)), NDOGBANOL (1.22a(iv)), LOGNANGA(1.22a(v)), ELING(1.22a(vi)), ITUNDU (1.22a(vii)), and BONƐK (1.22b) (Ponek). Flanking it to the north is NYƆ́'Ɔ́ (1.22d) and to the east,

BANTU LANGUAGES

YAMBETA (1.22e) and MANDI (1.22c) (Lemande) which are linguistically closely linked to BANƐN.[1]

Most of the names mentioned are merely place or clan designations, since we were able to study only two of the numerous dialects: BONƐK and NYƆ́'Ɔ́ (Nyokon).

Population. 24,426 *I.E.S.C.* (BANƐN proper).
1,916 *I.E.S.C.* (MANDI).
1,984 *I.E.S.C.* (YAMBETA).

BONƐK (1.22b) (ɔtaŋg) atɔmb (Ponek)

Locality. (F.C.) Village of Bonek on the Ndikiniméki–Bafia road, just within the limits of Bafia S.D.

Population. Not more than 50.[2]

Relationships. Professor Guthrie, who studied MANDI during the survey, considers that BONƐK is sufficiently close to it to be classed as a dialectal variant.

NYƆ́'Ɔ́ (1.22d) (Nyokon)

Locality. (F.C.) Rég. Mbam, north-west of S.D. of Ndikiniméki, also Rég. Moungo, west of S.D. of Yabassi.

Population. 3,900 *C.E.C.*

Relationships. There is another dialect of this language, called FUD at Kinding. They are mutually intelligible. Although NYƆ́'Ɔ́ is closely related to BANƐN there can be no question of intercomprehension. BANƐN is used for normal intercourse between the Nyokon and their neighbours.

6. THE BAFIA GROUP

The area north, south, and west of the town of Bafia is inhabited by tribes whose history has not encouraged the cultivation of a unified language. Repeated enslavements, flights, invasions have only too clearly left their mark on the linguistics of the region. These languages are as full of problems as their demography is of fallacious names and titles. Far more information would be needed than the Survey was able to amass during its short stay in this locality, before our classification could be scientifically justified. Suffice it to say that the general 'feel' of the material to hand causes us to mention in the same breath such languages as FA' (1.23) (Balom), KPA (1.24) (Bafia), DGAYABA (1.26) (Djanti), DGƆRƆ[3] (1.27a), CIDGA (1.28), YAMBASA (1.29), and 'SANAGA' (1.30).

Of these, NGƆRƆ, CIDGA, and YAMBASA are particularly closely related. They are in fact dialects of the same idiom. 'SANAGA' is here a linguistic device (just as

---

[1] Although there are some violent divergences between these dialects, the missions and the administration use a standard form of BANƐN which has become the lingua franca of a large part of this area.
[2] The language is spoken only by the village elders now. This figure is an estimate given by the village chief who said that the younger inhabitants now speak BANƐN.
[3] This is almost identical with Johnston's No. 216, Ba-ti (Baceŋga).

'les Sanaga' is an administrative one), used to cover numerous heterogeneous sub-tribes who employ roughly the same language. MAƊGISA (1.30a) is one of the better known dialects; BƐTSIƊGA (1.30b) (not to be confused with CIƊGA) is another. Some of these are well on the way to being Sub-Bantu due to the partial break-down of the system of class agreements. Similarly for various reasons the other languages of this group, it could be argued, behave in a strange manner for Bantu languages. Some irregularity of agreement and considerable unpredictability as regards comparative structure would tend to put them in the category of 'doubtful Bantu' in view of the fragmentary evidence of our material.

As regards the relationship of the group as a whole to other groups, indications are so confusing, pointing as they do to all the main Bantu languages of the immediate vicinity, that it would perhaps be preferable to abstain from comment.

FA' (1.23) (Balom)

Locality. (F.C.) On both banks of the Mbam at its confluence with the Noun.

Population. 3,846 *I.E.S.C.*

As no material for this language was recorded, it is to Professor Guthrie that we are indebted for this classification. He also worked on KAALOƊ (1.25), a language related to FA' and spoken by only 50 people. It is located on the right bank of the Mbam below the Noun confluence.

KPA (1.24) (ʈə) kpa (Bafia)

Locality. (F.C.) Rég. Mbam, S.D. Bafia. The township of Bafia and the immediate surroundings.

Population. 12,093 *I.E.S.C.*

Our material was recorded under the name of 'Bafia' by M. Jacquot and would seem to be a mixture of FA' and KPA, from the standpoint both of vocabulary and class prefixes. This is not surprising, as the informant was a student who had come from Bafia township to the École Régionale at Nkongsamba, and whose speech had presumably taken to itself many elements foreign to KPA. Only vocabulary was taken down.

ƊGAYABA (1.26) (Djanti)

Locality. (F.C.) S.D. of Bafia. Seven villages on the eastern slopes of the Djanti and Niabidi mountains.

Population. Less than 1,000 *I.E.S.C.*

The only available informant for this language was not very well suited to the task, his comprehension of what was required of him being very imperfect. For this reason our ƊGAYABA material may be unsound in several respects, especially in verbal forms.

ƊGƆRƆ (1.27a)

Locality. (F.C.) S.D. of Bafia on the left bank of the Mbam in the valley formed by its affluent the River Ngoro.

Population. Eight villages *I.E.S.C.*

CIDGA (1.28) tʃiŋga (Bundum)[1] (Kombe)

Locality. (F.C.) S.D. Bafia. On both banks of the Mbam just above its confluence with the Sanaga east of Bafia township. (This is the location of the informant's village and immediate vicinity.) Dugast, Johnston, and Tessmann include CIDGA in 'Bati' (1.27b) which, they say, extends to various localities between 11° 30′–12° E. and 3° 30′–4° 30′ N. It is hard to say from the evidence to hand where CIDGA ends and 'Sanaga' begins.[2] The Kombe speak like the Tʃiŋga, said our informant. There is a great similarity between CIDGA and DGƆRƆ.

7. SOME LANGUAGES OF THE EWONDO[3]—BULU GROUP

This section deals only with some of the outlying members of the group, which are located on or near the northern Bantu borderline. It is by no means intended to be exhaustive or final. Indeed, in such an area, where relationships are so close, where language names are so numerous, varied, and bogus, and tribal history and geography so chequered, it is doubtful whether any complete and incontestably correct demographic statement will ever be made.

The area covered by the whole group is vast, stretching almost to the southern frontier of F.C., occupying most of its central forest belt and even extending north into the wooded grassland beyond the Middle Sanaga.

A strange feature of this area is the unreliability of statements on intercomprehension of languages and dialects. While it is appreciated that the densely forested country does not tend to facilitate social intercourse, it is felt that several informants (particularly village and 'canton' chiefs) have exaggerated, probably for political reasons, the linguistic differences which exist between related peoples. On the other hand, in this same area, other informants have claimed that neighbouring languages—which looked most unlike their own on paper—were really quite intelligible to them! It is indeed very difficult to know exactly how much credence to place in the most solemn affirmations of informants when they compare their own language with, say, 'Yesoum populaire' or 'Ewondo populaire'. A possibility which must not be disregarded when considering degrees of intercomprehension, is that when the speakers of the various EWONDO–BULU languages meet, probably only the most conservative or least ingenious of them speak the pure form of their own local idiom, the others lapsing almost subconsciously into a bastardized form which submerges the salient local differences and emphasizes the family likenesses, rather as on the West Coast the various forms of regional English have to be standardized into Pidgin if intercomprehension with the African is to be effected.

With these facts in mind, remarks on relationships have been limited almost entirely to quotations of statements by informants, several of which may seem quite contradictory.

---

[1] This is the village name. Yɛbɛkolo was also given by the informant, but this is so misleading that it has not been used here.
[2] Mme Dugast gives 15,562 as the total population for CIDGA and BETSIDGA.
[3] Yaunde, Yaoundé, Jaunde.

YƐZUM (1.31) (Mvëlë)

Locality. (F.C.) Rég. Nyong et Sanaga. S.D. Nanga Eboko. The extreme southwest corner of the Sub-division between 12°–12° 30′ E. and 4° 10′–4° 30′ N.

Population. 8,075 I.E.S.C.

Relationships. The Yezum are said to understand the Yekaba, Bulu, and Ewondo. In spite of the chief's denial of comprehension of other surrounding languages, it is thought that the similarity of AVƏK vocabulary is too great for inter-intelligibility not to exist between these two dialects.

(i) AVƏK (1.32) (Bavek, Bafök, Bafuk); LEPƏK (1.32a) (? MƐDGAD); YAṢƐM (1.32b)

(ii) YADGAFUK' (1.33)

Locality. (F.C.) Rég. Nyong et Sanaga.

(i) S.D. Nanga Eboko. Three small enclaves to the north-east of Nanga Eboko. Enclaves in Rég. Mbam, S.D. Yoko, to the north of Yoko at Lena (50 km. away); to the south-east of Yoko at Mengang (10 km.) and at Medjamboum (20 km.); west-south-west of Yoko at Yassem (100 km.); at Issandja in the Bafia area, 120 km. south of Yoko on the main road.

(ii) S.D. Nanga Eboko. Due west of the chief-lieu on the right bank of the Sanaga. Rég. Mbam, due east of Bafia in the extreme eastern corner of the Sub-division on the road to Yoko. Two small enclaves to the north of Bafia. The Sanaga area is difficult to define owing to long-standing ethnic confusion between the Bavek and Yangafuk.

Population. 5,352[1] I.E.S.C.

Relationships. It is with extreme hesitancy that AVƏK, &c. and YADGAFUK' have been separated, as on paper they appear to be almost identical. Informants from the Nanga Eboko area, however, insisted on making the most of existing linguistic differences and would not admit to intercomprehension. This state of affairs would perhaps be admissible were it not for the following circumstances. After having recorded some AVƏK and YADGAFUK' at Nanga Eboko, an investigation was conducted into the speeches of the Bavek enclaves to the north-west. The dialect of the two enclaves nearest Yoko (LEPƏK) was almost identical with AVƏK—but the Yoko informant insisted that the Bavek of Nanga Eboko spoke YADGAFUK'. When a discrepancy of vocabulary occurred during the LEPƏK–AVƏK comparison and the word recorded in the latter language was suggested to the LEPƏK informant, he immediately said that this word was EWONDO. In view of this it will be realized that information on this district should be treated with the greatest reserve.

Both (i) and (ii) have a particularly strong vocabulary resemblance to GBÏGBÏL (Bobili) and, according to the chief of Issandja, AVƏK and his village speech are identical. All find YAṢƐM more difficult to understand 'although it is still the same language'. There is conflicting evidence on the inter-intelligibility of YAṢƐM and MƐDGAD, the chief of the former saying that his people speak 'Bafok' with those of Mengang and that each understands the other. A 'moniteur' from Mengang, however, states that there is little intercomprehension between his compatriots and the Yassem

---

[1] This figure comprises speakers of all Bavek–Yangafuk dialects.

villagers. The latter have intermarried extensively with the Djanti. Some Djanti words occur in YAṢƐM, the latter being only just recognizable as a version of AVƏK.

GBÏGBÏL (1.34) (Bobili, Bobilis)

Locality. (F.C.) Rég. Lom et Kadei, S.D. Bertoua. The area enclosed by the Rivers Sanaga, Sesse, Long, and Do, to the north-west of Bertoua.

Population. 6,247 *I.E.S.C.*

Relationships. Despite the close vocabulary resemblance, the informant would not admit that he could understand YAƉGAFUK'. Reasonable intercomprehension exists with the Bamvele (who speak BËBËLË[1] (1.35) according to Professor Guthrie), but there is no close affinity to the neighbouring languages POL or MÄKAA.

ÈKÍ[2] (1.36) (Omvang, Mvang, Badjia)

As regards the names given to languages spoken by the Mvang, it is pointless to argue which is the more correct, since the various branches of this tribe no longer speak the same language. Moreover, they have repeatedly been lumped together with other ethnic unities, some closely related and others not, and labelled amongst other things as Badjia. This name is of doubtful linguistic significance in relation to ÈKÍ. The latter was listened to and classified, the former was never encountered and is probably linguistically as well as ethnically an omnibus term for numerous small entities.

In Nanga Eboko S.D. there are two villages inhabited by Mvang (Biwong and Mimbele). Here ÈKÍ is spoken. The total population given by the local administrator is 621.

There are numerous sub-chefferies or clans in the Sub-division which speak the same language, said the ÈKÍ informant. He could give no speech names, however. These clans, &c. are notably Yebanda (1,182), Yengong (350), Yembani and Yetchoa (746). (The figures were given by the Administration.) The two last are on the south-east confines of the Sub-division and probably form the north-west portion of the Omvang area in *C.E.C.*[3]

In S.D. Doumé, said our Nanga Eboko informant, the original language of the Mvang (i.e. the Mvang Makona), already limited to the oldest members of the tribe (1.36a), is fast disappearing owing to intermarriage with the Makaa, whose language is being adopted (1.38a).

In S.D. Akonolinga the Mvang are said by the same informant to have adopted the language of their neighbours, both enclaves (*C.E.C.*) speaking MAKE (1.37).

8. MÄKAA AND EAST CAMEROONS GROUP

This is a most loosely knit and unbalanced conglomeration of languages, spoken by people who for the most part dwell in localities scattered in the depths of virgin rain-forest. MÄKAA is by far the most extensive and its speakers the most numerous.

---

[1] This language was not investigated. Professor Guthrie's researches in this direction have led him to place it very close to EWONDO and BULU.

[2] This was the name given by the chief of one of the two villages claiming to speak 'l'Omvang pur'!

[3] This linguistic group can be extended by the criterion of inter-intelligibility to the Bamvele, Yebekanga, Yessamba, and Yekaba, also more loosely and with an inferior degree of comprehension to YAƉGAFUK', AVƏK, and 'Yesoum populaire'.

Only the northern fringe was investigated, i.e. the Mboans variety of MÄKAA,[1] and also BAAGƏTO (MƐDJIME) and MPIƐMƆ (Bidjuki), but hearsay evidence was obtained for languages which would have been otherwise inaccessible.

MÄKAA (1.38) (Maka)

Locality. (F.C.) S.D.s Bertoua, Doumé, Abong-Mbang, Mbalmayo, Akonolinga, Sangmelima, &c. The area covered is of a straggling irregular shape but the main locality is between 12° 30′–13° 35′ E. by 3° 50′–4° 35′ N. Enclaves occur at 13° 35′ E. by 4° 45′ N. and at 12° 35′ E. by 4° 15′ N. Other scattered enclaves are to be found between 12°–12° 25′ E. and 3° 20′–3° 45′ N. This information is largely taken from I.E.S.C.

Population. 51,633 I.E.S.C.

Relationships. Many widely divergent dialects exist in this language, so much so that our informant had, in conjunction with a few friends, drawn up a very tentative grammar in the hope that it would help the Makaa to attain linguistic (and political?) unity. Its vocabulary relates it to NDJEM (1.39) and the languages above-mentioned.

BAAGƏTO (1.40b) ɓaayəto (N. Bangantu); MƐDJIME (1.40a) mɛɖime[2] (Medzime)

Locality. (F.C.) Rég. Lom et Kadeï. The valley of the River Doumé above its confluence with the Kadeï. Also spoken by the Medjime (whose language it is said really to be) on the right bank of the Doumé, west of the River Mbang.

Population. 1,711 (N. Bangantu)+2,684 (Medjime) I.E.S.C.

Relationships. Totally unrelated linguistically to 'S. Bangantu' near Mouloundou which is a Non-Bantu language. Similarly it bears only a general family likeness to the speech of the Bangando of O.C. It would seem to fall between MÄKAA and MPIƐMƆ as regards its classification. Lexical similarity is noticeable particularly to Guthrie's NDJEM (1.39) vocabulary and also to MÄKAA. It is easily understood, according to our Bidjuki informant, by the Bidjuki, Mpiɛmɔ, Konabemb, and Mpə̃mpɔ̃ (Boumboum, Bombo, Mpombo, Pumpum, &c.). NDJEM, he stated, was the common language of all these tribes, who have been grouped together with several others under the name of Kozime. It is doubtful whether the informant's statement regarding easy intercomprehensibility can be accepted unreservedly in view of the recorded versions of BAAGƏTO and MPIƐMƆ. Sound correspondences are often peculiar though regular, and would not tend to make the two languages mutually intelligible, closely related as they are.

MPIƐMƆ (1.41) (Mbimu)

Locality. (F.C., O.C.) According to our informant, the Mpiɛmɔ and Bidjuki speak the same language, Bidjuki, Biakumbo, Bikum, and Kpabili being clans of the Mpiɛmɔ tribe. The Mpiɛmɔ proper inhabit villages immediately to the north of

---

[1] S.D. Doumé.

[2] Mme Dugast says that the N. Bangantu speak NDJEM. This is only a half-truth, according to our informant, who stated that NDJEM is only used as a lingua franca. The N. Bangantu and Medjime share the same language but call it BAAGƏTO and MƐDJIME respectively.

Yokadouma on the road leading to Batouri. The Bidjuki live in Rég. Lom et Kadeï (S.D. Yokadouma) and in Rég. Haute Sangha (D. Nola). Their villages line the track leading from Yokadouma over the border to Nola.

Population. Mpiɛmɔ proper 3,977 *I.E.S.C.*
Bidjuki 3,419 *I.E.S.C.*[1]

No figures are available for the remainder of the tribe.

Relationships. In the absence of any linguistic evidence from the other clans, the statement of the Bidjuki informant regarding the similarity of all MPIƐMƆ speeches must be accepted. The same informant, however, said that MPIƐMƆ was easily understood by the speakers of KONABEMB (1.43) (1.43a), MPÕMPÕ (1.42), and MƐDJIME, a fact which was doubted by one MƐDJIME informant. Vocabulary relationships with MÄKAA, MƐDJIME, and BƐKWIL[2] were especially strong, while POL and MPIƐMƆ offered some interesting comparisons.

9. KAKƆ AND POL

In eastern F.C. and western O.C., on the northern fringe of the forest belt and in enclaves in the savannah country, are to be found speakers of Sub-Bantu languages which, while showing at times marked affinities to the MÄKAA-NDJEM complex, are sufficiently far removed from normal Bantu grammatical procedure to warrant their inclusion in a separate group. The Survey examined KAKƆ and POL in this group, to which, on the authority of Professor Guthrie, may be added the Sub-Bantu languages of KWAKUM (1.48) and PƆMƆ (1.47).

KAKƆ (1.45) (Kaka)

Locality. (F.C., O.C.) Rég. Lom et Kadeï, S.D. Batouri; Rég. Haute Sangha, D. Berbérati; approximately between 13° 40'–15° 30' E. and 4°–4° 35' N.[3]

Population. 36,932 *I.E.S.C.*

Relationships. Between the KAKƆ of F.C. and O.C. there are merely dialectal differences. The vocabulary is for the most part Bantu with special similarities to the MÄKAA-NDJEM complex. Several GBAYA loan words have been identified in KAKƆ.

POL (1.46) **poli** (Pul)

Locality. (F.C.) (i) S.D. Bertoua. To the extreme north of the Bertoua–Deng Deng track in the villages of Ona, Mansa, and Mambaya (chef-lieu).[4] (ii) S.D. Doumé, the

---

[1] This may or may not include the O.C. Bidjuki, who are, says Mme Dugast, more numerous than those of F.C.

[2] From Professor Guthrie's material.

[3] Mme Dugast speaks of Kakɔ enclaves amongst the Gbaya of Bertoua, to the number of 1,824, but inquiries yielded no information on this subject. This figure is not included in the total population given above. The five Kako villages which she situates south-west of Ngaoundéré around 7° N. by 13° E. no longer speak KAKƆ owing to intermarriage with the neighbouring Mbum. The vocabulary for this area given by Strümpel in 'Wörterverzeichnis der Heidensprachen Adamauas', *Zeitschrift für Ethnologie*, xlii, Berlin, 1910, is almost identical with our KAKƆ material recorded at Batouri.

[4] This information can be considered as of the utmost reliability. It came from the chief of the area. All the other villages in the 'Pol' canton speak different languages. Kano, Mbombi, Yambing, Viali, and

right bank of the Doumé to the east of Doumé, in the villages of Petit Pol and Grand Pol. (iii) S.D. Batouri, 7 miles south of Batouri at the village of Kombo.

Population. 2,200 *I.E.S.C.* This figure appears to include AZƆM speakers.

Relationships. The POL of Doumé and of Deng Deng have merely dialectal differences. Batouri POL was not the subject of an inquiry and no information on this speech is available. The Deng Deng Pol do not understand BƐTHƐN (βɛthɛn) (4.4) at all, and their comprehension of AZƆM (4.3) is very imperfect. Professor Guthrie has noted a striking similarity between Doumé POL and PƆMƆ (1.47), a language he investigated on the River Sangha between Bayanga and Ouesso. Further less striking comparisons can be made with members of the MÄKAA–NDJEM group. The vocabulary is of Bantu origin.

10. THE PANDE–MBOMOTABA GROUP (O.C., M.C.)

It was found impossible to obtain conclusive evidence regarding the languages of this group owing to (i) the very nature of this sparsely populated, inaccessible, and largely unknown forest region, (ii) the confusion of names of speeches and localities which exists not only amongst Europeans but also in the minds of neighbouring Africans. It seems certain that linguistically 'Pande' has both a general and a limited application. In its general sense it is synonymous with NDJƐLI (1.49) (Ndzali, Lindjeli) and covers all those languages which are felt to be 'similar', i.e. ŊGONDI (1.49b), PANDE proper (1.49a), BOGƆŊGƆ (1.49c), and perhaps others which have up to the present been miscalled PANDE, &c.

Professor Guthrie associates these in the main group with MBOMOTABA and BOŊGILI (both spoken farther south), the former being a collection of dialects which he states are not inter-intelligible though all claim the title of MBOMOTABA. The only languages pertaining to this group which were examined by us were PANDE proper (of Bania) and ŊGONDI (of Ngoundi and Ndélé).

ŊGONDI (1.49b) (Ŋgundi, Pande)

Professor Guthrie recorded some ŊGONDI at Nola, which forms the most northerly point of a long belt of ŊGONDI speakers stretching down the River Sangha, as far as Bayanga. He states that this is a Sub-Bantu language, closely related to PANDE.

Were it not for this evidence the Survey would have grave doubts of the Bantu nature of ŊGONDI. The material which it took down from a self-styled Ŋgondi— the only available informant—proved to be a mixture of GBAYA, GBOFI, ALI, PANDE, and ŊGBAKA MABO with a great preponderance of non-Bantu vocabulary. The informant admitted that his mother was of Gbofi stock, which may in part account for the extraordinary material he produced. He stated that this language was spoken only at the villages of Ngoundi and Ndélé on the River Bodengué, D. Boda, Rég. de la Lobaye. Its real name according to him was IŊGONDI (3.11), but it was

Dondi speak AZƆM (which was not investigated, no informant being available) (4.3). This may be a dialect of KWAKUM (1.48) since some maps show in this area an enclave of KWAKUM for which we have been unable to account. The speech of Nolam Bethen is said to be BƐTHƐN (4.4), a transitional language between AZƆM and MÄKAA which is spoken in the remaining villages of the canton: Yoko–Betougou and Koundi.

often called 'Pande' by neighbours. The population of this area, and in fact the total figure for all ŊGONDI speakers, would be most difficult to establish as the Ŋgondi are always confused physically and otherwise with the Pande, and furthermore at least two distinct languages bearing the name ŊGONDI are in existence, i.e. that of D. Boda, and the Sub-Bantu one of Nola. A third enclave was hinted at in M.C., Department de Likouala, D. Dongou in part of Ancien Bera Njoko on the River Ibengué. In any case it is doubtful whether the total figure of speakers of all varieties of ŊGONDI will exceed 3,000.

The wildest statements were made concerning intercomprehensibility. Two informants (Pande and Bakota) said that the Ŋgondi understand the Mondjembo very easily. Our material offers no support to this statement. Our ŊGONDI informant said that his people could all speak PANDE but that 'a Pande would take three days to learn ŊGONDI'. Probably the strangest piece of evidence came from a Pande who said that the Ŋgondi spoke 'like the Mangala and the Mondjembo' (!) These statements may be accepted as reasonably accurate, however, if one allows that the informants were thinking of two types of ŊGONDI at one and the same time.

PANDE (1.49a) (i)ɸande (Ŋgundi)

Locality. Numerous small enclaves. Rég. Haute Sangha, D. Berbérati at Bania on the Mambéré; also around Nola; also in several villages on the Bania–Nola road.[1] Rég. Lobaye, D. Boda, round Bambio and Boungué on the Mbaéré; also at Ndio on the Bodengué.

(M.C.) D. Dongou at Ancien Bera Njoko on the Ibengué, (these are called Koŋgwala), also at Makaou on the Motaba (called Ikɛŋga by some tribes).

Population. 1,000.[2]

Relationships. The version recorded agrees well with Johnston's PANDE vocabulary. The chief at Bania stated that his people speak rather like those of Enyellé (whence they claim to originate). The speeches of Bambio and Bania were compared and found to be virtually identical. At Bera Njoko—a cosmopolitan centre—the Pande 'speak much more slowly' said our Bambio informant. To judge by the few examples the latter gave us, the language of Bera Njoko may be less indeterminate than the PANDE of Bambio and Bania, i.e. the class system seems less fragmentary. Related by vocabulary content to all languages of the main group.

11. THE ŊGANDO–KOTA GROUP

ŊGANDO (1.50a) (d'i)ŋgando (Bangandou, Bagandou)⎫
KOTA   (1.50b) (d'i)kota   (Bakota)   ⎬ (Bodzanga)
                                                     ⎭

Locality. (O.C.) Rég. de la Lobaye, D. Mbaïki, on the right bank of the Lobaye between 17° 40′–18° (ŊGANDO), and 17° 30′–17° 40′ (KOTA).

---

[1] It would seem that in this instance the informant was using PANDE in its general sense. Professor Guthrie has identified the Bania–Nola road enclave as BOGƆŊGƆ (1.49c). Bruel calls this Bongili in his *L'Afrique Équatoriale Française*, Paris, 1918. Guthrie's material for this area has several non-Bantu loan words which appear to come from the neighbouring Banda-Yangere.

[2] From the *Rapport Politique*, Rég. de la Lobaye, 1949. The figure refers only to Pande in D. Boda. No other figures were obtainable.

Population. 2,893.[1]

Relationships. These are two dialects which are almost identical. Bodzanga is a family name common to the two groups. This is the last true Bantu linguistic outpost in this area. The language is said by informants to be closely related to those of the Dongou locality (M.C.) The vocabulary relates it to BOBAŊGI and LƆI. The other tribes of similar name in F.C. and M.C., i.e. north and south Bangantu and Bakota (Shake—Guthrie's B. 25) should not be confused with the Bodzanga. Again Guthrie's C. 63 (ŊGANDO) in the Belgian Congo does not appear to be particularly closely related. The Bakota claim to understand MBATI without learning it, but state that the converse is not true.

MBATI (1.51) (Isongo, Lissongo)

Locality. (O.C.) Rég. Lobaye, Ds. Mbaïki and Boda. The left bank of the Lobaye between 17° 25' and 18° 10' E. extending north to as far as 4° 10' N. in one place.

Population. 15,208 D. Mbaïki, 241 D. Boda.[2]

Relationships. Not particularly closely related to any language in the immediate vicinity, although the vocabulary resemblance to BOBAŊGI, LƆI, and MAŊGALA is at times striking. Fifty per cent. of our ŊGANDO material resembles MBATI, which also contains words from GBAYA (ALI) and vehicular SAŊGO. Tradition has it that the Isongo (or Mbati) came from the Belgian Congo as invaders less than a century ago and that there exists over the Oubangui a language which they still understand. A ŊGBAKA informant said that this would be ŊGƆMBE. Similarities exist indeed—this also applies to POTO—but they are not sufficiently striking to substantiate this theory. MBATI appears to be an ancestral name. Slight dialectal variants of the language are centred round the important villages of Bonaka, Bolemba, Zanga, and the chef-lieu Ndéa.

[1] Bodzanga. Extracted from *Rapport Politique*, Rég. Lobaye, 1949, Mbaïki.
[2] *Rapport Politique.*

Section B

BANTOID LANGUAGES

No claim is made that this section deals exhaustively with all languages falling into this category. It is hoped, however, that the more characteristic varieties of Bantoid spoken in the area covered by the western team have been dealt with.

BANDƐM (2.1)

Locality. (F.C.) Between 10°–10° 25′ E. and 4° 30′–4° 50′ N. on the Upper Wouri, north-east of Yabassi.

Population. 7,713 I.E.S.C.

Relationships. The vocabulary has unmistakable Bantu traits, although it is impossible to attach this language to any particular group in the vicinity. The Bandem say they are descended from the Bamileke.

The Survey did not encounter BANDƐM but Professor Guthrie kindly put some material at its disposal and it is on this evidence that these remarks are based.

Mme Dugast mentions the wide difference between various forms of BANDƐM, and therefore in the absence of personal experience in the area no further comment will be made on this one sample of the language.

NYAƉG (2.2) (kɛ)**nyaŋg** (Banyangi)[1]

Locality. (Br.C.) D. Mamfe. From the right bank of the Cross River north-west of Mamfe, to the Bambuto mountains on the eastern boundary of Cameroons.

Population. 14,269 Talbot[2]; about 10,000 Ittmann.[3]

Relationships. Most uncertain. Apart from a very close bond with KITW̊II it is difficult to attach this language to any group. Its vocabulary has an undoubtedly extensive Bantu content. Some correspondences with Guthrie's starred forms of Common Bantu are regular, but in the light of inadequate material it must be said that far more are not. Ittmann[3] has written a grammar and word-list of this speech in the introduction to which he says that in the western part of the area the language tends to resemble that of the coast, but that east and west NYAƉG are not very different from each other. There is considerable doubt as to the origin of several genders, while in many points of grammar there is evidence of un-Bantu behaviour. It is for these reasons that NYAƉG and KITW̊II have been classified as Bantoid.

[1] N.B. not 'ANYANG' which, from a comparison of ethnic maps, would seem to include the area in which TAKAMANDA, MENKA, and AṢUMBO are spoken. Johnston confuses Banyangi with BAMUM; he says that the former appears to be a variant of the latter. This confusion probably dates from the period of German influence. They constantly referred to the Bamum as Banyangi, and Bufe says that the latter speech is interwoven with that of the Grassfield natives, a statement which would be hard to prove if the language at issue were NYAƉG. There is little difference between our NYAƉG and Johnston's MANYAƉ (234) and KOƉGWAN (234*a*).
[2] Talbot's Banyangi area does not entirely correspond with later maps.
[3] *Z.f.E.S.* xxvi, pp. 2–35, 97–133, 174–202.

KITWII (2.3) (kítwîî (Manyɛmɛn, N. Balong)[1]

Locality. (Br.C.) D. Kumba. The north-east slopes of the Rumpi mountains extending beyond the Kumba–Mamfe road.

Population. Not more than 5,000 (a personal estimate based on the size of the N. Balong tribal area as compared with those inhabited by tribes whose numbers are known).

Relationships. This language is so closely and regularly related to NYAŊG that it is not proposed to give any linguistic details. Differences from NYAŊG are merely dialectal. The S. Balong, although originating from the Manyɛmɛn area, no longer speak the same language as their northern cousins. Our informant stated, however, that some of the very old men of the S. Balong still understood him. This we found hard to believe, unless the language of the 'old country' has been artificially preserved in the south, e.g. for the purposes of ritual.

TAKAMANDA (2.4)

MEDKA (2.5)

AṢUMBO (2.6)

AMASI (2.7)

These languages, spoken in the extreme west of Mamfe and Bamenda divisions, and probably in Nigeria too, were marked by Fr. Bruens on a map which he showed to Professor Guthrie at the School of Oriental and African Studies. During the Survey they were not investigated owing to the non-availability of informants within a reasonable radius of our main points of operation. No second-hand information on these languages was obtained in the field, but as they are surrounded by Bantoid languages, e.g. the ŊKƆM group, KEAQƏ, NYAŊG, and have TIV to the north-west, it is not improbable that they may have some of the characteristics already observed in their neighbours.

KIŊKWA (2.8) (? Mangen Konkwa)

Locality. (Br.C.) D. Mamfe. To the east of the Kumba–Mamfe road, roughly in the triangle which it forms with the divisional limit and 9° 30' E.

Population. Talbot has no figures for this area, although he has marked 'Mangen Konkwa' where we have Kiŋkwa. At the most there can be only a few villages speaking this language.

Relationships. Probably Talbot's Mangen Konkwa and our KIŊKWA are one and the same in view of an affinity in our material (almost entirely recorded by M. Jacquot) with languages of the MBO group—which are sometimes known as Ŋgɛn. At the same time it has many aspects reminiscent of ŊWƐ (Bangwa), which in its turn is part of the Dschang complex of Bamileke languages and dialects. Similarly it resembles

[1] Manyɛmɛn, according to our informant, is a general geographical locality in this area. N. Balong is, of course, an administrative label which at the same time attaches them to and differentiates them from the S. Balong.

in some respects NYAŊG and KEAQƏ. By the very number of its various relationships the classification of KIŊKWA is rendered difficult, and for this reason it is placed on its own as a Bantoid language.

TIKAR (2.9) (Ndob, Tumu[1])

Locality. (F.C., Br.C.) The area to the north of the River Mvi, stretching into the extreme north-east corner of Br.C. and along the course of the upper Mbam and the Kim.

Population. In French territory 10,500 *I.E.S.C.*; 12,500 *C.E.C.*[2]

Relationships. The language examined was the TIKAR of Ngambé. The River Mbam divides TIKAR into two main dialects which are not readily inter-intelligible. The vocabulary has a definite Bantu content without showing regular correspondences. The Non-Bantu words seem not to have a striking affinity with any neighbouring language, and the speech as a whole appears to be unclassifiable beyond the general heading of Bantoid.

KEAQƏ (2.10) (2.11) (2.12) (Keaka, Kejaka)

Locality. (Br.C., N.) The south-west corner of D. Mamfe extending over the Rivers Cross and Akpa far into Nigeria.

Although KEAQƏ is loosely used by the people of this area for their language, they say that this is a NYAŊG word meaning 'the salt-panners'—a reference to their chief article of trade in the past. As most government clerks under both German and British administrations appear to have been Banyaŋg, this explanation may be correct.

There are three main dialects of this language: (i) ƐDJAGAM (2.10), ɛdʒaɡam, (ii) ƐKƆI (ƐKWƐ) (2.11), (iii) ƆBAŊG (2.12). They are located in the KEAQƏ area as follows: (i) North-east and west; (ii) the extreme west extending into the Oban district of Nigeria over the Cross River; (iii) the south of the area. It is impossible to break down Talbot's figures with any degree of accuracy. As far as can be ascertained the total KEAQƏ speakers number about 12,000—(i) 7,500, (ii) 2,000, (iii) 2,500. This does not take into account ƐKWƐ in Nigeria.[3]

Relationships. Problematic. The dialects are intercomprehensible in Br.C. but there are probably violent divergences in the ƐKWƐ of Nigeria. Slight vocabulary relationships have been noted with all the surrounding Bantoid languages, including TIV. Although the vocabulary has much in common with Bantu, there are no regular correspondences. Several EFIK loan words were recorded. Grammatically the class system is unrelatable in shape and function to those of true Bantu languages (cf. NYAŊG).

[1] Johnston's 237 and 237a respectively. These so closely resemble our material that they must be dialects of TIKAR.

[2] Dr. Kaberry gives 10,500 for the Tikar population in French Cameroons and 175,000 in the Bamenda Province of British Cameroons. Unfortunately these figures are linguistically unacceptable owing to the striking difference between the languages spoken in French and British territory by 'Tikar' populations (see 'Land tenure among the Nsaw of the British Cameroons', *Africa*, xx, No. 4, pp. 307–23, October, 1950).

[3] Total Ekoi figures are given as about 90,000 by Dr. Abraham in his book *The Tiv People* (2nd edition), Crown Agents, 1940. This, however, would appear to include all the KEAQƏ and probably NYAŊG.

KƆRƆP (2.13) (Ododop)

Locality. (Br.C., N.) The western confines of Br.C. along the banks of the River Akpa and in the south-east part of the Oban hills.

Population. ?

Relationship. No linguistic material was recorded. Johnston has a vocabulary (No. 244) which has many points of similarity with surrounding Bantoid languages as recorded by the Survey, with particularly strong resemblances to OKII. Grammatically too it is related to the neighbouring Bantoid type speeches. Johnston, who lists twenty prefixes and one suffix adds: 'In any case the assignments to Bantu classes are arbitrary and not always convincing.'

2. THE ŊKƆM GROUP (2.14 to 2.25)

This name has been bestowed on the widely differing languages spoken over the larger part of Bamenda Division and the north of Mamfe Division[1] because it is felt that these form a linguistic entity having many of the features of ŊKƆM as described by Fr. Bruens.[2] At times the relationship is very obscure, but after careful examination of a great deal of confusing material, languages which at first were thought to be distinct have begun to show many common characteristics[3]—which are often, be it admitted, more easy to savour than to define. ŊKƆM has been chosen as a label since it is a language which has received more attention than the others, and has been more publicized, in a manner of speaking. Apart from this there has been little linguistic work attempted or even projected within this group.

In the early days of the Survey local tradition was followed by dividing the area into the Widekum group, the Tikar group, and the Katsina group; later it was found that much of this subdivision was artificial from a linguistic viewpoint as it is based on ethnic and historical data and theories. It was impossible to record examples of all these languages; it was even too arduous a task to ascertain their names, number, and location. An attempt was made to this end by means of the official government interpreter, but he could only give general statements as to the ability of people from certain areas to understand those of adjoining districts. This information is submitted only where first-hand material was not obtainable, and follows the account of this group.

It is not the purpose of this report to enter into ethnic details, but to clarify a most obscure linguistic situation; it would be useful, however, to give a very brief account of the demographic context. The entire area covered by this group, and indeed the territory extending southwards into Kumba Division and south-eastwards into F.C., has been the scene of repeated migrations, invasions, scissions, and secessions in which have taken part tribes of various speeches. Nothing is known for certain of the original inhabitants, and very little of subsequent human cross-currents. In only

---

[1] Dr. Abraham (*The Tiv People*) gives 139,000 as the population of the Bafumbun–Bansaw group which covers most of the area included in my Dkom group apart from OKII. This figure seems out of proportion with the total for Bamenda Province (301,000).

[2] 'The structure of Nkom and its Relations to Bantu and Sudanic', *Anthropos*, xxxvii–xl, pp. 826–66, 1942–5.

[3] It is not inconceivable that a relationship exists between these languages and TIV.

three villages do the inhabitants claim to be autochthonous; i.e. Bebe Jatto and Bebe Ketti (on Mount Kinka in the north-east of Misaji tribal area), and Lu (near Ndu, Nsungli area). Linguistically, however, there is little evidence in support of their claim. In comparatively recent times incursions have been made by Bantu and non-Bantu peoples and by mixtures of both. In such circumstances it is misleading to mention the names of individual tribes, since constant migrations may well have changed their original language too. An example of such change of language is to be found among the 'Tikar migration' tribes who cover the eastern part of the ŊKƆM group. Linguistically it is impossible to relate these to modern TIKAR, except in a vague generic sense. Similarly the language spoken at Bali Town near Bamenda has no point of contact with that in use in the former tribal habitat near the French border, where the language brought from Chamba country still survives despite a long sojourn on the fringe of the Tikar area. Yet the Bali Town language has little in common with the surrounding ŊKƆM type speeches.

The area of comprehension of any language of the group is limited to a very few villages, PIDGIN being used as the vehicular language.

ŊKƆM (2.14) (Bikom)

Locality. (Br.C.) Bamenda Province, centrally situated around Laakom, the chef-lieu.

Population. 15,492 (administrative figures quoted by Bruens, p. 827).

Relationships. No material was taken down. Bruens says that it is related to the speeches of the Nsungli tribal area[1] and our LAMSƆ' informant stated that his language was 'similar' to that of Babanki and Bikom.

IYIRIKUM (2.15) (Tiwirkum, Widikum)

Locality. (Br.C.) D. Mamfe. East of Mamfe on the Bamenda road, bounded in the north by the border of the administrative division.

Population. ?

Relationships. There is considerable linguistic evidence for the ethnic theory that the Mogamo farther north originated from Widikum.

ŊGAMAMBO[2] (2.16a) or MƎGAMO (2.16) (Mitaa)

Locality. (Br.C.) The south-west of Bamenda Division in the villages of Bafawchu, Bafawkom, and Babo II in South Ngemba tribal area; also in the Mogamo tribal area and the village of Babossa near Bali Town.

Population. 4,326 T.P. These figures were given by Miss M. A. Bryan and probably do not refer exactly to the localities defined.

Relationships. Related to IYIRIKUM, also MƐTA (2.17) or MENEMO (20,291 Talbot, 2,892 T.P.), NGI[3] (2.18) (7,367 Talbot), NGEMBA[3] (2.19a and b) (5,158 T.P.), and to ŊGWƆ (2.20) which is found in some parts of the Ngono area. It should be

[1] He further states that the village speech of MME closely resembles it.
[2] Strictly speaking this is the name used in the first three villages mentioned as it was there that our investigation was made.
[3] In the absence of the real language name, the tribal area name is given.

noted that several of these names cover territory in which unrelated languages may be spoken. Between the two Ngemba areas it appears that there is considerable dialectal difference, the northern version and BAFUT (2.21) (6,300 T.P.) being mutually intelligible. MENEMO is said not to be understood by the people of Bafut. In the minute tribal area of Ngono (1,463 Talbot) it was stated that six interpreters were used in the local court.

OSO[1] (2.22a) or FUŊGƆM (2.22)

Locality. (Br.C.) Bamenda Province, in the Fungom tribal area (south of the River Katsina) at Fungom, Jua, Esu, Kumfulu, We, Ketehumbuk, Zongunvon, Melang, Iwa, and Tukisson; also at Wum in the Aghem tribal area. Farther east in Fungom tribal area a version of this language is used as a lingua franca.

Population. ?

Relationships. The villages mentioned each speak intercomprehensible dialectal variants of the language investigated (OSO).

LAMSƆ' (2.23) (Banso, Bansaw, Lamnso)

Locality. (Br.C.) The east of Bamenda Division in the Kumbo area.

Population. Talbot's figure of 22,000 is suspect as it includes many other tribal areas.[2]

Relationships. According to some informants there are villages in the Ndop and Mbaw tribal areas which speak similar languages to LAMSƆ' as do Babanki and Bikom. There are some points of similarity with TIV.

OKII (2.24) (Boki)

Locality. (Br.C., N.) D. Mamfe. On the left bank of the Cross River, north-west of Mamfe, extending beyond the frontier into Nigeria. Johnston says that the northern dialects, DAMA, GAYI, and YAKORO[3] extend its range to the verge of Tiv territory.

Population. Talbot's figure of 962 appears to be hopelessly small.[4]

Relationships. KEAQƏ, TIV, and Johnston's NDE (Atam, &c.), BORITSU, and KƆRƆP. Also Meek's BITARE, ABÔ (*not* BAŊKON), and BATU. In most cases the vocabulary constitutes the chief point of resemblance, although prefix shapes in KƆRƆP correspond fairly well. OKII is probably on the fringe of two linguistic areas.

GENERAL INFORMATION (OBTAINED AT SECOND-HAND) ON NATIVE AUTHORITY AREAS IN BAMENDA DIVISION

No material was recorded for any of these areas other than as previously stated, consequently most statements made in this section should be treated with considerable reserve as they have not been checked against linguistic evidence.

---

[1] This is the name of the language spoken at Esu.
[2] Dr. Kaberry ('Land Tenure . . .') gives 32,000 but this is based presumably on ethnic rather than linguistic considerations.
[3] These are the names as given by Johnston.
[4] Dr. Abraham (*The Tiv People*) gives about 90,000 which includes the Boki in Nigeria.

BANTOID LANGUAGES

BIBA-BEFANG[1]

Spoken in a narrow belt north-west of Bamenda. It stretches south-west from the Menchem River near Modelle almost to the Mamfe administrative border.

Population. ?

Relationships. The people of this area are akin to the Widekum group, but their language is unrelated to MƆGAMO and surrounding idioms (government interpreter). Another informant, however, said that the Biba-Befang understand the Aghem.

ESIMBI[1]

North-west of Bamenda on the Nigerian border.

Population. 1,040 T.P.

Relationships. Said by the government interpreter to be a distinct language which is the same throughout the native authority area. Another informant states that they understand the Aghem but that they are not understood by people of the MƆGAMO complex.

FUNGOM[1] (2.22)

The north-west corner of the Division on both banks of the Katsina River.

Population. ?

Relationships. North of the Katsina, where the inhabitants are said to be of Jukun origin, the language used is incomprehensible to those living south of the river. JUKUN is used in the north as the vehicular language. Villages in the centre and east of the area would appear to have widely differing speech forms, the means of intercourse being a lingua franca form of the languages used in the western villages and at Wum in Aghem Territory.

BUM[1]

Centred round Laabum, north-north-east of Bamenda and 40 miles away, extending north for about 20 miles.

Population. ?

Relationships. Said by the government interpreter to be related to DKƆM. He states that the language of the chef-lieu (Laabum) is used as the means of intercourse throughout the N.A. area, as many of the villages have languages which are not mutually intelligible.

MISAJE[1] (2.25)

North-east of Bamenda about 50 miles away in a direct line, stretching north in a narrow belt for about 25 miles.

Population. About 4,000 (estimate).[2]

[1] The names are the administrative ones for the N.A. areas as marked on the Bamenda Division map of 1949. This map was copied from Nigerian Survey Records Map XVIII/440 and XVIII/480.
[2] Information obtained from Mr. Boyce, an Administrative officer on leave from this area.

Relationships. In the south localization is not prominent; the villages in the north-west of Banso authority share the language of southern Misaje. The settlements of Ekwe, Dumbo, and Biusa (pron. Bisa) on the projected new road to N. Cameroons constitute a linguistic unit which differs from the speech of the southern area (4.2). The languages of Bebe Jatto and of Bebe Ketti (4.1) are said to resemble each other very closely but to be different from that of N. Misaje.

NSUNGLI[1] (Nsugni)

North-east of Bamenda about 60 miles away.

Population. 15,000 (estimate).[2]

Relationships. Notes on this area, chiefly of ethnological importance, by Dr. M. D. W. Jeffreys and Dr. Phyllis Kaberry are to be found in *Africa* of January 1952.[3] The contents are far too complicated to summarize here, and give some idea of the extent and intricacy of the problems in this part of the world. The name *NSUNGLI* is said to be a nickname meaning 'the chatterers'. It is applied to the speakers of numerous village languages and dialects. According to Dr. Jeffreys, WIYA (or Ndu), WAR (Wa or Mbwat), and TAD are three distinct groups included under this cognomen. In the article quoted reference is made to the relationship between the inhabitants of Nsungli Territory and the Bansɔ, Bamum, and Tikar, a topic which in itself might well form the subject of a prolonged inquiry. Mr. Boyce divides Nsungli speeches roughly as follows: TAD[4] at Tala, Ngarum, Binka, and the new village of Tang Nunken; WIYA (the most important economically) at the chef-lieu of Ndu and at Konchep, Ngulu, and Lu; WAR (very scattered but numerically the stronger) at Mbwat, Kowngi, Nkambe, Njap, Binshua, Wat, Ntumbaw, and Nsop. Although Dr. Jeffreys states that these are three distinct groups, apparently they are quite able to converse together—perhaps in a kind of 'Union version' of the three speeches. A further curious factor in view of this alleged distinctness of languages is that all the Nsungli, regardless of their sub-grouping, are said to be able to understand their neighbours quite easily. The people of Ndu have close ethnic relationships with those of Ntem (Mbaw native authority) and Rom (Mbem native authority), and the War (of Mbwat) claim that some of their number have emigrated to the Kom area. As remarked under *NFUMTE*, some measure of intercomprehension exists between them and the Nsungli of all groups.

The government interpreter's information here seems to be at variance with the remarks of other observers. He stated that the same language was spoken throughout that area and was unrelated to its neighbours.

NFUMTE[5]

The extreme east of the Division.

Population. ?

---

[1] The names are administrative and refer to the N.A. Areas.
[2] Information obtained from Mr. Boyce, an Administrative Officer on leave from this village.
[3] 'Nsaw History and Social Categories', *Africa*, xxii, No. 1, pp. 71–75.
[4] This appellation gives rise to much absorbing but fruitless conjecture in an area where so many language and place names are of the pattern: alveolar consonant+vowel+velar nasal.
[5] Native authority or tribal name.

Relationships. To the north of the area the village of Aderi speaks NDALE. It should be noted that Ntere, marked on the administrative map of the Division as being just inside the Nfumte northern border, was moved over the boundary to its parent tribe some considerable time ago as its inhabitants were Mambila. The remaining territory is occupied by people claiming Tikar descent. They speak one language together; this may be a lingua franca. Those who live towards Nsungli N.A. 'hear' (i.e. understand) but cannot speak the languages used there.

MBEM[1]

The eastern corner of the Division.

Population. ?

Relationships. In the extreme north-east of the area are two villages, Saam and Ntem, where MAMBILA is spoken. In the centre Ntong, Ngung, Fam Si, Kwak, and Bom share the same speech which may be closely related to that used in the south at Mvwe, Gom, Nkot, Rom, Mbem, Nwa, and Yang where the inhabitants claim to be of Tikar stock. The Mbem are said to 'hear' the language of the Nfumte but to be unable to speak it.

MBAW[1]

The extreme eastern corner of the Division.

Population. ?

Relationships. Each village has a different language according to the interpreter. These do not resemble other Br.C. languages. FULANI is used as the medium of intercourse. Mambila influence is said to be noticeable in the north and Tikar in the south. Other information points to a common language which may be the TIKAR now spoken in F.C.

NDOP[1]

The south-east part of the Division.

Population. 17,963.[2]

Relationships. To the south-west, NDAGAM (Bali Kumbat) and 'Babanki' are spoken (government interpreter). The remaining part is a mass of scarcely mutually intelligible dialects with DGAAKA (Bali of Bali Town) and BAMUM used as vehicular languages in the centre and south-west respectively.

BAFUT[1] (2.21)

North of Bamenda around Bafut, stretching north-west along the Menchem.

Population. 6,300 T.P.

Relationships. The speech of N. Ngemba and *BAFUT* are said to be mutually intelligible.

In conclusion it cannot be too emphatically stated that in this area accurate population figures on a linguistic basis are not only unavailable but also unobtainable. Where

---

[1] Native authority or tribal name.
[2] Given by Talbot for 'Melamba' which on his map approximates to the Ndop N.A. area.

localization is so prevalent and linguistic 'shading-off' so baffling, it is doubtful whether even the number and exact location of *languages* may be satisfactorily determined without a very lengthy survey of the minutiae of regions which are difficult of access.

The total population figures[1] for the four divisions visited are: Bamenda 301,000, Mamfe 73,400, Kumba 65,000, and Victoria 47,600.

3. THE BAMILEKE GROUP (2.27)

No commonly accepted native name for this group was discovered. The name BAMILEKE is loosely used by the speakers themselves, although, as R. P. Stoll has remarked, it is 'un monstre de corruption'. The PIDGIN term 'Grafil' (Grassfield) is also employed for the languages and populations which occur both sides of the international border in this part of Africa, being used for languages of the ŊKƆM type too.

Locality. (F.C., Br.C.) The whole of the mountainous area of western F.C. comprised in the Bamileke administrative region, apart from a small patch in the extreme south-east (DIBUM), and one to the west of S.D. Dschang (MBO). It is hard to say how far over the Br.C. border it extends. ŊWƐ (Bangwa) definitely forms part of this group, but other frontier languages present difficulties regarding delimitation,[2] e.g. MBO and ŊKƆM.

Population. (F.C.) Total for Rég. Bamiléke 425,900[3] plus 40–50,000 'emigrés'[4] to other parts of F.C. (Br.C.) 9,222 Talbot (for Bangwa, or 'Bamileke').

The French figures can be further analysed:

S.D. Dschang	158,000	'Chefferies' of S.D. Bafoussam[5]	
„ Bafoussam	133,700	Bandjoun	27,000
„ Bafang	67,500	Bamougoum	14,000
„ Bangangté	66,700	Baham	13,000
	425,900	Bamendjou	11,000
		Baleng	9,000
		Batié	8,000
		Bayangam	8,000
		Bangou	8,000
		Bafoussam	7,000
		Baméka	6,000

In view of the lack of material in Br.C. where 'shading-off' may occur, we are unable to say whether the figure quoted from Talbot may be considered to be sufficiently high.

---

[1] From the United Nations Report on Mandated Territories, 1948.

[2] Apart from the fundamental problem of detecting linguistic systems and classifying by them in an area where indeterminacy is the rule, other difficulties which presented themselves throughout the Grassfields were: (*a*) the comparative inaccessibility of many districts in the given time, (*b*) the fragmentary documentation of this field in the past, (*c*) the gradual shading-off and admixture of languages and dialects.

[3] From *Memento, Cameroun 1949.* Service de Press et d'Information du Cameroun, Yaoundé.

[4] Estimate based on figures in *I.E.S.C.*

[5] Information from Subdivision administrative office Bafoussam. No attempt should be made to reconcile these figures with the totals as they are from different sources. The names are administrative ones.

BANTOID LANGUAGES 49

      Batoufam 4,000
      Bahouan 3,000
      Bandenkop 3,000
      Bangam 2,000
      Bapi 1,000
      Bandréfam 1,000
      Bandeng 700
      Fongou. No figures available as this is a new colony in the act of being set up on the left bank of the Noun. It is composed of representatives of all chefferies.

Relationships. This group is an easily recognizable Bantoid linguistic entity having little in common with its neighbours except where 'shading-off' occurs. BAMILEKE languages are regarded by Africans and Europeans alike as being virtually 'unlearnable' without spending a lifetime in the locality. It is impossible to estimate accurately the number of variants there are in the group even on an intercomprehension basis. Seldom do two informants agree on the inter-intelligibility of languages spoken a few miles away from their own village. Often distinctly contradictory statements are made as to the means of intercourse at market, one informant naming a local speech and another insisting that the omnipresent PIDGIN is used. It is a fact that Bamileke from villages often only two or three miles apart frequently prefer PIDGIN to BAMILEKE in their dealings with each other. It can safely be said that adjoining village speeches generally display considerable dialectal difference. A tentative grouping has been made, however, with the help of the interpreter of S.D. Bafoussam and other informants, of dialects which present no serious difficulties of intercomprehension. The names given are not applicable throughout the sub-groups. As each village boasts its own language or dialect and names it after the locality, we have generally taken the administrative name[1] of the best-known locality as the sub-group linguistic reference. When known, the language names as recorded by the Survey follow. Although BAMUM and ŊGAAKA appear to be closely related in several respects, they will receive separate mention after the BAMILEKE section. The main sub-groups are then:

DSCHANG–BANGWA (2.27a) ATSAŊG (asuŋ li)[2] atsaŋg (Dschangtalk,
      Dschang)
      ŊWƐ (Bangwa)

 The localities include Foreke Dschang, Djuttitsa, Baleveng, Bafou, Bamendou, Fotoména, Fontsingla, Fonsa Touala, Mankan, Fombap, Fokoué, and Fonopéa. Other informants place ŊWƐ (Br.C.) in this sub-group and our material supports such a classification, ŊWƐ and ATSAŊG being almost identical in our notes. Some village speeches to the north-east are said to be very similar to ATSAŊG; these, however, do not include that of Babadjou.

---

[1] Spelt according to the usage of the territory in which it occurs.
[2] 'language' or 'language of'.

Probably one fifth of the total population of S.D. Dschang (158,000) falls into this sub-group together with 9,222 inhabitants of the Bangwa area (D. Mamfe).

BABADJOU (2.27*b*) TSASO (ε)tsaso (from the native name of Babadjou village).

Spoken in the chefferie of this name and in nearby villages on the main road from Dschang to Bamenda. *Population*: five or six villages. An informant from the 'chefferie' contradicted the statement of another Bamileke who placed the language of Batchoum in this sub-group.

BAGAM (2.27*c*) (not to be confused with *Baham*) TSOGAP, (tso)γap¹.

Spoken in Bagam chefferie and in neighbouring localities in the north-east corner of S.D. Dschang. *Population*: about twelve villages. Several points of resemblance to BAMUM were noted in this language.

BAMOUGOUM–BAMENDJOU (2.27*d*) PAMUŊGUUP (nεγa)¹ pamuŋguup¹ (Bamougoum), MUNDJU (nεγa) mundʒu (Bamendjou).

There is a close affinity to the speech of Bameka (S.D. Bafoussam) and of Bansoa and Balessing (S.D. Dschang). *Population*: 31,000 (S.D. Bafoussam) plus the inhabitants of the two last-named localities in S.D. Dschang, for which no detailed figures were obtained.

BAFOUSSAM (2.27*e*) FULSAP fulsap¹

Spoken in and around the chef-lieu of the S.D. *Population*: 7,000+the chefferie of Baleng.

BANDJOUN–BAHAM (2.27*f*) MANDJŨ (ŋgɔ)¹ mandʒũ (Bandjoun), MAHŨM, (ngo) mahũm (Baham).

Spoken in S.D. Bafoussam at the chefferie and sub-chefferies of Bandjoun. Only slight differences occur between MANDJŨ and the speech of Bahouang, Baham, Bayangam, and Bamoudjo. Intercomprehension exists between these people and the inhabitants of Bandenkop, Batié, and Bapa. *Population*: 60–70,000 (estimated).

BABOUANTOU (2.27*g*) PAPWANTU (γö pa)¹ papwantu.

Spoken at Babouantou just within the north-east limits of S.D. Bafang. It is closely related to FƐ'ƐFƐ' (see 2.27*h*) and also to languages to the north-west and north-east extending into S.D.s Dschang and Bafoussam. *Population*: two villages.

BAFANG (2.27*h*) FA', (γεε)¹ fa', (Bafang), KUU (γəə) kuu (Bakou), more loosely (i.e. for the less localized speech) FƐ'ƐFƐ'.

FA' and KUU appear to be almost identical. They are close to PAPWANTU and also to the speech of Bana and Bankwett as recorded by M. Léger,[2] a French administrator. *Population*: about twenty villages+the township of Bafang.

---

[1] 'language' or 'language of'.
[2] 'Contribution à l'étude de la langue bamiléké', *Journal de la Société des Africanistes*, 1932, pp. 209–27.

BANTOID LANGUAGES

BANGOU-BATCHINGOU-BAMANA[1] (2.27*i*)

This sub-group was only encountered via general statements from informants. No speech names were recorded. Spoken in the south of S.D. Bafoussam and west of S.D. Bangangté. *Population*: 10–15,000 (estimated).

BANGOUA-BATOUFAM[1] (2.27*j*)

No first-hand linguistic information was available. Spoken in four villages astride the S.D. border of Bafoussam in the extreme south-east. *Population*: between 10,000 and 15,000 (estimated).

BANGANGTE (2.27*k*) NDJUBOGA ndʒuboya (Bangangté)

Used at the chefferie of this name, and also throughout the S.D. in native commerce. The surrounding chefferies speak this language more or less well but have retained their own idioms which, though Bamileke, differ greatly from NDJUBOGA. The figure of 66,700 is given in *Memento, Cameroun* for the whole S.D., from which should be deducted the Batongtou[2] and several settlements already accounted for in Sub-groups 27*i* and 27*j*. Pastor Bergeret, who has many years experience in this area, estimates that about 40,000 should be added to Banganté figures to cover large-scale emigration to S.D.s Bafoussam and Bafang and to the larger centres in general. This seems to be rather too generous an estimate to square with the other Bamileke statistics.

BATONGTOU (2.27*l*)

No first-hand linguistic material was recorded for this sub-group which occurs in the extreme south of the Bamileke area. Informants state that this language is very different from NJUBOGA.

(2.27*m*)

This locality has been separated from the rest since it is a newly founded[3] Bamileke colony in what was formerly Bamum territory on the left bank of River Noun. No information is held as to the speech of the area, but since the settlement is composed of elements drawn from all the chefferies of S.D. Bafoussam, it is quite likely that the original village speeches will be perpetuated for some time in small closely related groups while PIDGIN will serve for general intercourse.

Of the languages recorded, BAMUM and ŊGAAKA tend to fall outside the BAMILEKE periphery. The former has affinities with the both the DKƆM group and the one at present under consideration; the latter, while definitely not belonging to the DKƆM group, differs considerably from BAMILEKE too in many respects. It is stressed then that although they are mentioned in this section, they are considered as being merely on the fringe of BAMILEKE.

---

[1] Each of these sub-groups has at least one language which tends towards the *Bangangte* sub-group.
[2] A S.D. map showing 23 villages and the chef-lieu of Bangangté was divided by an informant thus: 6 Bangangté and 17 Batongtou.
[3] It is believed that this venture may have been undertaken as late as 1948.

BAMUM (2.28) ʃüpamʌm (Bamun)

Locality. (F.C., Br.C.) Rég. Bamoun, roughly the triangle formed by the Rivers Noun and Mbam and the Br.C. frontier. Mme Dugast (*I.E.S.C.*) says that eight chefferies have been transferred to Br.C. and lie between Bali Town and Banso mainly in the Ndop area.

Population. (F.C.) 74,848 *I.E.S.C*; (Br.C.) ? eight villages.

Relationships. The vocabulary has many points of contact with that of ŊGAAKA and the north-east BAMILEKE languages, especially TSOGAP. It seems to be of Bantu origin but without regular correspondences to Common Bantu forms. Grammatically it may be related both to DKƆM and BAMILEKE.

ŊGAAKA (2.26) (Muŋgaaka, Ba'ni, Bali of Bali Town)

Locality. (Br.C.) The township of Bali on the main road south-west from Bamenda. In view of the extreme linguistic localization throughout the Province, an attempt has been made by the Swiss Basel Mission and the Administration (following the example set by German colonizers) to impose this language as a lingua franca in Bamenda Division. Failure has, however, greeted these efforts, largely because of the antipathy of other tribes to the Bali, who were armed by the German commander and used to subdue their neighbours—who already regarded them as interlopers and invaders.[1]

Population. ?

Relationships. Although the Bali are kinsfolk of the Bali of Bali Kumbat, the two languages are absolutely dissimilar. ŊGAAKA has many features reminiscent of various BAMILEKE languages from both a lexical and a grammatical viewpoint. Phonetically it appears to be far less complicated—indeed were it otherwise one could hardly imagine such a language being chosen as a potential vehicular speech by Europeans. The general impression formed of it in our very cursory examination was of a 'simplified' and somewhat 'pidgin' version of BAMILEKE with by far the most rudimentary set of prefixes encountered in the area.

Before leaving the Bantoid section we would reiterate that no claim is made to have solved the numerous linguistic problems of the W. Cameroons highlands. As far as this region is concerned, the term 'Bantu Line' can only lead to misconceptions. If we consider it to be that which prevents the Bantu languages from mixing with the others we may as well abandon our search for it. If, on the other hand, we are prepared to admit that the term may at times have the meaning 'transitional area', 'plage de mélange', or even 'no-man's land', then we have no farther to go in quest of it, for the Bantoid languages of W. Cameroons constitute the southern edge of a Bantu Line several hundred miles wide. Subsequent researches will prove that in the west the sharp linear delimitation obtaining elsewhere has become a shaded area extending into Nigeria and changing shape, size, and colour with the slightest variation of linguistic classificatory criteria.

It is felt that, if nothing more, the Survey has indicated a few of the problems of the

---

[1] They originate from Chamba (Yola) in Nigeria and prior to arriving at their present location lived farther east at Bali Kumbat, &c., see NDAGAM (3.2).

north-west Bantu borderland. They are problems which merit examination by those who deny the existence of mixed languages.

Lastly, in view of the very nature of the subject it is emphasized that many statements on the Bantoid field may be incorrect, and many may be only half-truths. In evaluating the reliability of the material it should be remembered that much of it was gathered by investigators who were untried in this field, from informants who, by normal standards, would not have been considered suitable, in conditions which often were not conducive to accurate work of this nature. Furthermore, owing to pressure of work sometimes only two or three hours could be allocated to a language. Consequently it is hoped that no ambitious classification of the languages of Africa will be built on the Bantoid material herein. In this area caution is a greater asset than an active intuition.

Section C

NON-BANTU LANGUAGES

Perhaps it would be opportune at the outset of this section to point out the different implications of the terms Bantu and Non-Bantu as applied to languages. The former indicates a linguistic group which has certain well-defined characteristics peculiar to itself. The latter label was given to languages whose only link might well be the negative criterion of *not possessing Bantu features*. We must not then expect to find in this field anything approaching the unity of Bantu.

1. MISCELLANEOUS LANGUAGES

SILQADƐT (3.1) (Isaŋgɛlɛ)

Locality. (Br.C., N.) D. Kumba and Calabar. On both sides of the lower Akpa River, just to the north of Rio del Rey.

Population. No figures available.

Relationships. Classified by Bruens as EFIK. No linguistic material was recorded. An informant stated that this speech originated from Calabar and was a dialect of IBIBIO.

NDAGAM (3.2) **ndaɢam**[1] (MUBAKO, Bali of Bali Kumbat, &c.)

Locality. (Br.C.) Bamenda Province. South-east of Bamenda on the international frontier, at the villages of Bali Kumbat, Bali Gaso, Bali Gangsi, and Bali Bagam.

Population. ?

Relationships. Unrelated to ŊGAAKA (Bali of Bali Town). The language of Bali Bagam should not be confused with that of Bagam mentioned in the BAMILEKE group. The inhabitants of these villages hail from the Chamba area of Nigeria and have preserved their original speech to a great extent. A comparison of our material with Meek's vocabularies shows great similarity to DOŊGA and some resemblance to LEKON, WOM, and MUMBAKE. In some respects it is reminiscent of KANURI though here the relationship is slight.

NƉALE (3.3) **nðale** (Mbembe, Izare)

Locality. (Br.C.) The north-east corner of Bamenda Province. The Mbembe N.A. area, excluding the village of Ndaka.[2] In Nfumte the village of Aderi is said to speak NƉALE.

Population. 2,893 T.P. (M.A.B.) Note that the Mbembe in Talbot are not the same tribe.

---
[1] This may be the Bali Bagam name only, since our informant lived there.
[2] The informant stated that at Ndaka the language was 'more like JUKUN'. We hardly know how to reconcile this statement with the more recent discovery of the connexion between NƉALE and JUKUN.

Relationships. Unrelated to any language examined by us, but definitely connected by vocabulary with JUKUN.[1] The inhabitants are said to originate from Tiv country.

WUTE (3.4)

So many names have been bestowed on the Wute in the past that the choice becomes an arbitrary one. It would seem that **Mfute** (= 'man') is also the name of the tribe which is called Bute or Babude by western neighbours.[2] Mme Dugast, however, says that Wute is the singular and Wutere the plural. This may be the version of a neighbouring tribe.

Locality. (F.C.) Apart from two small enclaves in the south to the east and west of Nanga Eboko, this language is spoken exclusively north of the Sanaga on both sides of the road from Bafia to beyond Tibati, Yoko being fairly centrally situated in the area, which is bounded in the north by 7° N. and in the east by the Djerem and approximately 13° E. To the north-west, 12° E. forms a rough boundary, although in the west the territory extends to about 11° 20' E. round the headwaters of River Ndschim. This area also contains enclaves of AVƏK, TIKAR, and GBAYA.

Population. 16,121 *I.E.S.C.*

Relationships. Unrelated to any of the languages examined.

KƐPƐRƐ (3.5) (Duisburg,[3] apart from the generic name of MBUM, gives Keperre, Wuna, Buna, Bürre, Mberre, and Pẹri, which all refer to the particular area in question, but may be tribal names.)

Locality. (F.C.) Rég. Lom et Kadeï, in the north of S.D. Bertoua on both sides of the Sanaga around Boutchaba and Deng Deng. (This is, of course, the locality for KƐPƐRƐ and not the whole linguistic group.)

Population. 2,700 ('Inventaire ethnique du Cameroun' by H. de Pedrals, *Bulletin de la Société d'Études Camerounaises*, xv–xvi, September–December 1946).

Relationships. This is the most southerly dialect of the MBUM group which occurs on the Ngaoundéré Plateau beyond the scope of this survey. Tessmann[4] includes in his 'Mbumgruppe', Mbum, Kepere, Mbere (including Mbere-Mbere and Laka-Mbere), Kare, and Pani-Dui. Duisburg distinguishes between Mberre and Pẹri (= E. Mbum and S. Mbum respectively). He says that they show similarity, however, where they tend to deviate from N. Mbum, which he considers to be the 'true' MBUM. WUTE has probably had some influence on KƐPƐRƐ due to intermarriage.

---

[1] The vocabulary of JUKUN used is by W. K. Fraser. It was printed by the Government Printing Office, Zungeru, in 1908, and may not be particularly accurate.

[2] Most of the information on this language comes from Hofmeister's article in *ZfK*, ix, pp. 1–19, 1918.

[3] In *Untersuchungen über die Mbum-Sprache in Adamaua (Kamerun)*, by A. von Duisburg, M.S.O.S., xxviii, 3, pp. 132–74, 1925, from which comes most of our information on this language. Kɛpɛrɛ is supposed to mean simply, 'It is a person'. Be this as it may, our informant insisted that this was the name of the language he spoke.

[4] 'Die Völker und Sprachen Kameruns', by Gunther Tessman, *Peterman's Geographische Mitteilungen*, lxxviii, 1932, with map.

No particular affinity was observed between the vocabulary of this and other Non-Bantu languages recorded, although several words which might be Bantu loans were noted.

2. GBAYA–ŊGBAKA MANDJIA GROUP (3.6)

This is a very large isolated linguistic unit which occupies the eastern part of the Adamawa plateau, a large portion of Oubangui Chari, and extends into the north-west of the Belgian Congo. It has various names in the different areas it covers, notably GBAYA (**gɓaya** or **ɡɓāya**) in F.C. and O.C., and MANDJIA or ŊGBAKA MANDJIA (**ŋgɓaka mandʒia**) in the Belgian Congo and parts of O.C. It is a scattered group whose numbers are very difficult to estimate. Mme Dugast (*I.E.S.C.*) gives 71,464 for F.C.; the administrative figures for Gbaya in Rég. Lobaye (O.C.) are about 31,000. Basing an estimate on this information it is assumed that the Gbaya of F.C. and O.C. will be certainly not less than 140,000–150,000 strong.

Professor Van Bulck of our eastern team travelled extensively in the whole GBAYA, &c. area on his recent visit to Lake Chad, and stated on his return that the total figure for the whole group (all territories) wonld be in the region of half a million. Several informants have asserted that throughout the area inter-intelligibility exists to a greater or less degree. A comparison of Cameroun and Belgian Congo material gave abundant support to these statements.

Remarks will be confined to the area covered by the western team. ŊGBAKA MANDJIA is more fully treated in the eastern section of the report. In a field where such great similarity obtains, even had it been possible it would have proved unprofitable for our purposes to take down material for each sub-dialect. Consequently many dialects are known to us merely by indirect observation and a shaded area on a map. Some have been located after comparison of the maps by Tessmann and Mme Dugast. Where no detailed investigation of linguistic material was made, it cannot be considered an established fact that these divisions into sub-tribes and clans correspond *ipso facto* with dialectal differences.

It is not proposed to give geographical indications for dialects not investigated when their location, in so far as it was possible to ascertain it, is shown on the linguistic map included in this report. In the list of GBAYA speeches which follows, an asterisk indicates that the dialect concerned was the subject of an investigation.

GBAYA KARA (KALA) (3.6*a*) (F.C., O.C.) = Tessmann's Baja-Baja 125*b*.
GBAYA BODOMO (3.6*b*) (F.C.)
GBAYA LAI (3.6*c*) (F.C.)
*GBAYA BULI (3.6*d*) (F.C., O.C.) Investigated at Banga, near Bania, District de Berbérati (Haute-Sangha)
*YAŊGƐLƐ (3.6*j*) (F.C., O.C.)
BOKARI (3.6*k*) (O.C.) = Tessmann's Bokari 192   ⎫ These may be other
SOMO (3.6*j*?) (F.C. or O.C.), ? = Tessmann's Bessóm 191 ⎬ names for the Yangele.
*BAŊGANDO (3.6*m*) (F.C.)
ŊGOMBE KAKA (3.6*l*) (O.C.)
GBAYA BULI BUKUM (3.6*e*) (O.C.)
GBAYA KAKA (3.6*f*) (O.C.) (near Carnot)

NON-BANTU LANGUAGES

GBAYA BIANDA (3.6g) (O.C.)
GBAYA BOKOTO (3.6h) (O.C.)
'GBAYA BOFI' (3.6i) (O.C.)—see GBOFI.
'GBAYA KAKA' (4.6) (O.C.) = ?
*GBOFI (3.6n) (O.C.)
*ALI (3.6p) (O.C.)
MANDJIA (O.C.) Called NGBAKA MANDJIA (3.6q) by R. P. Van Bulck, who says that they are really Ɗgbaka 'but do not accept the name'. They are situated to the north of Bangui and around Diuma.
GBANU (3.6r) (O.C.)—spoken around Bossembele and Yaloke.
BUDIGRI (O.C.)—The area between Bossangoa and Bouka.[1]
BAGBA (O.C.)—Between Bossangoa and Bogangolo.

There is no relationship between ƊGBAKA MANDJIA and ƊGBAKA MABO. The practice of mis-calling languages by ethnic names is responsible for several confused issues in this area. It becomes normal to prefix Gbaya-to any ethnic designation, e.g. 'Gbaya Bofi', 'Gbaya Kaka', 'Gbaya Ali', and when this name is extended to the language it assumes a different implication. The Gbofi, for example, though of Gbaya stock, refuse to call their language 'Gbaya Bofi'. This, they say, is the mixed jargon spoken in a neighbouring region where Gbofi have intermarried with other Gbaya clans. Worse still, the language of the so-called 'Gbaya Kaka' (near Bambio in D. Boda) is so far from being GBAYA that they use the local lingua franca, SAƊGO, in their dealings with GBAYA-speaking neighbours. Its actual nature is not known as no informant was available, but in any case it is only spoken in two or three small villages.

GBOFI (3.6n) (Bofi, Baya Boffi)

Locality. (O.C.) Rég. Lobaye, D. Boda. Between 17°–17° 40' E. and 4°–4° 10' N., extending north to beyond Boda and south along the right bank of the Lobaye for about 10 miles.[2]

Population. 9,542 (under the heading 'Boffi'—*Rapport Politique*, 1949).

Relationships. In daily intercourse the Bokoto and Gbofi each speak their own language and understand each other easily. The Gbofi understand the Ali fairly well but, unlike the latter, prefer to use vehicular SAƊGO when they meet.

YAƊGƐLƐ (3.6j) (? Bokari, ? Bessom, ? Somo)

Locality. (F.C., O.C.) Rég. Lom et Kadeï and Rég. Haute Sangha. Along the road from Yokadouma to Batouri, extending over the F.C.–O.C. frontier. Also two enclaves,[3] one on the Batouri–Kentzou road and the other at 14° 45' E. by 4° 15' N.

---
[1] Professor Van Bulck has some administrative figures (5,059) for this clan. We are indebted to him for the names of the last three GBAYA speeches listed.

[2] Along the Carnot road just outside Boda begins a 40-mile stretch of villages inhabited, says our informant, by 'Gɓaya Bofi' who speak a mixture of GBAYA and GBOFI—no doubt a mixed population. It is not thought that these are included in the GBOFI figures.

[3] No investigation was held on the speech of these ethnic enclaves which are indicated by Mme Dugast (*I.E.S.C.*); unless the second enclave is the MBOPALƆ referred to by our BAƊGANDO informant, they may be Gɓaya in ethnic composition only.

Population. 2,752 I.E.S.C.

Relationships. This language must not be confused with 'Banda-Yangere' (of O.C.) which is related to BANDA. Intercomprehension exists between YADGƐLƐ, BAD-GANDO, DGOMBE-KAKA, and several other neighbouring GBAYA speeches.

A comparison with GBAYA (of Banga) showed only slight dialectal variants.

ALI (3.6*p*) (Baya Ali)

Locality. (O.C.) Rég. Lobaye, Ds. Boda and Mbaïki, on the right bank of the Mpama between 17° 30' and 17° 50' E., stretching to approximately 4° 25' N.; Rég. Ombella Mpoko, on the left bank of the Mpama between 17° 30' and 18° 30', extending almost to 5° N.

Population. Lobaye 2,184, *Rapport Politique*, 1949; Ombella Mpoko = ?

Relationships. The informant stated that ALI, GBAYA, and MANDJIA were easily inter-intelligible.

BADGANDO (3.6*m*), **ɓaŋgando** (South Bangantu)

Locality. (F.C.) Rég. Lom et Kadeï, S.D. Mouloundou. Six villages on the track from Mouloundou to Yokadouma, extending for about 50 miles north of Mouloundou.

Population. 2,736 I.E.S.C.[1]

Relationships. The informant stated that this language and GBAYA BULI, DGOMBE-KAKA, and YADGƐLƐ[2] were inter-intelligible, also the language called MBOPALƆ (3.6*s*?) south of Batouri. We did not succeed in locating the latter dialect; its speakers are not very numerous (*see* YADGƐLƐ). There is no obvious relationship between BADGANDO, KAKƆ, and DGBAKA MABO, contrary to classifications quoted by Mme Dugast.[3]

3. THE BANDA GROUP

This group covers a large part of north-eastern A.E.F. and extends into the Belgian Congo and Anglo-Egyptian Sudan, territories which were beyond our scope. Although there can be no doubt of its basic unity, it comprises languages which differ widely and are often mutually unintelligible. The main body of the group will be dealt with in the report of the eastern team. This will include MBANDJA, GÖBU, MƆNƆ, (C.B.); DAKPA, LADGBA (A.E.F.); YAKPA, DGBUGU, TƆGBƆ, LADGBASE (A.E.F. and C.B.) The only BANDA listened to by us was YADGERE, for which only sufficient material was recorded to enable us to classify it.

YADGERE (3.7) **kra**[4] (Banda-Yanguéré)

Locality. (O.C.) Rég. Haute Sangha, Rég. Lobaye. Between 4° 40' and 3° 55' N., and the Rivers Mbaéré and Mambéré, stretching westwards to the south of Berbérati

---

[1] This figure would seem rather large for six forest villages.
[2] Statement checked against material and found to be possibly correct.
[3] I.E.S.C., p. 143. It should be noted that this is a misquotation of Tessmann's classification. He placed BADGANDO with GBOFI in the GBAYA group and *not* with DGBAKA MABO.
[4] The true implication of this name is doubtful. According to our somewhat unreliable schoolboy informant it may equally well mean BANDA as distinct from YADGERE.

as far as 15° 40' E. An 'arm' descends to 3° 55' N. in the south of the area between 16° 40'–50' E. There are also various villages scattered along the main roads of this district.

Population. Rég. Lobaye 3,460 (*Rapport Politique*); Rég. Haute Sangha 10,000 (estimated). Professor Tucker does not include this figure in his total for BANDA speakers (180,000–200,000) given in *The Eastern Sudanic Languages*, p. 19.

Relationships. All Banda-Yangere speak in exactly the same way, said our informant. They do not understand the DAKPA of Grimari and Bakala; similarly the BANDA of Damara and other localities in the far north is incomprehensible to them. There is absolutely no linguistic relationship between the GBAYA-speaking Yangɛlɛ and the Banda-Yangere.

4. THE ŊGBAKA MABO GROUP

This group itself forms part of Professor Tucker's SERE-MUNDU languages, spoken in two widely separated areas: (1) NE. Belgian Congo and SW. Anglo-Egyptian Sudan; (2) NW. Belgian Congo and on the right bank of the middle Oubangui. ŊGBAKA MABO (3.8) and MƆNDJOMBO (3.9) were the only languages listened to in this group. The eastern team encountered far more members of this unit and it is to this section of the report that reference should be made for greater detail on this subject.

ŊGBAKA MABO (3.8) **ŋgɓaka maɓo** (Ngouaka, Mbaka Limba, Gmbwaĝa)

Locality. (O.C., C.B.) Rég. Lobaye, D. Mbaïki, and D. Mongoumba. Roughly between the Rivers Lobaye, Mpama, and Oubangui, bounded to the west by 17° 45' E. and to the south-west by the Boda–Mongoumba road. Also in the north-west of the Belgian Congo on the left bank of the Oubangui, descending to Libenge.[1]

Population. Rég. Lobaye, 17,323 (*Rapport Politique*); Belgian Congo = ?

Relationships. MƆNDJOMBO and MBUNDJO (3.10) were said to be inter-intelligible with ŊGBAKA MABO by our informant for the former language. The similarity of vocabulary between ŊGBAKA MABO and BANDA already noted by Tessmann was observed during our investigations—which were only sufficiently extensive to enable a classification to be made in the light of material supplied by Professor Tucker[2] before our departure for Africa. No close linguistic relationship exists between ŊGBAKA MANDJIA (i.e. GBAYA) and ŊGBAKA MABO.

MƆNDJOMBO (3.9) **məndʒombo** (Mondjembo)

Locality. (O.C., M.C., C.B.) Rég. Lobaye, Rég. Likouala. The right bank of the Oubangui from 3° 40' to 3° 25' N. For the exact location of those on the Belgian Congo side of the river see the eastern section of this report.

[1] The Ŋgɓaka on either side of the Oubangui call their opposite numbers 'Ŋgɓaka Limba'; each insists that its own name is 'Ŋgɓaka Mabo'. Perfect intercomprehension is said to exist between both sections.

[2] Much of the information given on this language is based on statements (published and otherwise) made by him.

Population. Rég. Lobaye, 582 (*Rapport Politique*).

Rég. Likouala, 200–300 (estimate).

Belgian Congo, see the report of the eastern team.

Relationships. See ƊGBAKA MABO. The informant said that the Mbundjo who live immediately to the south on the right bank speak a language which is identical with her own. The eastern team believe 'Mbundjo' to be a mere pseudonym (it means 'European' in vehicular SAƊGO). On their side of the river they had never encountered this term. Tessmann made no mention of the Mbundjo in his map, but his MƆNDJOMBO area extends southwards to beyond Impfondo. This would seem to take in the Mbundjo[1] region as described by the MƆNDJOMBO informant. GBANZIRI and ƊGBAKA appear to be closely related to MƆNDJOMBO from a comparison of vocabulary. The actual investigation of this language was carried out by means of a SAƊGO interpreter (speaking SAƊGO proper, not the lingua franca). All Mɔndjombo are said to be able to understand this speech.

MƆNDJOMBO will be referred to at greater length together with other members of this group in the second part of this volume.

---

[1] They may be more numerous than the Mɔndjombo.

KEY TO MAP AND INDEX OF LANGUAGES WESTERN SECTION

Map No.	Language	Page
	Bantu Languages	
1.1	LUNDU	19
2	EKUMBƐ	20
3	MBƆŊGƐ	20
4	BATAŊGA	20
5a	BIMA	20
b	BIMA of the Balundu Badiku	20
6	BAKUNDU	19
7	ŊGORO	19
8	BARUE	20
9	DUALA	21
10	MOKPE (Bakwiri)	21
11	BOMBOKO	21
12	SU (Isubu, Bimbia)	21
13	OLI (Wouri)	21
14	POŊGO	21
15	MUŊGO	22
16	BODIMAN	22
17	BAFƆ	25
18	BALONDO	24
19	BABƆŊG	24
20a	MBO of British Cameroons	25
b	MBO of Mbouroukou	25
c	MBO of Dschang	25
d	MBO (Bareko)	24
e*	BANEKA	24
f	KAA (Bakaka)	25
g	MWAHƐT (Manehas)	23
h	AKƆƆSƏ (Muamenam)	24
i	AKƆƆSƏ (Bakosi)	25
j	NSWƆSƏ (Basosi)	25
k	ELƆŊ	25
l	NNENÛ (Ninong)	25
21a	BALUŊ	26
b	BƆŊKƐŊ	26
c	BAKOKO	27
d	BAŊKON (Abo)	27
e	LƆMBI	27
f*	NDOKBELE	28
g	YABASI	28
h*	NDOKPENDA	28
i*	NYAMTAM	28
j*	DIBENG	28
k*	NDOKAMA	28
l*	BAKEM	28
m	MBAŊG	28
n	DIBUM	28
22a	BANEN	28
i*	NDOKBIAKAT	28
ii*	NDOKTUNA	28
iii*	NDOGBANG	28
iv*	NDOGBANOL	28
v*	LOGNANGA	28
vi*	ELING	28
vii*	ITUNDU	28
1.22b	BONƐK	29
c	MANDI	29
d	NYƆ̃'Ɔ̃ (Nyokon)	28–29
e	YAMBETA	29
23	FA' (Balom)	30
24	KPA (Bafia)	30
25	KAALƆŊ	30
26	ŊGAYABA (Djanti)	29, 30
27a	ŊGƆRƆ	30
b	BATI[1]	
28	CIŊGA	29, 31
29	YAMBASA	29
30	'SANAGA'	29
30a	MAŊGISA	30
b	BƐTSIŊGA	30
31	YƐZUM (MVĔLĔ)	32
32	AVƏK (BAFOK)	32
32a	LEPƏK	32
b	YAS͡EM	32
33	YAŊGAFUK'	32, 33
34	GBĬGBĬL (Bobili)	33
35	BĔBĔLĔ (Bamvele)	33
36	ĔKĬ (Badjia, Mvang, Omvang)	33
36a	ĔKĬ of the Mvang Makona	33
37	'MAKE'[2] of the Mvang Makona (probably MVĔLĔ)	33
38	MĂKAA	34
38a	MĂKAA of the Mvang Makona	33
39	NDJEM	34
40a	MƐDJIME	34
b	BAAGƏTO	34
41	MPIƐ̃MƆ (Mbimu, Bidjuki)	34–35
42	MPƆ̃MPƆ́ (Mbumbum, &c.)	35
43	KONABEMB	35
43a	KONABEMB of the Boman	35
44	NDJEM of the S. Konabemb	
45	KAKƆ (Kaka)	35
46	POL	35–36
47	PƆMƆ	35
48	KWAKUM	35
49	PANDE or NDJƐLI	36
49a	PANDE proper	37
b	ŊGONDI	36
c	BOGƆŊGƆ	36
50a	ŊGANDO ⎫ (Bodzanga)	37
b	KOTA ⎭	
51	MBATI (Isongo)	38
	Bantoid Languages	
2.1	BANDƐM	39
2	NYAŊG (Kenyang)	39
3	KITW̃II (N. Balong)	40
4	TAKAMANDA	40
5	MEDKA	40
6	AS͡UMBO	40

KEY TO MAP AND INDEX OF LANGUAGES WESTERN SECTION (cont.)

Map No.	Language	Page
Bantoid Languages (cont.)		
2.7	AMASI	40
8	KIƊKWA	40
9	TIKAR	41
10	ƐDJAGAM ⎫	
11	ƐKOI (ƐKWE) ⎬ KEAQə	41
12	ƆBAƊG ⎭	
13	KƆRƆP	42
14	ƊKƆM	42–43
15	IYIRIKUM (Widikum)	43
16	MƏGAMO	43
16a	ƊGAMAMBO	43
17	MƐTA (MENEMO)	43–44
18	NGI³ (AƊGIE)	43
19a	NGEMBA³	43
b	N. NGEMBA³	43
20	ƊGWƆ⁴	43
21	BAFUT³	44, 47
22	FUƊGƆM	44, 45
22a	OSO	44
b	FUƊGOM proper	44
23	LAMSƆ	44
24	OKII (Boki)	44
25*	MISAJE⁵	45
26	ƊGAAKA (Bali of Bali Town)	49, 51, 52
27	BAMILEKE⁶	49, 51
27a	Dschang-Bangwa	49
b	Babadjou	50
c	Bagam	50
d	Bamougoum-Bamendjou	50
e	Bafoussam	50
f	Bandjoun-Baham	50
g	Babouantou	50
h	Bafang	50
i	Bangou-Batchingou-Bamana	51
j	Bangoua-Batoufam	51
k	Bangangté	51
l	Batongtou	51
m	(a new colony on the left bank of the River Noun)	51
28	BAMUM	52

Map No.	Language	Page
Non-Bantu Languages		
3.1	SILQADƐT (Isangele)	54
2	NDAGAM (or MUBAKO)	54
3	NƊALE	54
4	WUTE	55
5	KƐPƐRƐ	55
6	GBAYA, &c.	56
6a*	GBAYA KARA (or KALA)	56
b*	„ BODOMO	56
c*	„ LAI	56
d*	„ BULI	56
e*	„ BULI BUKUM	56
f*	„ KAKA	56
g*	„ BIANDA	57
h*	„ BOKOTO	57
i*	'GBAYA BOFI'	57
j	YAƊGƐLƐ	56–57
k	BOKARI	56
l*	ƊGOMBE-KAKA	56
m	BAƊGANDO	56
n	GBOFI	57
p	ALI	58
q*	NGBAKA MANDJIA	57
r	GBANU	57
s	MBOPALƆ?	58
7	YAƊGERE (Banda-Yangere)	58
8	ƊGBAKA MABO (Mbaka Limba)	59
9	MƆNDJOMBO	59–60
10	MBUNDJO	59
11	IƊGONDI (see 1.49b)	

Unclassified Languages

4.1	Language of Bebe Jatto and Bebe Ketti: probably non-Bantu	
2	Language of Dumbo, Biusa, and Ekwe: probably non-Bantu	
3	AZƆM (perhaps a dialect of WUTE)	
4	BETHƐN	
5*	MBOA (may be a mixture of MBUM and GBAYA)	
6	'GBAYA KAKA'	

NOTES

* Probably not a language name, but a clan or sub-tribal name distinguishing groups speaking virtually the same language.

(1) Classification based on Johnston's BATI (216) vocabulary, locality as in Dugast's *I.E.S.C.* The speech of the Bundju and of the Kombe noted by Dugast seems to be identical with CIƊGA (see p. 31).

(2) This name is suspect as it refers to a speech characteristic found over a wide area.

(3) Administrative names.

(4) See p. 43 (ƊKƆM group).

(5) The administrative name is given here to related languages of S. Misaje and NW. Banso N.A. areas.

(6) Names 27a–m refer to localities not languages; see pp. 49 ff.

Part II
REPORT OF THE EASTERN TEAM
OUBANGUI TO NILE

CONTENTS

1. THE LINGUISTIC INVESTIGATION
    - I. Itinerary — 65
    - II. Method of Investigation — 66
    - III. The Results Obtained — 68

2. THE BANTU LANGUAGES
    - A. Extreme West Group — 69
    - B. Western Group — 69
        - Western Group Transition Languages — 73
    - C. Extreme North Group — 74
        - Extreme North Group Transition Languages — 75
    - D. Northern Group — 76
        - Northern Group Transition Languages — 81
    - E. Eastern Group — 82
        - Eastern Group Transition Languages — 84
    - F. Extreme East Group — 85
        - Extreme East Group Transition Languages — 89
    - G. Central Language — 90

3. THE NON-BANTU LANGUAGES
    - A. Nilotic Language — 90
    - B. Nilo-Hamitic Languages — 91
    - C. Central Sudanic Languages — 91
    - D. Eastern Sudanic Languages — 92
    - E. Southern Sudanic Languages — 99
    - F. Gbaya-Ngbaka Languages — 106
    - G. Equatorial Languages — 107
    - H. Unclassified Language Group—Meegye — 110
    - I. Equatorial Bantoid Language — 113

4. PYGMY GROUPS — 114

5. INDEX OF ETHNIC AND LINGUISTIC NAMES — 116

1. THE LINGUISTIC INVESTIGATION

THE Eastern Team of the Bantu Line Survey was entrusted with the task of investigating the linguistic frontier between the Bantu and the non-Bantu languages in the area between Lake Albert in the East and the Ubangi River in the West. After six months' preparation in London at the School of Oriental and African Studies, the team left Southampton by air on 25 June 1949, joining Professor A. N. Tucker at Malakal (S. Sudan) on 28 June, and continued the same day to Juba.

I. ITINERARY[1]

28 June–3 July. Work at Juba.

3–18 July. In the Anglo-Egyptian Sudan, via Loka, Lui, Amadi, Mundri, Meridi, and Rimenzi to Yambio. After ten days' study at Yambio (Bogoro, Pambia, Kredj, Baka) the team left for Aba (Belgian Congo) via Meridi and Yei.

18 July–20 August. General survey of all languages spoken in the north-eastern corner of the Belgian Congo; preliminary soundings at Aba, Faradje, Dungu, Aru, Nyrambe, Rethy, Vieux-Kilo, Bunia, Badia Lolwa, Oitshia, and Mwenda. From Fort Portal (Uganda), Professor Tucker left for Kampala, and the team returned to Mutwanga to begin the linguistic investigation in detail.

21 August–6 October. From Beni to Uvira; along the western shores of Lakes Edward and Kivu as far as Lake Tanganyika; through the territories of Beni, Lubero, Rutshuru, Masisi (Mutongo), and Kalehe to Costermansville, and thence via Walikale (Itebero) and the Territories of Kabare and Mwenga to Uvira.

6–31 October. Return northwards to Mbingi via the eastern shores of the lakes (through Ruanda-Urundi).

11 November 1949–20 February 1950. Investigation of the eastern borders of the Belgian Congo from Lake Edward northwards to Aba (through the territories of Rutshuru, Lubero, Beni, Mambasa, Djugu, Mahagi, and Faradje).

20 February–24 June. Investigation of Medje-Mangbetu and Zande-Vongara groups (through the territories of Watsa, Wamba, Paulis, Niangara, Dungu, and Poko to Avakubi).

24 June–23 August. Investigation of the Stanleyville area (through the territories of Bafwasende, Banalia, Isangi (Yangambi), and Opala (Yanonge) to Stanleyville).

23 August–14 September. Investigation of the central region to the east of Buta (territories of Banalia, Buta and Ango). Illness detained Mr. Hackett at Buta from 9 to 18 September.

14 September–14 October. Professor Tucker rejoined the team and, together, the team investigated the central region to the West of Buta (through the territories of Bondo, Aketi, and Bumba as far as Lisala). On 14 October Professor Tucker left for Uganda via Stanleyville.

14 October–21 November. Investigations in the north of the Ubangi District (territories of Bumba, Banzyville, Bosobolo, and Libenge).

[1] Résumé of *Quinze Rapports de la Mission Linguistique Bantoue-Soudanaise*, written in the course of the expedition and forwarded to the International African Institute through I.R.S.A.C. (Institut de Recherche Scientifique en Afrique Centrale), Costermansville.

22 November–23 December. Investigations in the south of the Ubangi District (territories of Libenge, Gemena, Lisala, Budjala, and Bomboma). By skirting the northern limits of the Ngiri marshlands it was possible to find informants representing nearly all the languages spoken in the territory of Nouvelle-Anvers. On 2 January 1951 Mr. Hackett left by air for London. The following day Professor Van Bulck left via Zongo for French Oubangui-Chari and the Tchad in order to make a general linguistic investigation of the entire Tchad Territory. He returned to Europe on 31 May 1951.

While the team was in the Anglo-Egyptian Sudan, the Government provided a lorry for transport. In the Belgian Congo the team used a kit-car which was placed at our disposal by I.R.S.A.C. of Costermansville. We take this opportunity of recording our sincere appreciation. Thanks to this assistance the team was able to cover some 27,000 km. and continue its studies without interruption for a period of nineteen months.

In preference to an independent and self-contained expedition, the team chose to call at each government post and avail itself of the hospitality of each mission station, whether Protestant or Roman Catholic, whence it could investigate the languages spoken in the surrounding regions. This method proved to be far more satisfactory, as we were thus enabled to take advantage of the experience of specialists who have worked for many years in the area, to visit the tribes on the spot instead of summoning them to a distant post, to work with the widest possible choice of informants, and to obtain many examples of dialectal variations. We should like to take this opportunity of once again thanking the bishops and other authorities who have made this method possible, and all the Superiors and missionaries who without exception welcomed us so warmly.

II. METHOD OF INVESTIGATION

1. THE LANGUAGE IN WHICH INQUIRIES WERE CONDUCTED

In a very few cases, when dealing with exceptional informants, it was possible to use French or English. In the majority of cases, however, it was necessary to use one or other of the trade languages: Kiswahili, Kingwana, Uele Bangala, Lingala as spoken in the Buta-Bondo area, Lingala as spoken in the Lisala area. Investigations made in the more remote villages, where informants were ignorant of the trade languages, necessitated the use of languages which we had already recorded in the course of previous investigations. This was always the case with the pygmies. We were nearly always able to avoid the use of an interpreter; at the outset experience showed that information obtained through interpreters was seldom reliable when dealing with precise gramatical details, while errors were frequent even in simple matters of vocabulary.

2. THE PHONETIC TRANSCRIPTION

All linguistic information was recorded by both members of the team, using, as far as possible, the International Phonetic Alphabet script, with careful indication of the tones.[1]

---

[1] In this Report, the spelling of names of languages and peoples follows the orthography given in Professor Van Bulck's *Orthographie des noms ethniques au Congo Belge*, Brussels, 1954.

3. THE CHOICE OF INFORMANTS

Wherever possible, work was carried out with a minimum of three informants, two of whom were youths and one an adult.

Our preference went to the young rather than the old. Scholars in their sixth or seventh year, or even schoolmasters, were found to be ideal. They are more open-minded and more receptive than the older members of the community and, having made some study of grammatical analysis, find it easier to give a faithful translation of phrases involving grammatical niceties. Furthermore, it should not be forgotten that they have greater reserves of patience than their elders. As for their knowledge of the language, although it may not yet be as wide as that of the older men, it was nevertheless amply sufficient to satisfy the requirements of this expedition, seeing that they live from day to day in their own native environment. Moreover, in case of doubt, they were able to refer on the spot to someone more experienced than they.

We preferred the method of two youths and one adult, because the young are better teachers. But the older man is necessary in order to correct them in cases of error or doubt.

As an investigation of this nature called for an extremely concentrated mental effort on the part of the informants, the sessions could not be prolonged for more than two and a half hours. After this lapse of time the team was replaced by another, thus requiring three teams of three informants daily (although the same informants could perhaps be used again on the following day). This change of team also offered certain other advantages, such as that of increasing the number of soundings possible for each of the villages. Thanks to the missionaries whom we met on our journeyings, who were experienced in linguistics and took an interest in our work, we were offered a really ideal choice of informants for languages of wide extension. Knowing the dialectal peculiarities, they were able to choose just those informants whose speech best reflected these differences. At Ingi, for example, for the language of Mamvu alone, we were provided with twenty-eight selected informants, each one of whom represented a dialectal variant.

We preferred to visit the Africans in their natural social context, rather than require that they should come to us. Such a method permits a better choice of informants, greater confidence on their part, and the certainty of being able to cross-check. Only in the case of the territory of Nouvelle-Anvers was it found necessary to make an exception to this rule; here, the swampy nature of the terrain would have required months of travel, and we had to content ourselves with a choice of informants from amongst those to be found concentrated in the college and middle schools.

4. THE EXTENT OF THE INQUIRIES

For each language we first took a fundamental vocabulary of some 400 to 450 substantives (parts of the body, terms of relationship, natural phenomena, animals, plants, and cultural elements): this with a view to phonology, tonology, and nominal classification. Next we examined the nominal accord (substantive plus substantive), the adjectival accord (substantive plus numeral, qualificative, quantitative, demonstrative, and interrogative adjectives) and the different pronominals. Then came the examination of the verbal system: the copula, 'to have', and a typical verb such as 'to eat', in the affirmative and negative throughout its conjugation. Finally we examined the derived forms of the verb (causatives, intensives, applicatives, &c.), with an eventual study of the different tonetic systems of the verb.

The time at our disposal and the mental capacity of our informants determined the extent to which the outline of this scheme was elaborated.

III. THE RESULTS OBTAINED

Our investigations covered 438 languages and dialects. Following each reference to a language or dialect in this Report will be found an initial and number referring to Professor Van Bulck's documentation:

N indicates a Nilotic language, 1 to 3,
NH indicates a Nilo-Hamitic language, 4 to 8,
S indicates a Non-Bantu language (Sudanic), 9 to 213,
B indicates a Bantu language, 220 to 479,
P indicates a language spoken by pygmies, 1 to 28.

It is true that time did not allow us to extend our investigations as far to the south as we could have wished in order to have a comprehensive view of each of the Bantu groups bordering the linguistic frontier. But our principal objective—to determine the frontier and obtain grammatical data for each of the languages spoken along it—has been fully realized.

During the journey information concerning the linguistic frontier was taken village by village. It has thus been possible for Professor Van Bulck to record this information on maps to the scale of 1/200,000, and subsequently on maps of each chefferie. A general map on which all these details have been recorded is annexed to the present Report.

The complete documentation will require at least two years of preparation before it can be published, and will comprise 30 sections, of which 16 deal with Bantu grammar, 1 with Nilotic, 1 with Nilo-Hamitic, 10 with Sudanic, and 2 with Bantoid. This work would be completed by 10 further sections, in which Professor Van Bulck will publish the linguistic material he has collected on the languages and dialects of the Tchad Territory.

This present Report should properly have followed rather than preceded the publication of the documentation, so as to provide the summary and the conclusions. It is with reluctance that, in deference to repeated requests, we have adopted the inverse procedure. Perhaps we may therefore be excused for speaking of 'unclassified languages' and 'transition languages'. Until we have completed the detailed comparative examination of our documentation it will remain impossible to resolve many of the questions which have arisen in the course of our investigations and to determine the reliability of certain hypotheses which, while still requiring complete justification, we have used as provisional guides. Rather than court error by launching into risky hypotheses which we might later have to rectify, we have preferred to indicate plainly those results which are beyond doubt and those which must for the moment remain uncertain. Later we hope to be able to complete this Report by showing what solution our documentation offers for the classification of those languages which we have for the moment had to term unclassified or transitional. Meanwhile, we hope to have the opportunity of publishing the documentation, so that others, too, may decide for themselves whether there exists a better solution than our own.

2. THE BANTU LANGUAGES

A. EXTREME WEST GROUP

(A) PYGMY GROUP

We met with two groups of Bambinga pygmoids, one to the north of Libenge, the other to the south of Mawuya, both belonging to the 'Pygmoïdes Négrilles' of the French Congo. It is only recently that they parted from their brothers who still live on the right bank of the Ubangi. Their language, Limbinga, is related to a Bantu language spoken on the right bank of the Ubangi (P. 26, 27).

(B) FRENCH CONGO GROUP

Three languages spoken in the territory of Bomboma may likewise be related to the languages of the right bank of the Ubangi. They are: (*a*) Ndaanda (B. 478), the speakers of which are called Kpàlà by their neighbours the Bomboli; (*b*) Lobala (B. 477), which lies to the north-west, neighbouring the Monjombo; (*c*) it is probably correct to add Bomboli, a dialect of Lobala (B. 479). It is also called Bombongo. This dialect seems to have affinities with both Lobala and Budjaba.

B. WESTERN GROUP

We are proposing to call this group the Western Group of Riverines. It will include:

in the West: the Congo River sub-group;
             the Ngiri sub-group;
             the Saw sub-group;
in the centre: the Lokele;
in the East: the Aruwimi River sub-group;
            the Middle Congo River sub-group.

(A) WESTERN SECTOR

Time did not permit us to take to the water in search of these river fishermen dwelling on islands or in the swamps; but, by skirting the swamps on the northern side, we were able to collect specimens of their principal languages. These can be divided into three sub-groups:

I. *The Congo River Sub-group*

Judging from our inquiries and the material we were able to obtain on the spot, we include the following in this sub-group:

1. The Mabaale dialects in the territory of Nouvelle Anvers:
(*a*) the Mabaale groupement at Nouvelle Anvers;

(b) the Mabembe groupement to the east of Nouvelle Anvers, and the Limpandja groupement to the west of Nouvelle Anvers;
(c) the Mabanza groupement opposite Nouvelle Anvers (B. 460);
(d) the dialect called Mbinga, spoken in the villages of Bibomba, Baba, and Bambutu;
(e) the dialect of the Balobo, comprising the Bodjinga in the north, the Bokula in the centre, and the Bonkembe in the south.

2. The dialect Dibaali, spoken amongst the Babaali of the River Duwa in the territory of Busu Mandji. We were able to obtain an example of this from the village of Liboko (B. 459).

3. Iboko, spoken by the Iboko of Nouvelle Anvers (formerly known as Mukandja) and of Dundu on the left bank of the river. This has been preserved for us in the *Essai sur la Langue Congolaise* by the Rev. Fr. Cambier (C.I.C.M.), Brussels, 1891.

4. The speech of the Boloki or Bologi. They live in the riverside villages of Mosembe, Emate Loa, and Bonjoku (B. 465a, b). They are also to be found farther up the River Congo at Bolombo on the left bank, Mobeka at the mouth of the Mongala, and Bokumbi opposite Mobeka.

5. The speech of the Ndobo along the Ndobo stream and in the village of Bongwanja on the Congo River.

Perhaps we should also include:

6. the speech of the Likila in the villages Mobena, Ndobo, Gundu, and Myongo. They are called Bangele or Balobo by their neighbours (about 500 inhabitants).

II. *The Ngiri Sub-group*

We include here:

1. the speech of the Libinza:
(a) the Libinza of the Ngiri River;
(b) the Libinza of the River Congo in the villages of Libanda and Boboko (B. 466–7).

2. The speech of the Baloi or 'Baato 'ba Loi ('People of the Ngiri river') (pop. about 700). At the present time these people live on the middle Ngiri River, but we know from tradition that their ancestors emigrated from the Libinza (B. 464).

III. *The Saw Sub-group*

Amongst the dwellers on the River Saw we were able to contact:

1. the Bolondo, living by the river from Budjala in the north down to the village of Monenge (B. 463) (pop. about 1,000);

2. the Ndoolo, scattered between Bokola and Tanda (B. 462) (pop. 5,000). They are also known as the 'Bondokoyi of the Ndoolo marshes. This common designation, however, is applied to a mixture of natives of diverse ethnic origin (Poto, Likaw, Bamwe, &c.), but who all speak Ndoolo nowadays.

With strong reservations, we think it possible that the speech of the post Likula on the Mongala River might also be attached to this sub-group.

Despite all our researches in this region, we were unable to find a tribe bearing the ethnic name of Bangala or Bamangala; nor did we find a village-language called Lingala. It is true that we find the majority of the grammatical elements of the vehicular Lingala languages distributed amongst the languages of this sub-group; but no single language presents all these characteristics together. The languages of the Mabaale and the Libinza bear the closest resemblance to Lingala.

(B) CENTRAL SECTOR

The central sector is best known to us for the *Lokele* language, but the importance of this language (spoken by some 14,000 people) has been greatly exaggerated. The Lokele owe their reputation to their indefatigable commercial activity and their incessant rovings on the upper reaches of the river. In this sector, then, we group:

1. *Lokele*, which is divided into two dialects: (a) the western dialect, spoken by the Yawembe (B. 419–21) (pop. 8,278), mostly in the neighbourhood of Yangambi and Isangi; (b) the eastern dialect, spoken by the Yaokandja (B. 420 and 422) (pop. 6,436) in the neighbourhood of Yakusu and Yanonge.

The speech of the *Lileko* is only Lokele; they are groups of Lokele who have settled on the left bank of the river (at Yatuka and to the east of Yanonge, amongst other places). Farther downstream several other Lokele settlements are to be found, e.g. in Bumba Territory (the Lokele-Mongabe between Bumba and Yambinga), and in Lisala Territory (the Lokele-Molwa to the west of Lisala).

2. The speech of the *Mbooso* (B. 423) and *Yalikoka* (B. 424) (pop. together, 6,902). The Mbooso group lives opposite Isangi, on the right bank of the Lomami. Formerly they inhabited the two villages of Lieki and Etambe only; but these villages joined those of their neighbours, the Yalikoka, a few years ago. The Yalikoka are of Topoke origin. Since then, both the Mbooso and the Yalikoka have adopted the Lokele language. Two other enclaves of Mbooso, at Yanonge and Mbelo, have been absorbed into the Fuma sector.

3. The *Fuma* (B. 425 and 426) have, for the most part, been known as pseudo-Bambole. It is true that they are of Mbole origin, but, under strong Lokele influence, they are quickly adopting the Lokele language. One can, however, still trace Mbole characteristics in their speech. The Fuma are divided into Yalihila (pop. 3,060) and Yalikanza (pop. 4,577).

It was not possible for us to follow the extension of Lokele influence father downstream amongst the Yanongo (Turumbu-Lukutu) and Moingi of Elisabetha.

(C) EASTERN SECTOR

The mere existence of a gong language is quite sufficient for the identification of those languages which belong in this sector. We will first follow the banks of the Lohale (Aruwimi), and afterwards those of the middle Congo.

I. *Along the Aruwimi*

1. Eduumbi or 'Litungu', spoken by the 'Watungu' riverines.

  (a) 'Wangbelima de l'eau', in the Panga region. Only the old people still speak Eduumbi; the young have adopted Napopoyi-ti;

(b) The 'Watungu' riverines of Banalia (B. 438). This comprises: the village of Bambamboli to the west of the River Longele (only the old people still speak Eduumbi here; the young speak Libwali); the Bombwa Group (Banalia clan); the Banalia fishermen; the river villages west of Banalia (Musegu, Ayonga, Amoti, amongst others).

In the last three cases, the young people speak Leangba or Leboro.

2. Various dialects in the villages of the lower Aruwimi, e.g.

(a) at Yambuya, Ekilo, Bokaku: a few individuals, but mixed with Bamanga (Mbayi) and Baangba;
(b) the speech of Mongandjo: same mixture;
(c) the speech of Likombe and Yambumba: certain likenesses to Olombo (B. 439);
(d) the speech of Ilongo (B. 440);
(e) the speech of Yangonde and Bomane;
(f) the speech of Baonde.

II. *Along the middle reaches of the Congo*

1. The dialect of the Basoa-Basoko (B. 442); at Yambese and Basoa; at Yoafo and at Basoko at the mouth of the Aruwimi; at Bomenge and in the villages of the lower Lulu; in a village on the left bank in Isangi Territory.

2. The dialect of the Baonga, spoken in a village on the left bank of the river in Isangi Territory.

3. The dialect of the Yamanongeri, Yaolema.

4. The villages of the Congo River to the east of the mouth of the Itimbiri.

5. Umbesa, the dialect of the Bombesa (known to the Administration as Mombesa) (B. 441).

6. Various dialects included under the common name of Upoto, e.g.

(a) Lipoto of Bumba (B. 453);
(b) Likele spoken by the Bokele of Umangi (B. 454): similar to Litembo.
(c) Lipoto-'Bumwangi of Umangi (B. 455);
(d) Lipoto-Empesa (B. 456);
(e) Ngundji, opposite Umangi, and 'Petit Ngundji' at Umangi;
(f) Kunda and Kumba, near Boyange;
(g) Mongo, below Lisala;
(h) Yakata, Yamongiri, Liombe, and Yambuya in Busu Djanga Territory;
(i) the island of Esumba, opposite Umangi;
(j) Lipoto above the mouth of the Mongala;
(k) Lipoto at Lusengo, below the mouth of the Mongala.

Should we also include the speech of the Yasanga? These river people formerly occupied the Stanley Falls, but were forced to move upon the arrival of the 'Baenya (known to the Administration as Wagenya). At the present day there remains nothing of the Yasanga beyond a clan name still used amongst the 'Baenya. Of the Yasanga language there remains no trace; as for that of the 'Baenya, it has hardly any relationship with the group at present under consideration.

OUBANGUI TO NILE 73

WESTERN GROUP TRANSITION LANGUAGES

(A) THE 'DOKO DIALECTS

Provisionally we shall divide these dialects into two sub-groups, according to the form of the nominal prefixes.

1. Dialects having a vocalic pre-prefix:
    (1) Ingbeele at Lisala (B. 443), plus Apindi, 'Bolongo, Bashwa, and Bobala;
    (2) Ndeke, Bweela, Mongombo, and Popolo;
    (3) 'Bokutu (B. 448) at Umangi, plus Dyobo (known to the Administration as Diobo);
    (4) Ingundji at Busu Mandji (B. 444);
    (5) 'Bumbiya at Busu Mandji (B. 445);
    (6) The dialect spoken in the area between Likimi (right bank of the Mongala) and Libayi (to the north) inclusive (B. 447).

2. Dialects having a pre-prefix of the form consonant plus vowel:
    (1) Gomba at Busu Mandji, under Ngombe influence (B. 446);
    (2) Mimbo in Budjala Territory (B. 452), plus Mundjinga and Dyobo (also in Budjala Territory).

(B) THE LITEMBO DIALECTS

This is a transition form between (A) 1 and (A) 2. Litembo-speaking groups are widely scattered.

(1) Motembo-Bosanga, on the Mongala River (B. 449);
(2) River Motembo, on the Mongala (at Mbinga in Lisala Territory) (B. 450);
(3) Motembo-Mokiri (i.e. Motembo of the interior) or Bombenga, in Bombangi chefferie of Lisala Territory (B. 451);
(4) Motembo enclaves in Budjala Territory: Libanza and Bokele villages on the Banga Melo;
(5) Motembo on the Mongala in Budjala Territory: Molendo, Bosengo, and Akula villages; and on the right bank, Popolo and Nzambe villages;
(6) Bosanga and Gwelenge villages at Banga Bolu;
(7) Motembo on Sumba Island;
(8) Motembo at Malundja, mixed with Ngombe-Bombele;
(9) Motembo on Ukaturaka Island.

(C) THE NGIRI 'DOKO DIALECTS IN BOMBOMA TERRITORY

1. Bamwe:
    (1) Lituuka (B. 468);
    (2) Moonya (B. 469);
    (3) Liboobi (B. 470);
    (4) Mundongo (B. 471).

2. Djandu (B. 472). The village of Bobonga speaks a dialect slightly different from the rest of the Djandu (Maliba, Bomanga, Ewaku, and Monia villages).

3. Ebuku (B. 473), and its related dialect, Lingunda.

With reserves we include provisionally:

4. Budjaba (B. 474). Although neighbours of the Lobala, they nevertheless do not speak the same language.

5. The speech of the Kutu of the Ngiri River (pop. upstream 700, downstream 1,100). We were unable to visit them.

C. EXTREME NORTH GROUP

(A) LANGUAGES HAVING VESTIGIAL SUFFIXES

1. Likarili (B. 226):
  (a) In the Belgian Congo, in Ango Territory, Sasa chefferie (pop. 1,000); only a few old people still know the language, the remainder having adopted Pazande.
  (b) In French Oubangui, north of Zemio (pop. 3,000–4,000). The Bakari are located between the Rivers Chinko and Warra, along the Mbomu as far as Karre. They are separated into two sections by the Biri.

2. The Pseudo-Bangba Group:
  (a) Nyangali, spoken by the Banyanga (pop. in 1931: 2,130) (B. 231, 232, 235). This language is still very well preserved in the ten villages of this little enclave in Watsa Territory, and we took samples of it at Edeya and Ingi.
  (b) Gbatiri, spoken by the Bagbati (pop. in 1931: 821) (B. 233). In the three villages of the Bagbati there only remain a few rare survivors who still speak the original language, which closely resembles Nyangali.
  (c) The Mabadi (pop. in five villages in 1931: 1,191) are nowadays completely Mangbetu-ized. This is easily understood, for they are a dynastic family. According to the Rev. Fr. Costermans, it has not been proved that the Mabadi ever had a language of their own, or that they ever constituted a separate ethnic entity. It may, then, be simply a clan group.
  (d) For the speech of the Mayeka we have been given a series of words (B. 234), but the exact place where the Mayeka used to live has eluded us. At the present time we have been unable to locate them.

3. Lingbee, spoken by the Bangbee (known to the Administration as Mangbele) (B. 230):
  (a) In Niangara Territory there are only a few elders (about 30) who still speak Lingbee;
  (b) At Gombari the Lingbee language was still in existence a few years ago (cf. Liesenborghs in 1936), but today all the Mangbele there speak either Namangbetu-ti or Mamvu.

(B) LANGUAGES HAVING PREFIXES, BUT NO SUFFIXES

1. The Bahr-el-Ghazal Group:
  (a) Homa (B. 220), spoken by the Bahoma-Babanga according to the Rev. Fr. Santandrea. There are still a few at Mopoi and Tombura;

(*b*) Bodo (B. 221). A few speakers in French Oubangui, and also, according to the Rev. Fr. Santandrea, at Dem-Zubir in Bahr-el-Ghazal.

(*c*) Boguru:

  (1) The speech of the 'Babukur (B. 222, 223) to the west of Yambio (Anglo-Egyptian Sudan) between the Rivers His and Kisi, affluents of the Sue. The language is in an advanced state of decay, and is only spoken by a few old men, the rest speaking Pazande.

  (2) Kogoro (B. 224), spoken by the Babogoro of Bangassou in French Oubangui. It was still in use a generation ago, and is spoken today amongst expatriates now residing in the north-east of the Belgian Congo.

  (3) Boguru (B. 225), spoken by the Bagbele, of which there are about seventy-five representatives in the two villages of Bapa and Babinguru to the north of the Garamba National Park. They are separated from the Baka by the stream Nambelima, an affluent of the Aka River.

2. Bungbinda, the language of the 'Bangbinda:

(1) spoken in the Anglo-Egyptian Sudan;
(2) spoken in a few scattered spots in the Uele region;
(3) spoken at the village of Kotele, 20 km. from Buta.

EXTREME NORTH GROUP TRANSITION LANGUAGES

1. Liliko (B. 279, 291)

The Baliko are grouped in two chefferies of Wamba Territory. The Toriko, under Chief Mangbukele (neighbourhood of Babondei) (pop. 25,962), have kept their language; but the so-called Maliko, under Chief Bangatsho, although of Liko origin, have for the greater part adopted Ebudu, the language of the Babudu, by whom they are completely encircled.

As for the Mabudu-Malika chefferie, under Chief Abusa, these are mainly 'Ba'budu with a few 'Baliko amongst them.

Liliko is also spoken by a group of Mabiti (B. 280) in the Gwatala chefferie of the territory of Paulis. The Mabiti clans are often erroneously classified as Mangbetu, because the Mangbetu dynastic family took their earliest warriors from amongst them.

2. Libaali

The 'Babaali are grouped in Bafwasende Territory (pop. 37,738). Four dialects may be distinguished, which roughly correspond to the four sectors of the territory:

(*a*) the dialect of the 'Bakundumu in the north-east (pop. 11,330) (B. 292, 293*a* and *b*, 294 and 296);

(*b*) the dialect of the Bekeni in the west (pop. 6,679). In 1949 the 'Babaali of Kondolole (mixture of Mbayi, Baangba, and Apopoyi) were added to the Bekeni Sector;

(*c*) the dialect of the Bemili (pop. 5,883);

(*d*) the dialect of the Bafwa Ndaka (pop. 13,246) (B. 297).

The Libaali language, with its multiple classes, has undergone a very marked development, in which one can recognize the influence of the recent Bwa bloc, but also that of an archaic Liko substratum.

D. NORTHERN GROUP

(A) KUNDA

This is the group of pseudo-riverines of the Saw and the Ngiri. In contrast to the true riverines of the Congo and its main tributaries, these people call themselves Kunda. Here we group:

1. The Diko ('Likaw') of the River Saw (B. 475). The Diko people who live on the Saw still speak their own language; but amongst those who live to the east of the Saw, in the village 'Petit Likaw', there remain only a few who speak it, the remainder having adopted Ngbandi.

2. The Bongambo of the Banga region ('Banga Likaw'), occupying the villages of Likaw, Modzuku, Epanga, and Keleku (B. 476).

3. The old Molegi population of Bongolo. Only two speakers of the language survive to this day.

4. The Bomboma group, which includes the Makengo, the Bomboma, and the Bokondji of Bomboma Territory.

(B) THE NGOMBE BLOC

Here we group Ngombe, Ebudja, Ebango, and Libinza.

I. *The Ngombe Dialects*

(a) Northern Ngombe:

(1) the Bosobolo enclave (B. 407);
(2) the five enclaves in Libenge Territory: Busu Mboma, Busu Bwamango, Lisingo, Sabe, and Singa (Betina);

(b) River Congo Ngombe:

1° Ngombe *sensu stricto*

(1) Lisala Ngombe: at Busu Godo, Mundingili (B. 414), Kalagba, and Ebongo-Moka;
(2) Mbinga Ngombe: at Busu Mokelu (B. 415), Mondunga, and Mbata; also among the Bomba at Bopeke and Bolubwa;
(3) Akula Ngombe (Ngombe Bombele): at Busu Nami, Gwenzale, Libona, Gwemba, Busu Gbweka, and Busu Muli;
(4) Mongala Ngombe: along the banks of the Mongala from Ikonongo and Bombele as far as Malundja, and on the island of Ukaturake;
(5) Banga Bolo Ngombe: between the River Saw and the River Ngiri in the villages Ndebo and Dama, &c.
(6) Ngombe north of Bomboma: Bobey, Kwala, and Busu Ndongo;

2° In addition there are two groups of Mbati-Ngombe in the Mawuya region of Libenge Territory:

(7) Mbati-Ngombe and Mosimba: between the Rivers Ubangi and Lua;
(8) Kipoto: a small Ngombe enclave to the north of Mawuya (B. 416);

OUBANGUI TO NILE 77

(c) Busu Mandji Ngombe:

(1) Lisena, the dialect of the Vulangba at Busu Mandji (B. 408): these are perhaps Wiinza who have undergone Ngombe influence;
(2) The dialect of the Ngombe Wiinza: at Busu Mandji in Lisala Territory (B. 409), at Busu Efuta and Mbundja in Budjala Territory (B. 411), and two small enclaves in the middle of the Mbanja in Budjala Territory (Busu Ngwele and Busa Kambo).

II. *The Budja Group*

We may divide the numerous Budja speeches into two groups, the language spoken by the Bombanga being in a category of its own.

(a) Southern dialects (Embudja):

Under this head come:

(1) Manga, Waisalaka, Bosanga (B. 401), and Bongoli;
(2) on the left bank of the Itimbiri in the Moenge area, Yanduku, and Yandunga (B. 406).

(b) Northern dialects (Ebudja):

(1) The Bosambi dialects (B. 400): Yamwando, Yamuwa, Botsholi, and the speech of the Yamoloto, Yaliambi, and Woonda.
(2) The dialect of the Yamiekoli (= Yamikeli), Yalokuli (B. 405);
(3) The dialect of the Libute-Yanzila (B. 404);
(4) The dialect of the Yamandika (B. 403).

(c) The Bombanga dialect, *see* the speech of Manga Bongolu (B. 402).

The Survey found it impossible to carry out investigations in the Ebango area because of floods. It is clear, however, from information from various sources that this language belongs to the Northern Budza dialect group.

III. *The Binza Group*

This is an immense group, the various dialects of which we found exceedingly difficult to classify. In it we place:

(a) Ibindja of the Aketi area, spoken by the Babindja, Baduumbi (B. 393), Maway (B. 394), and others.
(b) Libinza of the left bank at Ibembo; it was taken down among the Babinza Bokengele (B. 395) and Busayu.
(c) Ligendza of (1) Nioka, Yandongo, Bandi, Tshimbi (Sectors of the territory of Bumba), (2) the Yambuku area amongst the Western Bawiinza: Bokoyo (B. 396), Gongo, and the Eastern Bawiinza: Yalisika, Yambila (B. 397).
(d) Digendja spoken by the Bagendja or Bangendja of Lisala in the Boyange area, (1) in the following villages: Bokutu (B. 399), Motina Baweya, Boobi (B. 398), Bokapu; (2) in the seven Wiinza villages to the north of Umangi, Bangi, Bopwe, &c.; (3) farther west to the north of Umangi in four villages: B. Gope, B. Gope Moke, B. Kolo, and B. Gomani.

(e) Wiinza-Ngombe of B. Mandji (B. 410): (1) to the west, Bokapo; (2) to the east, B. Mandji, Mongiri, Monguba.

(f) Ligendza-dibaali on the River Duwa, Yambuku area, at the villages of Mondumba, Ngbengbe (= Digbi) (B. 457).

(g) Wiinza-dibaali on the Duwa, B. Mandji area, at the villages of Monzelenge and Ligongo (B. 458).

The speakers of these dialects should not be confused with the Babendja of the River Kalumete or the Bagenza of the left bank of the Ibembo, a splinter group which emigrated westwards. The two latter are Mabinza who have been submerged by the influence of the Bwa group (more especially of the Angba sub-section) of Banalia.

(C) THE BWA BLOC

The investigation of the Bobwa (popularly known as the Ababua) was rendered especially difficult by the extreme multiplicity of their languages, which have not only been superimposed but often completely intermingled. We believe that they may be divided into six groups whose evolution becomes progressively complex: I. Apagibeti; II. Benge and Baati; III. a transition group; IV. Yewu; V. Bwa; VI. pseudo-Bangelima.

I. *Apagibeti Group*

This group is the closest to Libenge. The name refers neither to a language nor to a clan but is merely a cognomen given to these people who habitually begin a conversation with the formula, 'He says that . . .' '*apa-gi beti* . . .'. By this means they are distinguished from the Napagisene (II), Napagibetini (IV), and the Napagitene (V). It goes without saying that this is the application of popular philology rather than of a rigorous scientific classification. What should be noted, however, is that in this first group we found it virtually impossible to discover a former common name such as was found to exist for the three others.

In the Apagibeti group we include:

(a) North-eastern Apagibeti, called Gezon by the Angbandi. Here we group (1) Egulu, spoken by the Babogulu of Ngaye (B. 375); (2) Ebugbuma, spoken by the Babugbuma of Ngaye (B. 376); these have undergone strong Libaati influence. (3) Gezon, spoken by the Kashi and the Lite in Coquilhatville Province.

(b) Egbuta, spoken by the Bagbuta, who dwell on the Itimbiri near Ibembo in Bumba Territory. We were unable to obtain a specimen of this.

(c) Apakebeti of Yambuku area; seven villages between Yambullu and the Duwa (B. 381).

(d) Ilombo of the River Duwa (formerly the village of Dundusana) now strongly influenced by Ligendja.

(e) Apakibeti (Gezon) of the Abumombazi area, spoken by the clans of Ndalangi, Bige, Ndunge, and Ngende (B. 382) (pop. 1,806).

(f) Apakabeti of the north of Lisala Territory. It is spoken by the Bodjame Bodjwambe (or Bonzwaambi) (B. 380), Mongongo (or Momongo), Mongwapere, Monveda, and Bokondji. They are called Ndaayi both by their southern neighbours the Ngoombe and also by the Vulangba.

It is said that the original Ligbe of the Bagbe was related to Apagibeti. It has now become extinct, and one is tempted to wonder whether the last traces of it are preserved in the Lingbee of the Mangbele (B. 230).

II. *Benge-Baati* (or Napagisene)

(*a*) The Libenge dialect (B. 373):

(1) One part has remained localized to the north of the Uele;
(2) another was found in the Aketi area. Most of the Babenge, however, have been overrun by the Bandia and Zande invasion.

(*b*) The dialect of the Babaati (B. 372, 374) in the sub-group of the Bolende.

(*c*) The dialect of the Babaati of Loomia:

(1) The speech of the Babaati of Loomia (the Lowama) (B. 370);
(2) Ligbaase of Ibembo (B. 377).

(*d*) The dialect of the Boganga:

(1) Boganga of Momie;
(2) Boyanga.

(*e*) The dialect of the Bagbe:

(1) Ligbe spoken by the Bagbe who are situated on the 'Vicinal' (local branch railway line) from Km. 140 to Km. 215 (B. 365*a*);
(2) the Bopandu;
(3) the Bobongono;
(4) Labibi at Ibembo (B. 379);
(5) the Bongongoli (B. 379) (Bongbongulu).

III. A transition group between groups II, IV, and V, known like IV as Napagibetini.

(*a*) The speech of the Mongingita, found to the west of the River Soombo and called Lingingita of Barisi (B. 367). It is similar to that of the Babalia, Bogongeya, and Bandingima.

(*b*) A group of Babaati who have come under Mongingita influence. They include:

(1) the Balisi, who speak Lelisi south of the Bangingita (B. 368);
(2) the Bolisi of Ngayi;
(3) the Bogbaasa of Likati;
(4) the Bunduli.

(*c*) The speech of the Bawiinza [= 'BaWeenza' of our maps]:

(1) on the Buta–Titule road between Kms. 25 and 35, north of the River Balinguunguli, where Liwiinza (B. 369) is spoken;
(2) the language of the Makere who have undergone the influence of the Bayewu to the north of Zobia.

(*d*) The speech of the Boganzulu, Liganzulu (B. 364), used between the Rivers Rubi and Tely. To this should be added the languages of

(1) the Bogbali, south-west of Buta;
(2) the Basali, west of the Bogbali, who have been influenced by the Babinza.

(e) The speech of the Bobwa-Bokipa of Kole, near the Protestant Mission of Bongandje (B. 365); Libwa-Kibuyi to the south of the River Tely.

(f) The speech of (1) the Bobwa of Moma (south), Ankpo, and Kagbo, (2) the Bobwa of Ibembo (B. 378).

IV. *The Yewu group* (known as Napagibetini) (B. 364). It is situated between the Rivers Bima and Ombo, and comprises the languages of the

(a) Bosanwa, west of River Bima, chefferie Aponsa.
(b) Bobita, west of the Bosanwa.
(c) Bogbawa of Zobia; chief André Ndabaguto.

V. *The Bwa group* (Libwali, known as Napagitene). This language is spoken east of the River Bima by the

(a) Bokete of Dingila and Bambili (B. 363).
(b) Bokapu of Angodia, east of Azanga (B. 362).
(c) Bokiba: Bombesa and Zobia, between the Bokapu and the Bodongbale.
(d) Bolongwa, in the Angodia area (B. 362).
(e) Bogongeya, Titule area.
(f) Bodongbale, Titule area, between the Bokiba and the River Bima.

VI. *The pseudo-Bangelima group of Banalia.*

(a) Leboro, spoken by the Baboro (B. 384);
(b) Leangba, spoken by the Baangba (B. 383);
(c) Lesalia, spoken by the Bosalia;
(d) Lelima, spoken by the Balima;
(e) Lebendia, spoken by the Bobendia between Motoma and Bolenge (B. 385).

Outside the territory of Banalia, the following also should be added to the group:

(f) Lehanga, spoken by the Bahanga in Basoko Territory to the west of the River Kalumete (B. 386);
(g) Lebendja, spoken by the Babendja in the Aruwimi Forest (B. 387);
(h) Legenza, spoken by the Bagenza, an enclave in Mabinza country, Aketi Territory. Their clan traditions suggest an origin not far from the River Lulu.

(D) THE BAKANGO (Riverine)

Along the lower Uele, the Api, the Bima, and the Bomokandi the fisherfolk all call themselves Bakango. They can hardly be said to have a common origin but are bound together by the similarity of their customs and way of life. They all claim to speak Likango but the diversity of these languages shows that this name merely designates a medium of intercomprehension obtained by deliberately deforming and degrading their various forms of speech. This explains the simplification and reduction of the noun classes to two in number in spite of the fact that other class prefixes survive. The languages described earlier (Apagibeti, Benge-Baati, Yewu, and Bwa) were the original forms which have been thus simplified. The various forms of Likango recorded by us are:

I. Likango of the River Uele, taken down at Angodia (B. 389);
II. Likango of the River Bima, taken down at Titule (B. 390);
III. Likango of the River Bomokandi, taken down at Poko (B. 391);
IV. Likango of the River Api, taken down at Api (B. 392);
V. Likango of the lower Uele and of the Likati taken down at Likati and from the capita Gbabu on the River Uele.

We were unable to verify whether the Bogala who live along the lower Uele downstream from Bondo also speak a Likango dialect. We do not mention here the Adiyo (on the River Bili) who for the most part speak Bandia.

NORTHERN GROUP TRANSITION LANGUAGES

A. OLOMBO (= Turumbu). These are all situated in Isangi Territory (10,395).

I. The greatest concentration is on the right bank of the Congo near the riverine Lokele. It includes the former chefferies of Yawenda, Weko, Yaelongo, Yambaw, Yangambi, Yaboni, and Awembe (B. 417). Eastern Turumbu (B. 418).

II. There are a few villages on the left bank (e.g. Yakutu near Yanonge). They originate from Busukutu on the right bank. As they mingled with the Lokele on the left bank they were influenced by them and became fisherfolk. Their version of Olombo shows considerable contamination when compared with that of the opposite bank.

III. We do not include the *Turumbu de l'eau* or Yanongo of Elisabetha. It would seem that they do not speak Olombo; we offer this remark with considerable hesitation, however, as we were unable to contact this people.

B. TOPOKE (= Eso) (45,958)

I. Topoke proper. These were formerly to be found in eight chefferies of Isangi Territory: Bohuma, Moendu, Logoge, Ihoa, Bolea, Ilongo, Yatyasoa, and Kombe, but have since been consolidated into four sectors: Luwete (7,930), Lukombe (4,236), Bambelota (7,846), and Kombe (7,637) (B. 427).

II. We also include two groups whose ethnic origins were probably diverse, but who now speak Topoke, i.e. the speeches of (a) the Liutwa (8,330), (b) the Baluombila (9,970) (B. 429).

III. Alombooki (11,165). These are known as pseudo-Lokele of the River Lomami. It should be noted that originally they consisted of two different groups and that since then both have undergone Lokele influence. They do not accept the name of Lokele or Topoke. In their speech the following features may be noticed: (a) a vocabulary which is basically Topoke, but with loan words from the 'Cuvette' (= Mongo area); (b) Lokele influence in the verbal system (B. 430).

IV. Likolo (Yanonge area). There are several villages in the sector of Yanongo calling themselves Likolo but only the village of Yawiko may rightfully claim this name (B. 428). At present Topoke is spoken there and the Topoke origin of the village can be proved. The other villages are composed of foreign immigrants who have been grouped together as 'floating' population in one and the same sector. They speak either Lokele or their own languages, such as Tsholo-Tsholo and Mongandu of the Mongandu, Likunda of the Elambo, Selenge and Sale of the Wangelima 'licenciés', and lastly Fundi-Heri of those with mixed Arab ancestry—the remnants of a former Arab outpost.

We have already spoken of the Yalikoka; they are of Topoke origin it is true, but they have been so strongly influenced by the Lokele, who are infiltrating on all sides round the Lomami estuary, that they now speak Lokele only (B. 424). This process was no doubt accelerated by the inclusion of the Mbooso (B. 423) in their sector.

C. LOMBOLE

If we attempt to group the Mbole dialects taking into account Lokele infiltration we obtain the following picture starting in the south and working northwards:

I. The purest group is Keembo of Opale.

II. The language of the Yaamba (which is still close to Keembo) (B. 430). It is also to be found amongst the following clans: Yasongi 22, Yalikanda 26, Yaotumbi 27, Yaeti 28, Yaeneru 30.

III. The language of the Yaisa and Yaikoli (B. 434), Yangonda and Botunga (B. 431, 432) and of the following clans: Yaongendja, Yatulema, Yataka, Yaenga, and Yalukulu. This variety of Lombole has been far more affected by Lokele than the other two. Botunga is particularly remarkable in this respect.

IV. Continuing northwards we reach the language called Fuma (B. 425), spoken by the Yalihila and Yalikandja; here the Mbole substratum has almost disappeared, so strong has been Lokele influence (B. 425, 426). Eastwards, however, Lombole has been influenced by Kibira, characteristics of the latter being clearly identifiable in the Lombole of the Bokuuwa (B. 433), at the villages of Ikutu and Yakamba which neighbour on the Babila area.

Unfortunately our information on this group is incomplete. As we were unable to get to either Opala or Yahuma, we cannot state precisely where the limits of the group fall. It seems, however, that we should classify as belonging to Lombole the following groups: Lobaye (e.g. Yaamba), Tooli, and Kembe. As far as Yahuma Territory, i.e. the Bongandu, the boundary is indefinite and the same degree of indeterminacy occurs on the south-western, southern, and eastern frontiers of this group.

E. EASTERN GROUP

We may bestow on this section the name KUUMU-BIRA. In our opinion the following languages should be included in it:

I. Ibuti; II. Ikaiku; III. Kibila of the forest; IV. Kikuumu; V. Ibili; VI. Ebugombe; VII. Kibira (Western); VIII. Kilengola and Kinya Mituku; IX. Kibira of the plain; X. Kibira of the Ruwenzori.

I. *Ibuti* ('Kimbuti')

This is the language of the Babuti ('Bambuti') pygmies who are scattered amongst the forest-dwelling Babila. Although it has certain peculiarities which render it easily identifiable (especially as regards pronunciation), it is obvious that it has all the characteristics of forest Ibila (P. 1, 4, 6, 9, 14, 28).

II. *Ikaiku*

The Bakaiku live in the Beni area on the Beni–Mambasa road. They will not accept the name Babila or Bakuumu. From a vocabulary point of view the Babuti consider that this language is the closest to their own. Unfortunately we were unable to finish our investigation of it.

III. *Forest Kibila*

The Babila live in Beni Territory (5,659) and in Epulu Territory. These are the facts which we were able to gather amongst the forest Babila: 1. Southern Babila (Oitshia), Beni Territory (B. 247–9); 2. Western Babila (Epulu), Epulu Territory: Babombi (B. 246); 3. Eastern Babila (Mambasa), Epulu Territory: Bakwaanza (B. 244); (Lolwa) Epulu Territory: Bayaku (B. 245)—Chief Apaligba. The pygmies who live with them say they speak Ibuti.

IV. *Kikuumu*

The Bakuumu cover a vast area of which the Survey was able to take in only the most northerly portions. Our documentation is merely fragmentary for the Bakuumu of Lubutu (34,383) (B. 250) and the Lowa River Bakuumu (B. 251). We were unable to continue the investigation amongst the Bakuumu of Opienge (B. 252), Bafwasende Territory, Angumu Region. They have two dialects with only very slight variations: that of the Kuumu Wanda to the east, and of the Kuumu Looya to the west. They live between the Rivers Tshopo and Maika. We were also able to contact the northern Bakuumu (11,752) to the north of Stanleyville (B. 253). With these should be included the Badoombi or Bakuumu of the River Tshopo (B. 254) living at Km. 29 on the Stanleyville–Benyamusa road. Previously they have been wrongly classified as Barumbi (i.e. Odyalombi).

We found it impossible to deal with the Bakuumu-Bazimba of the former territory of Masia now situated in Opienge Territory (3,370). In addition to these there are some 10,000 Bakuumu in Ponthierville Territory.

V. *Ibili*

The people known as Bapere (Babili) who live to the north of Biambi in Lubero Territory (5,139) have various dialects with only slight variations. We have noted:

1. Ibili, spoken by the Babili (B. 255, 256).
2. Eleedji, spoken by the Baleedji of Manguredzipa (B. 258).
3. Etike, spoken by the Batike (of Mount Mayi) (B. 257).

We were also told that other dialects exist, spoken by: 4. the Babaidumba of Avakubi; 5. the Babeka of Fungula Meso; 6. the Bahokohoko of Lubena.

VI. *Ebugombe* (12,304)

This is to be found in Beni Territory. The speech of the Babugombe is very similar to the preceding dialect and occurs (*a*) from Lubena as far as the Beni–Bela road (B. 260), (*b*) in an enclave on the River Semliki between Beni and Mutwanga (the village of Kitobi) (B. 259).

VII. *Western Babira*

The Survey was unable to reach the Western Babira, i.e. Babera, Stanleyville Territory, Babeda on the main railway line and Babila of Ponthierville (4,403).

VIII. *Kilengola and Kinya Mituku*

We were, however, able to get a little information on Kilengola spoken by the Balengola of Ponthierville (B. 261, 262) and on Kinya Mituku, the language of the Banya Mituku, in the same territory (B. 263).

IX. *Kibira of the Plain* (31,703)

There is a marked difference between the speech of the Forest Babila and that of the Babira of the plain. The latter are divided into five clans but this does not appear to correspond with any linguistic differences (B. 236–9).

X. *Ruwenzori Kibira*

We believe that the three following speeches found on the spurs of Mount Ruwenzori should be classed with Kibira of the plain: (*a*) Kihumu (called Kuamba in Uganda) (B. 242) for which our information was supplemented by that of Professor A. N. Tucker working in Uganda; (*b*) Kihianzi, spoken by the Bahianzi; (*c*) the speech of the Lega clan. Our information was gathered at Mwenda and Mutwanga (B. 240, 241).

EASTERN GROUP TRANSITION LANGUAGES

Here we insert a whole group of transition languages. Although they are clearly spread over three separate areas, there can be no doubt as to their unity. They are:

I. *Linyali*

Southern Banyali (Bunia, Geti Territory) 1,927.
Northern Banyali (Djugu Territory) 10,679.

The northern and southern sections are separated by the Lendu, but their linguistic unity is obvious.

(*a*) The southern Banyali speak Libvanuma (from the name of one of their clans). They live in Dzabi chefferie, Geti 'Poste' (B. 266) and extend southwards as far as Mboga and westwards to the Irumu–Beni road (at a village at Km. 74) (B. 267).

(*b*) The northern Banyali inhabit Djugu Territory in a Bantu enclave amongst Non-Bantu languages (Lendu to the south, Mamvu, Mangbutu, Mabendi to the northwest). We took down our example of it at Vieux Kilo (B. 264, 265).

(*c*) A group of the northern Banyali have emigrated to the Arebi area, Watsa Territory, and have retained their original language (called by them Libombi) up to the present time (B. 268*a* and *b*).

II. *Ebudu* (Wamba Territory, 83,329)

Between the northern Banyali and the Babudu stretches the vast forest, inhabited by Mamvu, Mangbutu, and Babila. No tradition exists which might throw light on migrations in the distant past between the two sections with related languages. Five dialects may be distinguished. They are spoken by:

(a) the Matta, north and south of Maboma (B. 269); this is the closest to Imbo;
(b) the Bafwakayi and Malamba, north of Bafwabaka (B. 270);
(c) the Bafwagada (Lega), between Bafwabalwe and Ibambe (B. 272);
(d) the Makoda, Wadimbisa, Timoniko of the Ibambi area (B. 271);
(e) the Balika in Malika-Mabudu chefferie, Wamba Territory (B. 273).

III. *Imbo* (or Kimbo according to the Babaali)

This is the speech of the Bambo, known as Bombo or Moondo, or Baambu in Epulu Territory (2,060) (B. 274, 275).

IV. *Indaaka* spoken by the Bandaaka (4,750), Epulu Territory

The speakers of this language live in the Avakubi area but stretch north of the Ituri as far as Abulu and Babudu country. The language is related to the speech of the Babeeke without, however, bearing all the latter's marks of external influence (B. 277, 278).

V. *Ibeeke*

There are now only two villages of Babeeke-speakers: (a) the village of Ibeke on the Avakubi–Irumu road, Km. 388 (B. 276); (b) the village of Ibeke south of the Ituri. It is a very mixed dialect of Imbo origin which has undergone Bila and Baale influence, or vice-versa.

F. EXTREME EAST GROUP

The Bantu of the extreme east of the Belgian Congo all belong to the Eastern Bantu Group.[1] Here we find representatives of four groups: I. Nyoro; II. Rwanda-Rundi; III. Yira (Nande); IV. Hunde.

A. THE NYORO GROUP

I. *Olunyoro*

The Survey merely touched on Olunyoro when passing through Fort Portal. Strictly speaking it does not extend as far as the Belgian Congo (B. 298).

II. *Olutoro*

The same is true of one of the dialects of this language (B. 299). According to tradition the Basongora originated from Butoro and used to speak the language. However, those Basongora encountered by the Survey between the River Semliki and the slopes of Mount Ruwenzori all spoke Kinande dialects.

III. *Kitalinge* (or Mawisi)

Spoken by 5,945 in Beni Territory. The Survey was unable to reach these in the Belgian Congo as, in the absence of a practicable road, an immense detour would

---

[1] This refers to Professor Van Bulck's 'Bantou de l'Est' group (v. his *Recherches linguistiques au Congo Belge*).

have had to be made south and east by rounding the Ruwenzori range and re-routing the expedition from Fort Portal onwards. We were able, however, to get sufficient information to justify the inclusion of this language in the Nyoro group and not in that of Nande as it has been erroneously classified in the past (B. 300, 300a).

IV. *Oruhima*

The Avahima shepherds who emigrated from Unyoro to the west of Lake Albert have almost all lost their original language. Our efforts to unearth a few remnants of it were, however, successful and we finally discovered a few enclaves:

- (a) Oruhema in Bunia Territory, at the Bagota chefferie of Sota, in the villages of Bundikase, Rusoke, Mbogo, and Mitega (B. 302) (2,925);
- (b) Oruhuma spoken by the clan of the Ababito who live round about Badia in Bunia Territory (B. 306);
- (c) Kihema in the extreme south of Djugu Territory, at the village of Chief Lovangira, the only one in the area which has not adopted Lendu (Southern Ndruna) as its language (1,450);
- (d) Oruhima in the extreme north of Rwanda, north of Biumba in Buberuko, Ndorwa, and Mutara (B. 303, 304).

V. *Runyambo* and *Rukaragwe* (Ururagwe)

On the eastern frontier of Kwanda, on the Mubari and Migongo, the existence of a few Karagwe and Nyambo hamlets was indicated, but these were found to be immigrants from Uganda and Tanganyika. The main body of them is not situated in Rwanda.

VI. *Etshihororo*

The same may be said of the Avahororo, who have settled north of Biumba on the Uganda boundary. Their settlements are, however, independent entities which have retained the original language (B. 305).

B. The Rwanda-Rundi Group

After a very close investigation pursued impartially both amongst Africans and Europeans, the Survey was able to establish that the unification of Ikinyarwanda and Ikirundi is eminently desirable and, moreover, capable of being achieved very rapidly if local collisions are avoided. It is a psychological rather than a linguistic problem.

I. *Ikinyarwanda* (1,976,234)

To the 1,870,410 Banyarwanda resident in Rwanda itself should be added 105,824 who are divided amongst the Belgian Congo territories as follows: Bwisha (Rutshuru) 68,742; Bukumu (Rutshuru) 10,991; Gishari (Masisi) 26,091. The investigation dealt with:

(a) Ikinyarwanda proper:

(1) Ikinyanduga, at Nyanza (B. 340, 340a);
(2) Indara, at Kisangala (B. 341);

(3) Iganza (southern Buganza) at Rwamagana (B. 342);
(4) Indorwa (Rukiga), at Biumba (B. 345).

(b) The language of Bwisha, Igikiga taken down at Rugari and Djomba (B. 344, 344a); the same language occurs in Mushari, Bukumu, and now, because of Rwanda immigration, is to be found as far off as Gishari (Kamuronza).

(c) The language of Bufumbwa in Uganda. No precise information.

(d) The language of the Bahutu. It is hard to obtain definite statements, as many informants avoid dialectal variants and try to speak Ikinyarwanda of Nduga which is supposed to be the most normal and the most correct dialect. Our information relates to Kihutu of:

(1) the Ndara, at Kisagala (B. 347);
(2) the Mulera: Urulera (or Ikihera) at Rwasa (B. 348);
(3) the Bogoyi: Ikishobyo, spoken by the Amashobyo at Nyundo (B. 349);
(4) Itshogo (or Kingogo), Igitshiga or Urukiga or Ikiga of the Batshiga who live in the mountains of Murunda (B. 346).

II. *Ikirundi* (2,024,925)

In Urundi there are 2,011,982 Barundi, to which should be added 12,943 who live in Uvira Territory. Of the combined labour force of 14,371 Banyarwanda and Barundi now employed in the Belgian Congo we are unable to say what proportion are Barundi. Our investigation of Kirundi was conducted at Kitega (B. 339).

C. THE YIRA GROUP

This group (256,748) is generally called Nande, although the origin of this cognomen is uncertain. Ekiyira languages have therefore been called Kinande (or Kindande). The natives insist that there are many localized dialects but the differences between them are very slight indeed.

I. The languages reputed to be the oldest: (a) Ekibito, spoken by the Ababito (B. 312); (b) Ekihira, spoken by the Avahira (B. 308); (c) Ekihomba, spoken by the Avahombo.

II. The languages of the northern Avanande: Batange of Chief Selimani (1,735) in Beni Territory.

III. The languages of the Avanande who arrived via the south of Lake Edward: (a) Ekimate (19,151), Lubero Territory (B. 322) taken down at Bingi; (b) Ekikumbule of the Ikoobo (3,293 in Masisi Territory). These were the advance-guard of the immigration which did not halt until it reached the mountains to the north-east of Masisi Territory (B. 323); (c) Ekitangi spoken by the Avatangi (30,830) in Lubero Territory, taken down at Mulo, south-east of the Nande bloc (B. 310).

IV. The language of the Avaswaga (121,246), in Lubero Territory:

(a) Ekiswaga. The speakers of this language, which was taken down at Mulo and Kyondo (B. 309), infiltrated between their forerunners and the Basu;

(b) Ekikira also belongs here (B. 311).

V. The language of the Avashu (64,689 in Beni Territory):

(a) Ekishu spoken over a vast area. We took it down at Kyondo and Bunyuka (B. 313, 314);

(b) It is not very likely that Ekishukaali, spoken by the Avashukaali (Bashu women), differs greatly from the foregoing. We were, however, unable to find an example of it (B. 315).

VI.

(a) Ekilega (B. 316, 317);
(b) Ekihambo (B. 320).

These have acquired a certain amount of celebrity as it was thought, from Johnston onwards, that in Lega could be seen le-dha (Bale-dha, the language of the northern Lendu). Be this as it may, at the present time their speech is clearly Ekinande.

VII. Ekisongoora, spoken by the Avasongoora (at the mouth of the River Semliki on the shores of Lake Edward), has already been mentioned. These people claim that formerly they spoke a Nyoro dialect; nowadays they speak a dialect of Ekinande; 1,266 in Beni Territory (B. 319).

VIII. Lastly there is Ekisanza, spoken by the Wanisanza, who are scattered around Beni, but who to the best of our knowledge speak one and the same dialect. This is used:

(a) in the central group: the people of Buleki and Beni (4,993 Wanisanza in Beni Territory);
(b) in very small settlements on the slopes of Mount Ruwenzori, including among others: (1) the Banga Ngala to the north (1,408); (2) the Bolema (5,661) and the Malambo (2,476) in the centre; (3) the Mumbatu and the Bavingulu to the south.

These are often called Bakondjo (B. 321)—the people with filed teeth—especially in the east of Uganda, where this name is used to distinguish them from the speakers of Kuamba (Bira Group).

D. THE HUNDE GROUP

At the present stage of our examination of the collected material we think that these should be divided into two sub-groups: I. Shi; II. Hunde.

I. *Shi Sub-group*

In this first sub-group we put two languages: Ekihaavu and Amashi. Our linguistic work in this area was greatly facilitated by the groundwork done by the White Fathers and especially Mgr. Cleire. For Amashi a very detailed grammar and a voluminous dictionary (both cyclostyled) enabled us to start off the very first day on the main body of the work. Moreover, a few months after our visit, Professor Am. Burssens, on the invitation of Mgr. Cleire, came to spend several months on the tonal study of this material. The Survey will therefore not base its remarks on its own documentation, gathered hastily in the field, but will instead compare its own results with those which accrued from Professor Burssens' methodical and exhaustive examination.

(a) Ekihaavu is only found in Kalehe Territory at the chefferies of Kashofu, Binga, Kaliba, and especially on the island of Kidzwi (50,000) (B. 326).

(b) Amashi. At the present stage of the analysis of our notes we believe that this may be divided into the following:

(1) Kabaare speech, reputedly the purest and most common, Kabare Territory, chefferie of Kabaare (80,000) (B. 329, 330).

(2) Burhale-Ngweshe speech, chefferie of Ngweshe (109,784), very close to the foregoing one (B. 331).
(3) Nyangeshi speech, south of Bukavu, has been influenced by the admixture of thousands of immigrants with the local population. The immigrants who can find nowhere to live in the Strangers' Quarter sleep at Nyangeshi and work in Bukavu.
(4) Amalindja, spoken by the Avalindja (4,601) in Kabare Territory (B. 332).
(5) Amaziba, spoken by the Avaziba (8,982), Kabare Territory (B. 333).
(6) Amahwindja (or Amalwindja) (8,193), Mwenga Territory (B. 334).
(7) Balonge-Longe speech in the north of Kabare Territory.

II. *Hunde Sub-group*

This group is to be found west of Lake Kivu, to the north and south of sub-group I.

(*a*) Tembo. We divide this into two dialects:

(1) Kitembo, spoken by the Batembo, which occurs especially in the Kalehe district (15,020). A few speakers may be found as far afield as Masisi Territory but there they have mingled with other tribes (B. 325, 326);
(2) Kihunde. In the east of Rutshuru Territory and a large part of Masisi Territory (33,583) (B. 324*a* and *b*).

(*b*) Nyindu. Two languages which diverge only slightly seem to contain archaic survivals, they are:

(1) Kinyindu of Lwindi (11,000 in Mwenga Territory) (B. 338);
(2) Ekirhinyi-Rhinyi of Burhinyi, which probably should be classified here, but we were unable to examine it (14,393 in Mwenga Territory) (B. 338*a*).

EXTREME EAST GROUP TRANSITION LANGUAGES

As the purpose of the Survey was simply to examine the languages spoken along the Bantu linguistic frontier we had to content ourselves with demarcating the eastern Bantu bloc from the Lega-speakers. Thus our investigation of Lega went no further than those languages adjacent to the frontier. These are:

1. Kinyanga, Masisi Territory (24,744) (B. 351, 352). It is spoken to the north of the administrative centre of Masisi and stretches as far as the Forest Wakumbule in the north-east corner (Avakumbule ba gbito). It is here that the transition occurs from the other Wakumbule who speak Ekinande.

2. Kikaanu (3,510), Masisi Territory (B. 353). Spoken in the Walikale area, forming the fringe of the Central Lega bloc.

3. The central Lega bloc. We were able to obtain examples of the following dialects:

(*a*) Kileega, spoken by the Shabunda Bakisi (33,444) (B. 354).
(*b*) Ileega Imuzimu (33,107), Mwenga Territory: (i) Ishile of Mwenga, Mungoombe, Kanutuya (B. 354, 354*a*); (ii) Iwanga Baale of Kituutu (B. 355).
(*c*) Ebeembe (2,326), Uvira Territory (B. 359, 359*a*).
(*d*) Etumbwe of Butumbwe (Mwenga 7,997) apparently differs but little from (*c*).

(e) Kileega kya Wakabango (B. 358) is very close to the Kileega of Pangi. Fr. Colle investigated the speech of Fundi Sadi (without publishing his findings) but the Survey was unable to reach it.

(f) Kesongola of the River Lowa to the west (B. 356 and 263). This language together with Kegengele is a transition from the Bila group of the River Lualaba.

(g) Probably Kisanzi of Baraka should be included here. Fr. Vyncke wrote a grammar of it as early as 1882 but it was never published (B. 337a). We say 'probably' because at this juncture in the Kabambare area another group has been mentioned, for which we have as yet no information. It includes Kibangu bangu and Kibuyu.

For reasons already given the Survey had to halt on these borders, and in any case the mountains prevented informants from reaching either Uvira or Lake Tanganyika.

G. CENTRAL LANGUAGE

ENYA

The group of 'Wagenia' (Baenya) fisherfolk of Stanleyville is often considered as part of the tribes of the middle reaches of the River Congo. Moreover their traditional history leads us to expect this to be the case. Indeed the 'Wagenia' found some Yasanga at the falls when they arrived. At the present day, however, only a few clan names survive. The investigation of the language spoken by the Baenya now shows clearly that its speakers are of foreign origin. It belongs to the central Bantu language bloc and is quite different from all the others spoken in the Stanleyville area.

3. THE NON-BANTU LANGUAGES

A. NILOTIC LANGUAGE

DHO ALUUR

The only Nilotic language spoken in the Belgian Congo is Dho Aluur. The Pamitu and Pandoro constituted the advance-guard of the Nilotic invaders. In Djugu Territory they are given their clan name of Mambisa; the Bale call them Go (4,093). The latter, however, have all adopted Bale-dha in preference to their original language. We will say more of this under the heading of Bale-dha.

The Aluur proper live in Mahagi Territory (72,542). They are called 'Aluur of the plain' (N. 1) to distinguish them from the 'Mountain Aluur' of the Okoro clan who dwell over the Uganda border (Nyapea N. 2).

Turning to those who have undergone Aluur influence we find in Mahagi Territory:

(a) Wahema, known as Djukot (16,507) (N. 3);
(b) Wanyoro, known as Mokambo (12,289) or Magongo (3,316).

The total number of Dho Aluur speakers in the Belgian Congo was in 1948 as high as 109,628.

B. NILO-HAMITIC LANGUAGES (BELGIAN CONGO)

I. KAKWA

The administrative territorial boundary divides the Kakwa (17,201) into two sections: Northern Kakwa (Aba) in Faradje Territory, Ima chefferie (4,937) (NH. 4), and Southern Kakwa (Adi) in Mahagi Territory, Diopa chefferie (12,264) (NH. 5). The language of the north has been preserved better than that of the south where indications of number and gender leave much to be desired.

II. FADJULU

There are, it is true, in Faradje Territory two Fadjulu villages (Yali near Mongwa, and Lama) with about 200 inhabitants, but they have almost all substituted Kakwa for their original language and a few speak Logo.

C. CENTRAL SUDANIC LANGUAGES

The vast area covered by the central Sudanic languages stretches from Lake Chad (western group: Barma, Kuka, Sara) to the Anglo-Egyptian Sudan (eastern group: Bongo, Baka) and some distance westwards (Kredj Gbaya). In the Belgian Congo there are only two of its members: I. Baka (eastern group); II. Furu-Gbaya (Kredj sub-group).

I. BAKA

The Survey was able to contact the Baka at Yambio in Anglo-Egyptian Sudan (S. 88) before encountering them in Faradje Territory on its arrival in the Belgian Congo. What few Baka there are (about 1,300 in all) are divided into two separate sections:

(*a*) the eastern section has no areas which are exclusively Baka. The speakers of this language are scattered amongst the Logo and Mundo. In fourteen villages there are about 500 (150 HAV).[1] The most important villages are Lalibe (34 HAV), Madri (30 HAV) and Aiwa (23 HAV) (S. 86, S. 87, S. 89).

(*b*) the western section lives in the Zande chefferie of Renzi east of Duru (Duru Territory). There they occupy seven villages (about 800, or 208 HAV) which are situated to the north of the River Aka extending eastwards from Bagbele. The stream Nambelima-Aka separates them from the Boguru (S. 90).

II. FURU-GBAYA

In the Belgian Congo they call themselves Gbaya but their Mbandja and Ngbandi neighbours bestow on them the name of Furu. They live in Bosobolo Territory near the River Ubangi and stretch a little beyond the Ubangi into French Oubangui Chari where they are known as Bafuru. In Belgian territory, apart from those who are scattered in neighbouring villages, the main body has remained united and forms a rather important entity in the Dula area, east of Bosobolo, close to the Gobu and Ngombe (S. 170).

---

[1] In official figures, *Hommes adultes valides* = able-bodied adult males.

D. EASTERN SUDANIC LANGUAGES

The distribution of these languages in Anglo-Egyptian Sudan and Uganda has already been described by Professor A. N. Tucker.[1] Here we are confronted by their continuation towards the south. We would divide this larger unit into three groups: (A) Moru-Madi, (B) Mamvu-Lese, (C) Lendu; the last is very different from the others and it is with all due reserve that we include it.

A. MORU-MADI

In this group we include the central dialects: I. Logo; II. Avokaya; III. Bari-Logo; IV. Kaliko; and V. the southern dialect Lugbara.

I. *Logo*

The Logo area is in Faradje Territory (50,356, i.e. 15,000 HAV). According to Fr. Costermans there are at least six dialects (S. 29–31, 34–35, 38–43).

(*a*) Logo of the Anglo-Egyptian Sudan border:

(1) Odjila, the dialect of 'those who live downstream'. These are almost all in Anglo-Egyptian Sudan, and in the Belgian Congo representatives of this people are hard to find. Their villages are to the north of those of the Odjiga.

(2) Odjiga, the dialect of 'those who live to the east'. Its speakers occupy the area north of the Rivers Utwa and Dungu, being therefore the southerly neighbours of the Odjila. They are not very numerous and are only to be found in a few villages.

(3) Akori. This dialect is intermediate between Odjiga and Odjila, and is probably closer linguistically to the latter. There are only a few scattered individuals who speak it in the Belgian Congo (S. 37).

(*b*) The main body of Logo who occupy the area bounded on the north by the River Dungu and on the south by the River Obi (officially known as the River Nzoro). These speak two dialects:

(1) Northern Logo or the dialect of the Ogamaaru (= 'northerners') who mainly inhabit the large chefferies of Chief Azile (S. 34) and Chief Matafa (S. 38).

(2) The central or River Obi dialect. These people have been classified according to their habitat as 'upstream' Tabuloba and 'downstream' Tabulaga (S. 35).

(*c*) Logo of the extreme south. These we will call Obi-Leba or 'people beyond the River Obi'. They are only 5,152 in number. We recorded this dialect at Todro (S. 41) and Makoro (S. 40).

II. *Avokaya*

We are unable to state their exact numbers as they are a scattered people, living between the Odjila in the north and the Odjiga in the south, i.e. to the north of the main Logo area, in the basin of the Rivers Utwa and Dungu (but only on the right bank of the latter). Their number may be estimated at 3,000. Fr. Costermans' detailed investigations have shown that Ogambi is not a separate language nor even

---

[1] *Eastern Sudanic Languages*, vol. i, 1940.

an ethnic entity, but merely the reigning dynasty of the Avokaya. Our examination was conducted both amongst the latter (S. 32) and also amongst the Ogambi (S. 33, 36).

III. *Bari*

The Bari, called officially Bari-Logo, reject all theories of a common origin with the Logo and will not intermarry with them. Nevertheless they now speak a related dialect, which is closer to Avokaya than to Logo. In the past they were blacksmiths and lived on the banks of the Garamba, being later driven away and installing themselves in an area reaching from Niangara in the west almost to Faradje in the east. We do not know what language they spoke at that time. Their present dispersed state is of recent date since, wherever we found survivors, they always spoke the same dialect which is related to Logo. Our information relates to:

(*a*) Chief Surur's group, south-west of Faradje. These are the most numerous (3,839) and live mainly in the three villages of Mele, Konzo Bari, and Motoba. Most of them still speak Bari (S. 45).

(*b*) A very small enclave in Watsa Territory, Gaduma chefferie, between Wanga and Ingi-Gombari (S. 47). Here there are no more than 970 divided between five villages, and among these there are scarcely ten old men who still speak their own language, i.e. Bari of Surur chefferie near Todra.

(*c*) A few old men, established as notables, in the villages under Matshaga domination in Niangara Territory. The investigation took place among the Midi-Midi near Ekibondo (S. 46). Apart from these few exceptions most of them have adopted either Bangba (the language of the substratum) or Namangbetu-ti (the language which reigning clans of the Matshaga-Duga prefer to their original Pamiangba, a Barambo dialect).

It still remains to be verified whether the Bere vocabulary taken down by Czekanowski does not refer to these Bari-Logo, as at the time of writing there is no trace of a Bere tribe in this area.

IV. *Kaliko*

The Kaliko dwell round the head-waters of the Obi in Mahagi Territory. Official statistics put their numbers as high as 12,231, but this figure should be reduced as it refers to an artificial territorial division which puts Kaliko and Lugbara in one and the same chefferie. We have then to distinguish two groups:

(*a*) Northern Kaliko who speak a dialect clearly related to Logo (S. 44);
(*b*) Southern Kaliko who live near the River Obi and speak only Lugbara.

V. *Lugbara*

The Belgian Congo Lugbara are the continuation of those who are to be found in Uganda. In the course of a conversation with Fr. Crazzolara, who is now writing a Lugbara grammar of the Lugbara-Padzulu dialect of Arua, we noted that between this dialect and those spoken in the Belgian Congo there are considerable differences, but not so great, however, as to preclude eventual unification.

All Lugbara of the Belgian Congo live in Mahagi Territory (58,147) between the Kaliko to the north and the Mumbi-Ndo (Okebo and Avare) to the south. There are five dialects: (*a*) Aluru (9,746) (S. 49); (*b*) Nyo (3,891) (S. 50); (*c*) Zaki-Lui (8,941) (S. 51, 52); (*d*) Oka (32,174) (S. 48); (*e*) Otso (3,396) (S. 53). The last-named which is used at the Aru Mission differs considerably from the other four.

B. THE MAMVU-LESE GROUP

The members of this group are clearly interrelated. Its position in regard to the Moru-Madi group will later be the subject of a close investigation. It includes: I. Mumbi-Ndo; II. Mangutu; III. Mamvu; IV. Amengi (very close to III); V. Efe-Lese; VI. Mabendi (very close to Lese).

I. *Mumbi-Ndo*

The name 'Mumbi' under which we group these people was given to us at Luga as a name which is common to both the Okebo and the Ndo, but later at Makoro this information was not confirmed. Moreover the name 'Ndo' is as common among the Ndo-Okebo as it is with the Ndo-Avare, but neither of these will accept the simple title of 'Ndo'. Their language seems to be transitional between Lugbara and Mangutu, being closer to the latter.

(*a*) Okebo. Blacksmiths by trade, they live in the mountains which lie between the Nile and the Congo, part of them being in Uganda and the others in Mahagi Territory of the Belgian Congo (8,996) (S. 55, 56, 57, 58). Later we will deal with those who are scattered in Djugu Territory (Oke, or Wafula-Yembe) but who now speak Bale-dha.

(*b*) Avare. Around Mahagi these are the western neighbours of the Okebo. They are situated between the Lugbara to the north, the Dongo to the west, the Mangutu to the south-west, and the Aluur to the south-east. As their total number is small (3,987) and the area they occupy is very large, the Administration has authorized Aluur shepherds to immigrate into the eastern part—the only region free from tsetse fly. Their dialect, from a purely linguistic and phonetic viewpoint, is almost identical with that of the Okebo (S. 59–60), but the Avare protest when their dialectal diversity is disregarded.

II. *Mangutu*

The following variants are heard: Mangutu, Mangbutu, Mongbutu—which explains why, in earlier ethnological publications (1880–1900) they were often confused with the Mangbetu, whom they call Mambettu or Mombuttu.

All the Mangutu inhabit Watsa Territory (8,705), in the two chefferies of Angwe, north of Watsa (3,428 under Chief Mangwangwe) and Arebi, south of Watsa (5,277 under Chief Makutana). According to Fr. Costermans, who for several years visited them in the forest round the head-waters of the Momokandi and the Ituri, they have at least five dialects with considerable lexical divergence:

(*a*) Mangutu proper, in the immediate vicinity of Watsa (S. 71);
(*b*) the dialect of the Mangutu-Karo ('upstream Mangutu'), on the left bank of the Kibali;
(*c*) the Mangutu-Lobe ('downstream Mangutu') dialect, on the left bank of the Kibali;

(d) the Awi-Meeri or A'i-meeri ('forest folk') dialect. Its speakers are called in the local trade language of Bangala 'Baatu na boondo';
(e) the Bamodo dialect.

There may be a sixth dialect, spoken by the Madandi, behind Mount Kilimanungo, but we could not obtain definite evidence of this.

III. *Mamvu*

The Mamvu, who have an enormous number of small clans which are individualistic and contiguous, all dwell in the almost impenetrable forest of Watsa Territory. This explains the incredible diversity of their regional speech variants. Just round Ingi alone we were able, thanks to Fr. Van den Wijngaert, to note down the lexical, grammatical, phonetic, and tonetic variants of no less than twenty-eight dialect forms. Together with those of Moto, Maboma, and Watsa we examined thirty-two. These, Professor Van Bulck thinks, may be reduced provisionally to six sections—which do not correspond to the administrative divisions as the latter were due to the contingencies of history rather than to tribal structure.

At the present time they are estimated at 23,855, spread over six chefferies: (i) Karuka-Lendu/Andikofa (5,108); (ii) Karuka-Lendu/Ateru (3,827); (iii) Mamvu Kebo (2,883); (iv) Mari-Minza (7,850); (v) Andobi (3,095); (vi) Bari and Mamvu Karo ('upstream') (1,092).

In the last chefferie the name 'Bari' may be confusing. They are all Mamvu with a ruling family which is Bari and has managed to retain its ascendancy, although the other Mamvu have been liberated from the domination of the Gombari Bari, the allies of the Mangbetu ruling clan.

To these we must add a small group of Mamvu to the north of Watsa Territory in Dungu Territory (*sous-chefferie* Kumba-Wando). After many upheavals, fratricidal strife, and attempts at conquest by the Mangbetu family, they are now completely scattered in the midst of remnants of various other tribes. In 1917 the Territorial Administrator Jorissen estimated their numbers at 2,000 HAV or 5,500 at the most.

The locality inhabited by the Mamvu may be roughly defined thus: the River Moto separates them from the Mangutu in the east, and in the south the River Nepoko divides them from the Lese; to the north the River Yelu forms their frontier with the Bangba-Mayogo—apart from the few Mamvu who remain in Dungu Territory; westwards there is no natural boundary line to separate them from the Babudu other than the vast virgin forest.

(a) Northern section (S. 63). This extends from the River Yebu in the north to the River Wanga in the south and is inhabited chiefly by Mamvu-Minza. Between them and the central and western sections are the Bari, the Banyanga, and the Bagbati, the last two tribes being Bantu in origin, but many of them have adopted Mangbetu during their period of subjection to the latter. This is the language which we recorded among the Ande-Kofa, Ande-Rungba, Menge, and Amandri.

Thus we come to another locality, bounded in the north by the River Obo, south by the River Bomokandi, and east by the River Moto. Linguistically it falls into two parts which we will call the central and eastern sections.

(b) Central section (S. 64). These are the dialects spoken in the Gambari area between the River Obo in the north and the River Bomokandi in the south, i.e. in part of the two Karuka-Lendu chefferies and in part of the Mamvu-Manzi chefferie (Andi-Ngombe-Tunsi). The main clans speaking these dialects are Ande-Kofa, Ande-Kori, Andi-Mbeli, Ateli, Anden, Atubi, Andi-Kilau, and Andi-Rimba.

(c) Eastern Section (S. 66, 70). It is mainly composed of Mamvu-Mari and comprises the whole Moku area up to the River Motu which separates them from the Mangutu. The main clans are: Andi-Ngba, Andi-Guli, Andi-Gori, Anda-Gbu, Anda-Gbi, Ande-Goti, Andi-Madu, Andi-Ntuli, Anda-Gbo.

Next comes the area south of the Bomokandi where we find two divergent groups of languages which we will call the western and south-western sections.

(d) Western section (S. 65). This includes the remainder of the dialects of the two chefferies of Karuka-Lendu which have not been classified in the central section.

(e) South-western section (S. 68, 69). The languages of this section are clearly closely related to the Lese spoken by their southern neighbours. The most important clans are the Awasu (south of the River Nepoko), the Andobi and the Abagufi of *sous-chefferie* Bere, and the Ande-Kere of Kebu chefferie.

(f) South-east section (S. 67). This occupies the extreme south-east area round the head-waters of the Bomokandi and the Ituri. Its dialects are close to Mangutu and especially to Lese. They are spoken by:

(1) in the Gamabo area, the Andi Komba, the Muli, and Ande Gofa (the last claim that they speak the Mamvu dialect which is the closest to the local Pygmy speech);

(2) in the Matapu area, the Andi-Bara, Andi-Kawu, Andi-Musi, Bali, and Andi-Mbororo.

Note: A very interesting piece of information worthy of being investigated was communicated to us at Ndoruma, north of the River Uele, in the village of the Zande Vongara chief Ukwatutu. A small enclave of Mamvu is said to exist north of the Uele in Dungu Territory, at Dika, chefferie of Chief Sadi, near the River Garba, where a few old men are still said to use their original language.

IV. *Amengi*

After the extreme multiplicity of Mamvu clan and speech names, the linguist feels disinclined to halt once more at minute villages on the boundary between Mamvu and Banga-Mayogo, but the inhabitants insist. They claim that they are all Amengi and not Mamvu.

(a) Muledre (S. 362). The first of these villages is situated on the road from Tora mines to Wanga at Km. 7. In spite of the natives' insistence to the contrary, this dialect seemed to us very close to Mamvu. Perhaps it is the proximity of the Bari-Logo on the one hand and their extremely isolated position on the northern edge of the Mamvu area on the other, which has confirmed them in their belief which to our mind is quite unjustifiable. A fresh investigation seems necessary.

(b) Maidjiru (now known as the Moodu). These are the southern neighbours of the Muledre. Their small enclave begins on the same road, south of the River Kandra, tributary of the Yebu, 20 km. south of Tora. Seven villages are said to use this language: Maidjiru, Molingba, Seu, Andube, Mayi, Ande-Lasi, and Moloku; in addition two villages in the Mazende area use it: Magai and Karikogu. According to the Muledre this dialect is very different from theirs. We arranged for numerous informants, but unfortunately they never materialized.

V. *The Efe and Lese Group*

We include in this group the Pygmy speech Efe (speakers estimated at 10,000) as well as Lese since, in spite of certain striking characteristics, the two languages are inseparable. The Lese are spread over five territories: Watsa 4,889; Epulu (Mombasa) 6,694; Bunya 7,018; Beni 1,480; Djugu(?). Total 20,081+. There seem to be five dialects, spoken by:

(*a*) The Balese-Otsodo. These are the Balese of Chief Bolayi, the successor of Arumbi in Watsa Territory. According to Fr. De Corte, they are known as Balese of the forest. Theirs is the dialect which is closest to Mangutu (S. 73, S. 81). A small group of these Balese, formerly the subjects of Chief Arumbi, extends into the northwest of Djugu Territory where they have as their southern limit the River Lodja. They now come under the authority of the local chief Sa Mununge.

(*b*) The Balese north of the River Nduye, better known in Epulu Territory as Walese-Dese or Lese-Ndese (chefferie Nikobayi) (S. 75). This group also includes the Andali who form an enclave of Lese-Dese in the Karo district at Apwayi (S. 76).

(*c*) The Baletse between the River Nduye and the River Epulu. They are often called Walese-Karo ('upstream people') (S. 74). The farther north one goes, the more one notices Mamvu influence. As we have seen above, there are a few Mamvu living in this locality beyond the River Nepoko.

(*d*) the Abvu-Nkootu, known to the Administration as Vonkutu. Those we questioned called themselves 'Obi'. They live in Bunya Territory (Chief Duge) and stretch into the vicinity of Gety where the forest borders on the plains of Lake Albert (Balese of Zunguluka) (S. 80). Their dialect is closer to Mvuba than to Dese or Karo.

(*e*) The Mvuba. Their language is used in the extreme south-east corner which extends almost to Beni. We found three groups:

(1) the main body of the Abaletse-Mvuba of Oytshia (S. 77, 78, 79);
(2) the north-eastern Mvuba who dwell between the Babira and the Watalinge (S. 82, 84, 85);
(3) the River Semliki enclave between Beni and the Ruwenzori at the village of Kilia (S. 83).

VI. *Mabendi*

The language of the Mabendi (called Ndra by the Bale) should be included in the Lese group. If we treat it separately here it is merely because the local natives do not confuse Lese and Mabendi though they consider them very close to each other. Those who have no close connexion with them sometimes, however, speak of them as though they were Lendu dialects. Confusion is caused by the fact that many Mabendi do indeed speak Bale-dha—as a second language—since on leaving the forest to live in the plains many of them took Bale wives.

They are to be found in Djuga Territory (2,299) under Chief Dengese who succeeded Buluba. Their dialect is very close to that of the Balese-Otsodo in the Arumbi area of Watsa Territory.

C. THE LENDU GROUP

The name 'Lendu' is probably derived from 'Lendru', the title bestowed on them by the Aluur. They call themselves Bale, whence the name of their language, Bale-dha. There are two distinct groups, speaking quite different languages: (I) those in the north, who speak Bale-dha; (II) those in the south who speak Ndru-na.

I. *Bale-dha*

The North Lendu area stretches over two territories: (i) a small group occupies the south of Mahagi Territory—the Wa-tsi clan under Chief Zangali (5,612); (ii) the main concentration extends to Djugu Territory—the Ru-tsi clan at Tsupu under Chief Libi (29,743), and the Biri-tsi clan under Chief Luka (30,052).

There are four dialects: (*a*) Bale-dha of the Fataki area (S. 20 and 21), the most widely used form; (*b*) Pi-dha to the north, i.e. around Kwandruma and Rety (S. 13); (*c*) the north-western dialect (found in Zangali chefferie) which shows signs of being influenced by Mumbi, the language spoken by neighbouring tribesmen who have mingled with the Lendu (S. 12); (*d*) Djo-dha which was the language spoken by the Bale of the forest (Djo). As this forest no longer exists we found it impossible to define the area over which the dialect extends or even to take down any examples of it.

Bale-dha is also spoken by various 'Lendu-ized' tribes which have lost their mother tongue and adopted some form or other of Lendu. True Bale (39,512) will always speak scornfully of the following dialects:

1. Ke-dha, used by the Ke, i.e. the Obebo whom we mentioned earlier when dealing with the Mumbi-Ndo. In Swahili they are referred to as 'Wafula-Yeembe' or 'forgers of hoes' because they pursue the trade of blacksmith in their small enclaves on mountain peaks. In Djugu Territory there are 4,920 of them under Chiefs Mangala and Dredza (S. 14).

2. Go-dha, used by the Mambisa who are known as Go because, at the time of the Pa-Mitu Nilotic invasion (in which some Pandoro Aluur joined) this advance-guard stopped first of all at Mount Goo after crossing the Nile. At present they occupy Mima and Pamitu chefferies in Djugu Territory (4,093). Their dialect is quite characteristic because it is better articulated and more virile than that of the Bale proper (S. 16).

3. { Djoo-dha (name used by the Wahema-Bangoyi).
    Dji-dha (name used by the Bale of Fataki).

The Wahema of Djugu Territory who speak this language number 30,499 (under Chief Kunga). Theirs is the dialect in use at Drodro and Lita. Apart from the Bangoyi clan (known as Banweki by the Administration) all these Wahema herdsmen have lost their pastoral customs and also their language, as they migrated from Unyoro via the southern plains (Boga) to the western shores of Lake Albert. As soon as one arrives at Blukwa one is in the Fataki dialect area (Dji-dha S. 15, 17; Blukwa S. 17; Drodro S. 19).

II. *Ndru-na*

This is the name bestowed on the language of the South Bale (or Lendu of the Bindi clan). They reside in the Gety area, Bunya Territory, Zadu chefferie under

Chief Kobvu (20,031). The speakers themselves claim that there are three dialects which they name after the chiefs of the area in which they are spoken (S. 22–25):

(a) Zadu dialect, used by the Buluba clan, Zadu chefferie (S. 25);
(b) Monobi dialect, *sous-chefferie* of Bamoko under Chief Monobi (S. 23);
(c) Kabona dialect, *sous-chefferie* of Bolomo (S. 24).

E. SOUTHERN SUDANIC LANGUAGES

Under this head we put the Zande, Mbaati, and Banda groups. It should be noted, however, that the relationship between the linguistic systems here is not so obvious as that which obtains in the previous groups. Therefore this is only a provisional classification pending the results of a more detailed investigation.

A. ZANDE GROUP

In this preliminary report one can hardly enter into a detailed discussion, but pending a fuller account of the matter let us confine ourselves to the following simple statement. In the opinion of Professor Van Bulck Pazande is not the real language of the wave of warlike Sudanic invaders who came from north of the River Mbomu, but was the language used by the various clans who dwelt in the area between the Rivers Uele and Mbomu at the time when this band of warriors confronted them and, in the Vongara clan, brought about the vast Zande conquest. We divide these languages into the following groups: I. Pambia; II. Pazande; III. Barambo.

I. Pambia

The main body of the Pambia group lives in the Anglo-Egyptian Sudan between the Tombara hills and the River Boko (2,900 taxpayers). The Survey encountered a few separate individuals at Yambio (S. 128–9). We have no information regarding the distribution or number of Pambia in Oubangui-Chari. In the Belgian Congo there are only a few survivors or immigrants, either in villages near the headwaters of the River Mbomu, e.g. at Tete-Bakuragba near Masombo, Ndoruma chefferie (S. 130), or at Yelepia, a Ketekpili hamlet at the fork of the Niangara–Ndoruma (or Yakuluku) road (5 HAV).

II. Pazande

This is spoken over a vast area by about 600,000 natives, but they have been split into three sections by colonial boundaries: Anglo-Egyptian Sudan 231,000; Oubangui-Chari 23,000; Belgian Congo 338,000.

(a) Pazande. The Survey had no opportunity of visiting the Azande of Oubangui-Chari, but at the outset a few days were spent among the Anglo-Egyptian Sudan Azande at Yambio. There the Avuru-Budwe speak the 'Sueh' dialect, which is the one described by the Rev. C. Gore in his grammar (S. 110). The same dialect extends into the Belgian Congo as far as the Avuru-Wando of Chief Gilima (the successor of Dekpi) in Dungu Territory. In the Belgian Congo the Azande proper (223,094) are spread over several territories: Dungu (the Avuru-Wando) 87,458; Niangara (the

Avuru-Wando and Avuru-Kipa [Ndeni]) 15,517; Buta (the Avuru-Mange) 8,466; Ango (the Anungo and Avuru-Ngindo) 57,703; Poko (the Avuru-Kipa) 59,950.

Such is the uniformity of Pazande that it is hard to speak of its *dialects* in the strict sense, in spite of the large area it covers. It is rather a question of local variants probably caused by differences of substratum. We believe, however, that the classification proposed by Fr. Van den Plas is justified subject to later completion. Apart from Bandia we distinguish under the head of Pazande the following dialects:

(1) Of the Sueh River, spoken in Anglo-Egyptian Sudan from Yambio to Meridie (S. 110, 112, 113, 114) and by the same group in the Belgian Congo, north of the River Uele between the Rivers Bwere and Aka (Dungu) (S. 111, 117, 118 Duru).

(2) Of the Bamboy, spoken in the south-east (i) between the Rivers Dungu on the north and Kibali on the south; (ii) on the left bank of the Kibali as far as the River Obi, Avuru Wando of Kumba-Wando *sous-chefferie*, Dungu Territory (S. 115, 116); (iii) on the right bank of the Dungu, east of the mouth of the Aka and as far as the Yei area.

(3) Of the Ambomu, spoken on the upper reaches of the Mbomu, the Api, the Gurba, and the Bwere. It is considered to be the purest form of Pazande and is used especially by the chefferies of Ndoruma (Chief Ukwatutu) and Ezo (Chief Yapwati) in Ango Territory (S. 119 Ndoruma, S. 120 Dakwa).

(4) Of the River Bomokandi, used particularly by the Avuru-Kipa who border on the Abarambo: (i) in Poko Territory, south of River Bomokandi in the Poko and Teli basin (S. 121); (ii) in Niangara Territory between the mouth of the Teli and Niangara, Bwemi chefferie.

(5) Of the Ambili or Abile. According to some traditions the Mbili language was that of the advance-guard composed of Abili, Embili (cf. Bambili). According to others Mbili was a Bantu language, related to Bungbinda. Their remnants have been submerged by the Bobwa or by the later waves of Azande invaders—it is no longer possible to distinguish between the various waves. Their language has imparted its characteristics to the Zande spoken by the Avuru-Mange of Buta Territory. A few settlements north of the River Uele in the Api area still use this dialect (S. 122). Here the term 'dialect' is really justified.

(6) Of the Anunga, spoken chiefly in Ango Territory which is occupied by the Avuru-Ngindo and Anungo (S. 123).

It is the superimposition of strata in this area which renders the study of it so difficult. Sometimes this characteristic shows itself in the Avongara class in the distinction between (i) Azande-Avongara; (ii) 'Just ordinary Azande', which they render in Bangala by the expression 'Azande pamba': these are vassals who accepted the ultimate expansion of the Avongara; and (iii) Auro, i.e. remnants of the tribes who refused to recognize or collaborate in the Vongara conquest.

At other times this stratification is shown by an opposition of tribe or language: (i) in Niangara Territory among the Avuru-Wando, a third declare that they are Amaadi; (ii) in Kembisa chefferie, Poko Territory, Chief Batenado is a Vongara but all his subjects are Abarambo; (iii) in Kumba-Wando *sous-chefferie*, Dungu Territory, we found 1,500 HAV Duga, 2,000 HAV Mamvu, 1,000 HAV Mayogo, 50 HAV Amaadi, 100 HAV Bakango; in Renzi chefferie of this territory there are 208 HAV Baka;

(iv) in Ango Territory, Sasa chefferie, there are 1,000 Bakari; in Mopoi chefferie there are about 2,000 Sele; one sixth of the population of the chefferie of the Embili Azande is composed of Abarambo and Bakango.

Are there any extant specimens of these substratum languages which differ from Pazande? We were told that in the Bili area (at Kende, Kalukulu, and Basekpio) there were still about thirty speakers of Angada (or Angodo), but we were unable to visit them. Similarly amongst the fisherfolk of the Uele there are supposed to be a few speakers of Adiyo (e.g. three at Km. 2 to the north of Bondo). Elsewhere on the Bili all the Adiyo are said to speak Pazande but we never encountered any of them.

(b) Bandia. There is scarcely any difference between Bandia and Pazande. As the Vongara conquest lasted only two or three years in this area, this similarity cannot be ascribed to Zande domination, though this has hitherto been asserted. Moreover, according to Bandia traditions, the Mbasa conquerors (descended from Luisia) who overran them did not speak Pazande. They adopted the vassal language. From this one can only conclude that modern Bandia was the substratum language of the River Uele (except for the Bangbinda and Babenge of the lower Uele) when the Bandia and Vongara conquests took place. The language name 'Bandia' was originally that of the ruling class. The 111,877 Bandia speakers include:

(1) The Abandia of Oubangui-Chari, north of the River Mbomu between Bangassou and Zemio whose numbers are not known to us.
(2) The Abandia of Bondo Territory (84,828). The division into chefferies is only significant from an administrative point of view (S. 126).
(3) The western Zande of Buta and Aketi Territories (27,049), including:

the Avuru-Ngulu (Chief Gatanga), Buta Territory (5,523) (S. 125);
the Avuru-Gatanga, Aketi Territory (15,049) (S. 124);
the Avuru-Nduma, Aketi Territory (6,477).

(c) Nzakara. This dialect is very close to Pazande (S. 127). Some Anzakara are to be found in Oubangui-Chari but the Survey was unable to contact them. In the Belgian Congo they occupy almost the whole of Soa chefferie (3,000) in Bondo Territory under Chief Gbatira. The area is bounded in the south by the village of Fakula on the Bangassou–Monga–Bondo road, in the east by the River Vungu, in the south-west by the River Pinga. Three Nzakara villages of Banzyville territory have been mentioned to us: Tongbo, Bonga, and Pamba. They now all speak Ngbandi.

(d) Patri. Three Patri-speaking villages were pointed out to the Survey on the right bank of the River Mbomu in Oubangui-Chari, but we were unable to obtain informants for this language, which seems to be a Zande dialect.

III. *The Barambo group*

(a) Barambo. The location of the Barambo enclaves indicates the route taken by the invaders:

(1) a small Barambo group still resides in Anglo-Egyptian Sudan in the Mopoi area. Fr. Giorgetti has done some work on them (S. 131);
(2) a few small settlements are situated on the other slope of the Congo-Nile ridge in Oubangui-Chari. These were not contacted by the Survey;

(3) the Belgian Congo Abarambo are located as follows:

(i) a few minute enclaves round the head-waters of the Mbomu in Dungu Territory near Pambia enclaves. The Survey encountered them in Ndoruma chefferie at Masomo near the source of the Duma (S. 135).

(ii) in Ango Territory among the Azande Embili, south of Dakwa, where they were estimated to form about one sixth of the population in 1913, i.e. 4,000 out of 24,000 (S. 136).

(iii) The main body occupies Poko Territory (35,457) where, except in the northwest, the River Bomokandi separates them from the Azande (Avuru-Kipa). On occasion the Kembisa sector has been lumped in with the Azande; this is an error. It is true that the chief of the Batenado sector is a Vongara, but all his subjects are Abarambo. Similarly one could be misled by the fact that Koronet, chief of Suronga sector, is Mabisanga while all his subjects, apart from a few Amaadi and Bakango, are Abarambo (S. 137 Mtadi, S. 138 Poko).

(b) Duga. Paamiangba (S. 133, 134) is a Barambo dialect with considerable variations. It is spoken by the Duga in the Dungu area (1500 HAV or 3,500) in the *sous-chefferie* of Kumba-Wando. The Duga formed the spearhead of the Barambo advance. They are also found elsewhere, but in these cases they have lost their language as a result of the influence of the ephemeral Mangbetu domination (1835–73), e.g. in the chefferies of Okondo I and II, Niangara Territory.

(c) As the Mangbetu Kingdom declined that of the Matshaga became powerful (1870–95). The name Matshaga is a Mangbetu deformation of a Duga clan name: Makpiga. This new ruling clan was then of Duga origin but most of its subjects were Bangba or Mayogo. At the present time five so-called Matshaga chefferies are all that remain of this Duga (or Matshaga) Kingdom. In them Mangbetu influence predominates and their composition is most extraordinary: 8,400 Bangba in Kopa chefferie under Chief Ekibondo, and in Bondo *sous-chefferie* (formerly Medi-medi chefferie); 10,000 Mayogo in Kereboro chefferie under Chief Badolo; 6,000 Mangbetu, Okondo II chefferie under Chief Okondo-Meka; 13,400 Madi and Duga in Okondo I chefferie, Chief Napangwe. This would make the Matshaga population of these chefferies: 42 (Kopa), 449 (Badolo), 20 (Okondo-Meka), 20 (Napangwe).

B. THE MBAATI GROUP

We bestow this name upon the group since this seems to have been their old name in so far as clans of such diverse origins will accept a title indicative of a common origin. Clan traditions show that formerly they lived north of the River Mbomu between its tributaries the Mbari and Chinko, and that their immediate neighbours were Bantu. In fact a few survivors are said to have remained on the right bank of the Mbomu in French Territory. In this respect mention is made of the Yakoma, Bangi, and Dendi (five villages) who are still supposed to speak their old language, while on the left bank of the upper Ubangi members of the same clans now speak only Ngbandi. In the Belgian Congo we included in this group:

I. *Sango*

Spoken by the fisherfolk of the Mobaye–Banzyville rapids (4,462 in Banzyville

Territory, Sango sector). A few Sango have come down the Ubangi and established themselves as fish-traders at the falls of Libenge and Motenge-Boma. The differences between their dialect and Ngbandi proper are few but clearly marked. A few fishermen, called Abasango or Sangoma, speaking the same dialect are located on the lower Uele upstream from Bondo.

II. *Ngbandi*

There are 49,495 speakers in Banzyville Territory but they belong to clans of various origins.

(*a*) The purest Ngbandi is said to be spoken by the Doondo of Kotakoli and the Bwaato of Abumombazi (S. 189 Yakoma; S. 188 Abomumbazi; S. 187, 190 Molegbwe). Ngbandi has resisted Mbandja encroachments but, at the moment, where it is in contact with Ngbaka it is giving way to it.

(*b*) North-west Ngbandi. Beyond the River Uele in Bondo Territory (Kasa chefferie, Chief Bela) in the angle formed by the Rivers Mbomu and Uele we find a small group of Ngbandi (525), neighbours of the Anzakara. Their dialect shows Nzakara influence (S. 186).

(*c*) Ngbandi-Gbeya, spoken by the Babugbuma. In Moma Territory, Ngaie sector, of Chief Gabia, on the one hand the Babogulu all speak Apagibeti, and on the other the Babugbuma are divided: some speak the Bantu Apagibeti (called Gezon by the Ngbandi), others use Ngbandi-Gbeya. Of the twenty Bugbuma capitas, all speak the latter language, but three of them also speak Apagibeti. This, they say, is their original language; Ngbandi would have been introduced later, and still more recently Libenge as used by their eastern neighbours gained the ascendancy. Ngbandi-Gbeya is a defective form of Ngbandi (S. 185).

(*d*) Ngbandi of Nzomboy. South of Banzyville Territory, in Businga Territory (Modjomboli Region) a slightly different dialect is spoken (S. 191). According to Fr. Mortier, its speakers, who are of Monjombo origin, have substituted Ngbandi for their own language, and have intermarried with the Mbaati.

III. *Mbaati*

On crossing the River Duwa at Businga, we come to the Mbaati area, Mombati chefferie, Lisala Territory. This is supposed to be the advance-guard of the thrust southwards. Their speech shows little difference from that of the Nzomboy of the right bank, which is explained by the fact that on the right bank the substratum was also composed of Mbaati (S. 193). Mbaati and Ngbandi of Nzomboy could be classified under the same head.

IV. *Mongwandi (South Ngbandi)*

The Ngbandi-bloc is split in the west by tribes of the Ngbaka, Mbandja-Banda, &c. invasions, but south of this wedge of invaders (i.e. south-westwards in relation to the Ngbandi bloc) we come upon those Ngbandi who were pushed back by the invaders. Here, mingled with the Bantu Kunda and Ngombe, they have, under Bantu influence, taken the name of Mongwandi. They occupy a wide strip stretching from east to west, in the north of Budjala and Bomboma Territories. At present in the north Mongwandi is in retreat before Ngbaka infiltration, but in the south on the other hand it is gaining ground from the Ngombe and those who live along the River Saw (S. 194/Mbaya, S. 195/Banga Bolu).

V. *Mbaati (south-west Ngbandi)*

Farther west between the mouths of the Rivers Luwa and Esobe (Esobe sector, Libenge Territory), the Ngbandi have retained their original name, still calling themselves Mbaati. There is little difference between their speech and that of the Mongwandi (S. 196). Further investigation will probably show that IV and V are really one and the same dialect.

The Kazibati and Mongoba enclave

We attach to the Ngbandi–Mbaati group the language of two villages—Kazibati and Mongoba—situated far away in the north-east of the Belgian Congo:

(*a*) Kazibati of Ara (S. 28) in Faradje Territory, near Arambau in the Makoro area (365 speakers);

(*b*) Mongoba (S. 27) in Watsa Territory near Arebi on the Watsa–Aumubi–Bunia road (50 speakers).

The Mongoba and Kazibati parted company only recently according to tradition. This whole group, we suggest, might have originated as an enclave of foreigners, porters who came from the west at the time of the great movements of peoples, but who instead of returning to their country of origin settled down in this area. Moreover their language differs so profoundly from Ngbandi that it is with difficulty that one finds those few traces which cause us to classify it with the latter.

C. THE BANDA GROUP

We found it impossible to divide the immense Banda group (321,000) into its dialects, as the largest part of it lies outside the Belgian Congo in Oubangui-Chari. South of the Ubangi only the outposts of the advance-guard of the invaders are to be found. Our documentation is limited to the Belgian Congo Banda, the dialects of which (apart from Mbandja) differ very little. They fall into the following divisions: (I) Togbo; (II) the Yakpa group: Yakpa and Mono; (III) the Langbase group: Langbase, Gbugo, Gobu, Langba; (IV) Ngbundu; (V) Mbandja.

I. *Togbo*

This is spoken in two Territories: (*a*) a vast group resides in Bosobolo Territory (S. 207); (*b*) a second group occupies the north-east of Libenge Territory. There are also three villages on the River Ubangi: Bura and Wuye to the north of Zongo, and Saratumbo to the south.

II. *The Yakpa Group*

(*a*) Yakpa. The administrative boundary has cut this group into two sections, one being in Banzyville Territory, in the Banza sector of the Bimbi River (1,605) near Molegbwe. The Yakpa are considerably intermingled with villages of other origins (S. 205). The second section is in Bosobolo Territory.

(*b*) Mono. Similarly, administrative limits have divided the Mono. One section is in Bosobolo Territory (S. 206) and the other in Libenge Territory.

III. *The Langbase Group*

(a) Langbase. The few Langbase who have crossed the Ubangi live in the north of Bosobolo Territory amidst Yakpa, Togbo, and Gobu (S. 203).

(b) Gobu. These, too, have penetrated but little into Belgian territory, and live in Bosobolo Territory (S. 208).

(c) Gbugo, also known as Gbugbu or, popularly, Boubou. We have here not an invasion wave but simply infiltration—a process which is still going on before our eyes between Banzyville and Molegbwe. In Banzyville Territory, along the Ubangi road, one finds a settlement of Gbugo alongside each Ngbandi village. Their numerical strength is impossible to estimate as they are really a 'floating population' (S. 204 and 204a).

(d) Langba. Here we have the exact opposite. In Bondo Territory, between the Rivers Mbomu and Uele, the Langba are talked of. In actual fact they *do* exist but are merely the descendants of Langba who, in the past, were brought into the area as captives of the Abandia (S. 202).

IV. *Ngbundu*

The Ngbundu form the most south-westerly point of the Banda advance. They advanced almost as far as the mouth of the Luwa. Enclaves of Ngbaga-Maabo, Kpala, and Ngombe are evidence of the populations who occupied these areas when they invaded it. In Libenge Territory, they have been divided into two sections by the Administration: North and South Ngbundu (S. 209).

V. *Mbandja*

This language has numerous Banda characteristics but nevertheless has so many distinctive features that one is inclined to regard it as separate. It has two dialects: (a) that of the south Mbandja, which is at the moment the most resistant to the influences of neighbouring languages; and (b) that of the eastern Mbandja, which has the purest forms but which has retreated before Ngbandi and is certain to lose even further ground to Ngbaka-Gbaya.

(a) *South Mbandja*

(1) The south Mbandja are situated in the south of Libenge Territory south of the River Esobe and the mouth of the Luwa. There are five groups of them: Mongondo, Wooro, Kungu, Gbalakpwa, and Luumba (S. 201).

(2) A Mbandja group exists between the Mbaati-Ngombe (to the south) and the south Ngbundu (to the north) in the Motengi-Boma area, Libenge Territory. In this area there are Kpala, Monjombo, and Ngombe enclaves.

(3) The Mbandja-Bango group is located east of the River Pongo, a tributary of the Luwa. The Ngbaka-Gbaya are penetrating into this area (S. 200).

(4) South-east Mbandja. Their dialect is almost identical with that of south Mbandja (S. 199); they form a narrow strip with the Ngbaka to the north and the Mongwandi to the south, whose languages are making inroads on south-east Mbandja which is visibly losing ground.

(b) *East Mbandja*

(1) The nucleus of these Mbandja (who speak the purest form of this language) is

situated in the Businga area (3,000) north of the River Duwa (S. 198). This is the dialect which formed the subject of a special study by Fr. Mortier.

(2) Farther north, north Mbandja is spoken along the Businga–Molegbwe road in certain villages with Ngbandi villages interspersed. In the past it has held its own with its Ngbandi neighbours but at present it is beginning to yield to the large-scale infiltration of its western Ngbaka neighbours. It is no longer to be found in its purest form; it has undergone the influence of Ngbandi and perhaps of other dialects which have been brought into the area more recently (S. 197).

(3) In spite of the hold which Ngbaka has on the area of its conquest a few Mbandja villages have preserved their identity. This is so in the case of three villages in the Bominenge area: Kalamba, Dambia, and Mbe, and six in Gemena Territory: Bowase-Bogbase chefferie.

(c) North-west Mbandja

The Survey was unable to verify what dialect was spoken in the small group which remained in the north-west near the River Bembe, the former gateway of the Ngbaka-Gbaya invasion of the Belgian Congo. They have as neighbours to the south the Ngbaga-Maabo. After later invasions the Ngbaka settled to the north of them and the Banda to the east.

F. THE GBAYA-NGBAKA LANGUAGES

What has just been said about the Banda is equally true for the Gbaya-Ngbaka. The Survey was only able to examine one salient in the south-east of the immense bloc of 500,000 Gbaya, located in Oubangui-Chari. It was not possible at that time to resolve it into its component parts. Later Professor Van Bulck, during his linguistic investigation in the Tchad, was able to touch on a few of these dialects while crossing the eastern zone of Gbaya-Mandja. He noted that the dialect which is clearly related to Ngbaka of the Belgian Congo is Mandja as spoken in the Districts of Buka, Batangafo, and Bosengwa (15,625). It is bounded in the west by the River Fafa, a tributary of the Ouham, in the north by the Sara, and in the east by the Banda. The western part of the area is dealt with in the western section of this report.

In the Belgian Congo the Ngbaka are almost all situated in Gemena Territory. They have been the subject of close investigation by Fr. Vedast Maes who is now writing a grammar and dictionary of this language. There are two main dialects:

I. The Eastern Dialect or Ngbaka

The speakers of this dialect, who live round Gemena, Bominenge, Karawa, and Gbosasa, claim to speak a purer dialect than that of the western Ngbaka on whom they bestow the derogatory title of Gbaya. It should be noted that among them throughout the southern area are to be found people of Furu origin as their clan association proves. These protest most vigorously when one tries to classify them with the Furu-Gbaya of Bosobolo (cf. *Eastern Sudanic Languages*). They state that they already spoke Ngbaka when, during their last migration, they crossed the Ubangi to occupy this area in the south-east (S. 212 Bominenge, S. 213 Gbosasa).

II. The Western Dialect or Ngbaka Gbaya

This we took down at Bobito where Fr. Vedast lives (S. 211). The difference between the two dialects is not really very remarkable. It can be seen, however, that the substratum languages—Mbandja, Furu, and Bokonwa—have all left their mark.

The western section too is located for the greater part in Gemena territory, but in the west encroaches on Libenge Territory. In the latter we find: (*a*) influenced by the Mandja substratum: (1) the Bunduru; (2) the Vulusi; (*b*) influenced by the Ngbaga-Maabo substratum: (1) the Bogilima; (2) the Bokiliyo; (*c*) influenced by the Bongo or Bokonwa: the Bokonwa.

According to Fr. Vedast's information, to these should be added two regional speech forms which are not so important: (1) Ngbaka-bi, spoken in the northern part of the Ngbaka bloc particularly in Libya chefferie (Bosobolo Territory) and in the north-west part of Gemena Territory (Bogose area); (2) Gbaya of Botili. In this village of Botili (Luwa Bolo chefferie, Libenge Territory) an archaic dialect is spoken which differs considerably from the Gbaya of the neighbouring villages.

G. EQUATORIAL LANGUAGES

We give this group the name 'Equatorial Languages' in memory of the Austrian linguist Fr. Müller, who was the first to make a study of it in his linguistic material gathered amongst tribes of the upper Uele: *Die Aequatoriale Sprachfamilie in central Afrika* (Sitz. der K. Akad. der Wiss. Wien, 1889). It should be noted, however, that we limit the application of the term and do not include the Azande, the Abarambo, or the Mangbetu. We divide it into (A) the River Mbomu section, (B) the Uele-Ubangi section.

A. Mbomu Section

This is the Ndogo-Sere group which has been studied in detail by Fr. Santandrea. He includes in this group Ndogo, Bai, Sere, Bvirig Tagba. Recently he has added Feroghe (Shayu dialect), Mongaiyat, Indri, and Togoyo. In the Belgian Congo we only encountered a fragment of the section, a group of Sele, known to the Administration as Basiri.

I. These form an enclave in the Banda area (Solo) in Ango Territory, Mopa chefferie. They are estimated at about 2,500 and are mixed with Azande. Unfortunately the only informants we could find were very unsatisfactory (S. 166).

II. A good number of Sele live farther north, scattered amongst the Azande in Ukwatutu chefferie in the River Gurba area. At Ndoruma the Survey encountered several of their notables who still had a perfect knowledge of their own language. According to some of these, the migration from the head-waters of the Mbomu took place only a generation ago (S. 165).

B. The Uele–Ubangi Section

We speak of 'Uele-Ubangi' to show how close is the relationship which binds together the two sectors of the Uele and the Ubangi. It is obvious that they are of common origin.

I. *The Uele Sector*

(*a*) Mundo. Fr. Santandrea has described the Mundo languages of Anglo-Egyptian Sudan (S. 91). In the north-east of the Belgian Congo we find the same Mundo. They are all located in Faradje Territory (2,798) (S. 92 to 95). Before the institution of the Garamba National Park they used to occupy both banks of the River Garamba. Now they are all on the left bank between the River Garamba and the River Dungu.

(*b*) Mayogo (50,061). The brief episode of Mangbetu rule tore the former Mayogo domain into shreds, but the resilience, high spirit, and fierce tenacity which characterize the Mayogo tribe have preserved it from annihilation. Whereas all the neighbouring tribes have yielded to Mangbetu influence, the Mayogo have opposed it most categorically and continue to scorn it. We found the following Mayogo enclaves:

(1) the Mayogo spoken at Isiro, Paulis Territory (29,881) which is the purest form (S. 97).

(2) Madyugu, spoken by the Mayogo of Matshaga chefferie of Kereboro (Chief Badolo) in Niangara Territory, is very close to the above, but there is some evidence of foreign influence (10,000) (S. 98).

(3) Mayogo as spoken south of the River Dungu in the Kumba-Wando *sous-chefferie*, Niangara Territory, where all the tribes are intermingled (e.g. at Seribongo) (1,000 HAV, or approximately 4,000 speakers) (S. 99 and 100).

(4) Maigo, spoken by Mayogo mixed with Bangba in the extreme north-east corner, i.e. between the Bari-Logo and the Mamvu, Watsa Territory, between Tora to the east and the River Yebu to the south. There are 987 Mayogo and 1,116 Bangba (S. 96).

(5) Maambi, formerly spoken by the Maambi. There are still a few rare survivors, e.g. at the villages of Mabaga and Mekara, east of Niangara on the left bank of the River Uele (S. 103).

(6) Paangai, spoken by the Angai (the 'Day' of Hutereau, Junker, Casati). There are still a few survivors (e.g. at the village of Wede) south of the River Uele between Niangara and Dungu. This dialect is very close to the Mayogo of Isiro.

(7) Likango, spoken by Bakango fisherfolk on the Bomokandi between Tely and Rungu—a Mayogo dialect (S. 102).

(8) Baleka, spoken by the Bakango fisherfolk of the River Uele at Niangara—also a Mayogo dialect (S. 101).

(9) Madjogo, spoken by the Mangbele in Wamba Territory (S. 104) at Mangbele-Mandai (2,266) and also in Isiro-Paulis Territory (2,927).

(10) The Maiko, indicated to us as inhabiting Watsa Territory between Watsa and Arumbi. Their dialect is said to be a mixture of Mayogo and Mangutu, but no speakers of it were encountered.

The Toro and Bere mentioned by Hutereau could not be located. Tradition has it that the Bere used to be neighbours of the Mamvu in the area south of the River Uele. They were driven out by the Mayogo and Bangba. Can these be the Bere in question, or did Hutereau really mean those who are now called Bari-Logo? The Toro then would be an advance-guard of the Bari-Logo. Up to the present time the Bari-Logo of Denis Survi live a few kms. from Tora.

(c) Bangba. The Bangba group (10,016) is by no means so well preserved. After crossing the Uele near Dungu they settled between that river and the Bomokandi.

(1) A portion of them was conquered by the Duga and now forms the substratum of the Matshaga chefferie of Kopa (Chief Ekibondo) and of the *sous-chefferie* of Bondo (Medi-Medi) (8,400 in Niangara Territory). These are the ones who have suffered the least change (S. 107).
(2) Those who took a more southerly direction are now mixed with remnants of various tribes in Kumba-Wando *sous-chefferie*, Dungu Territory (1,000 HAV, or about 3,500) (S. 108).
(3) Lastly a group is mingled with the Mayogo of the north-west enclave of Watsa Territory. There are 1,116 of them.

Fr. Costermans, who has studied in detail the Bangba of the Kumba-Wando *sous-chefferie*, believes that they speak four dialects which correspond to their various clans: (i) Koko, (ii) Mereyi, (iii) Alo, (iv) Makudu-Kudu. Perhaps to these should be added Modo and Tibu. The Survey was unable to verify this as there was insufficient time to engage in clan dialectology.

II. *The Ubangi Sector*

This sector is situated far to the west beyond Mobayi (i.e. Banzyville) and stretches along the River Ubangi. It includes:

(a) *Kpala-Bakpa*, the most easterly dialect and also the closest to Mayogo. Note, however, that the Kpala occur even farther to the south-west almost as far as the mouth of the Luwa. This language includes:

(1) Bakpa, spoken in the village of Bakpwa, near Molegbwe in Banzyville Territory (about 250 inhabitants). Nowadays only a few of the notables speak it (S. 178).
(2) Kpala of Libenge Territory. Only a few very small enclaves remain, scattered along the banks of the Ubangi between Libenge and Mawuya, e.g. at Likambo amongst the southern Mbandja, at the former village of Nzambe (near the Motenge-Boma plantation), in four villages near Kaia (S. 179), and in the Singa-Yaboi enclave.
(3) Gbendere. The users of this dialect are scattered among the South Mbandja, e.g. at the village of Gbendere (S. 183a) in Libenge Territory.
(4) Nyango, spoken at Gbendere too by the fisherfolk of the lower reaches of the Luwa and the Esobe. They are called Oyaango by the Gbaya and their dialect is almost identical with Gbendere (S. 183b).

(b) *Ngbaga Maabo*. This is a cognomen bestowed on Kunda clans (= 'I say that'). The group is situated on both banks of the middle Ubangi around the Bangui and Libenge areas.

(1) In French Equatorial Africa it is to be found, according to Professor Van Bulck's information, between the River Pama in the north and the River Lobaye in the south. It includes Ngbaga Maabo and Ngbaga Mapi (Ub. 1) and is also said to have slight local variations in the villages of Bumbangi, Yaka, Bugbwa, and Zende. The speech of Bukanga is said to show the most noticeable variations.

(2) In the Belgian Congo, Ngbaga Maabo are to be found along the River Ubangi from Zongo in the north to Libenge in the south. Their dialects are:
  (i) Libenge, considered to be the purest form, spoken just to the north of Libenge.
  (ii) Bandi, spoken in the chefferie of the same name.
  (iii) Djuma, spoken in the chefferie of that name.
  (iv) Grimma (Gilima), spoken at the village of Bakena in Djuma chefferie on the edge of Mbandja country.

There is a Ngbaga-Maabo enclave in the Banda-Mono area at the village of Buse Bwende, where the Libenge dialect is spoken.

The Bokiliyo and Bundulu of Libenge Territory are of Ngbaga Maabo origin but have now all adopted the Ngbaka-Gbaya language; the same is true of the Bozene in Gemena Territory.

(c) *Monjombo*. The Monjombo formerly were a fairly widespread group which lived on both banks of the Ubangi between Libenge to the north and Dongo to the south. At present there remain only a few settlements at the villages of Salebo, Mawoko, Isato, and Motenge-Boma. When the two plantations Motenge-Boma and Zambi were started many emigrated and settled on the right bank. There is a compact group of them at Beetu (S. 184).

(d) *The Buraka-Gbanziri dialect group*. These two speeches are so closely related that we treat them as dialects.

  (1) Buraka (715). This riverine group constitutes a Buraka chefferie in the Banza sector of the River Bumbi, Banzyville Territory (S. 180). There are also two small Buraka fishing villages far downstream on the Ubangi, one opposite Bangui not far from Zongo, and the other in the former Zambi chefferie near Motenge-Boma.

  (2) Gbanziri (about 150). There exists it is true a Gbanziri chefferie in Banzyville Territory near the Buraka, but almost all the inhabitants are either Buraka or Yakpa-Banda. It is only the ruling family which is Gbanziri and which speaks that language in the riverine communities of Dula, Bangi, and Bagiri (Bosobolo Territory)—45 HAV in all. The others use dialects of Banda, e.g. Yakpa, Mono, Togbo (S. 181).

The Gbanziri group is chiefly to be found on the right bank in Oubangui-Chari, around Kouango.

H. UNCLASSIFIED LANGUAGE GROUP—MEEGYE (121,703)

Since the languages of this group show Aka, Bantu, Bantoid, and Mamvu traits, we prefer to consider them apart as 'Unclassified', pending the results of a more detailed study. In this group we place: (A) the language of the Aka pygmies; (B) Nodyalombi-tu; (C) Naabulu-ti; (D) Namangbetu-ti; (E) Nameegye-ti; (F) Namakere-ti; (G) Namaele-ti; (H) Napopoyi-ti.

A. THE LANGUAGE OF THE AKA PYGMIES

The Survey took down this language at various points around the Niapu-Bomili forest, i.e. at Niakpu Kisanga in the Maele area (P. 15); at Medje in the Meegye area (P. 16); at Mangbaalu/Avakubi in the Abulu area (P. 14); at Ingelezi Panga in the

Popoyi area (P. 25). Far from being a corrupt form of Meegye, this language seems to be an earlier form of it.

B. NODYALOMBI-TU

This is spoken by the Odyalombi (8,133), known to the Administration as Barumbi, in the Opienge area of Bafwasende Territory. Now that the Wanumbi enclave of the River Tshopo has been included in the Lombi bloc of Opienge the total number of speakers has risen to 8,133. There are four groups: (I) Mabodi, (II) Bamulimu, (III) Bakorooyi, (IV) Babwangi—to the east, south, north, and north-east respectively of Opienge. Linguistic differences between these groups are, however, not very striking (S. 162, 163).

C. NAABULU-TI

It is spoken in the so-called Babeyru chefferie (Chief Mangbwalu) in Wamba Territory (1,452). According to tradition the founder of the short-lived Mangbetu dynasty was of Abulu stock (S. 160, 161). The language is still well preserved.

D. NAMANGBETU-TI

This was the court language of the Mangbetu dynasty during its short but brilliant existence (about 1836 to 1873 and then the years of its decline), and it has continued to spread during half a century of Mangbetu influence. Handicapped in the north by the presence of the Azande and later by the rival Matshaga-Duga power allied to the Bangba, Mangbetu influence could extend only south, east, and west. In the south first the Mayogo and then the Baliko and Babudu opposed it. In the east, thanks to the collaboration of Mabadi and Bari chiefs, it succeeded in gaining a foothold amongst the Mamvu as far as Gombari and even Wanga. In the north-east, the Abarambo group did not give way to it. In the west its influence was halted by the River Bima. At present it no longer seems to be gaining ground, but wherever it has taken root its prestige is enormous and its tenacity proverbial.

It is very probable that at the height of Mangbetu power the language was, if not artificially, at least traditionally preserved at court, to shield it from those deleterious influences which were undermining the Meegye dialect by the loss of its intervocalic consonants. This language has the following dialects:

I. *Mangbetu Proper*

The nucleus is in the Rungu area, Okondo II chefferie under Chief Okondo-Meka (5,965). There are, however, in the chefferie a few Amaadi and Duga-Barambo (S. 143, 144, 145). We were also told of a Mangbetu village called Ezo in Kumba-Wanda *sous-chefferie*, Dungu Territory, on the River Obe, a tributary of the Obo.

II. *Tribes which have undergone Mangbetu influence and now speak Namangbetu-ti* (18,175)

(*a*) Mabisanga. These have lost their former Bantu language and speak only Namangbetu-ti (S. 147). They occupy the old Ganzi chefferie which is now called Aduandra (Graffi) (4,035).

(b) Amaidjuwu, of the Madangba chefferie of Jos.Mbeli, Paulis Territory (8,215), which is a mixture of Mayogo, eastern Ameegye, and a few Amangbetu. The Mangbetu influence is very slight indeed (S. 146).

(c) Mangbele. The chief of the Mangbele and a group of old notables still speak their original Bantu language, Lingbee, but the younger people have substituted Namangbetu-ti for it. They form the chefferie of Gata in Niangara Territory (4,429). We have already mentioned two Mangbele groups who now speak Mayogo, the Mangbele-Mandei of Wamba (2,266) and the Mangbele of Isiro (2,927).

(d) Mangbele of Gombari sector. In this sector, whose chief (Mongiba) is himself Mangbele, there are 1,496 of his fellow tribesmen. The other members are Banyanga, Bari-Logo or Mamvu (Watsa Territory). They occupy six villages: Titi, Molendi, Djabulindi, Melo, Akeku, and Gina. Their mothers are of Mamvu origin and the men are descended from the Mangbele conquerors who collaborated with the Amangbetu and were Mangbetuized under their influence.

E. Nameegye-ti (67,451)

It is the Ameegye and not the Amangbetu who occupy the west of the so-called Mangbetu Territory, i.e. Paulis-Isiro Territory. They include:

I. Independent Ameegye who form the chefferie of Chief Ebandrumbi Achille (13,238) (S. 148 to 150).

II. Ameegye under Mangbetu chiefs (54,213):

(a) Mava-Ndei chefferie under Chief Ababu.
(b) Mongomasi chefferie under Chief Gbatala.
(c) Azanga chefferie under Chief Magwangasa.

F. Namakere-ti

The Amakere occupy the right bank of the Bima downstream from the Amaele as far as Zobia. In Buta Territory they number 17,488 (S. 151). In the north-east there are numerous Bakete and Bawunza, who are all of Bantu origin but have adopted as their language Namakere-ti. The same situation arises with the Bambese although they are considered to be true Amakere.

A dialect which is very close to the latter and also called Makere is spoken by the River Uele Bakango at Amadi (S. 152). It indicates a period of Makere settlement on the banks of the River Uele before the Mangbetu and Zande conquests.

G. Namaele-ti

The Amaele live south of the Amakere extending to the new Niapu (source of the River Rubi) Sasi chefferie, Poko Territory (13,055) (S. 153 and 154). They have numerous clans, at least ten of which claim to speak separate dialects, e.g. the dialects of the Makele (S. 157), Matsongu (or Bashobu) (S. 158), Maboko (S. 159), and Bamboko of Gwobo-Balele (S. 157). The differences between them, however, seem not to be very striking.

The dialect of the Maboko (clan of the old chief Adzapane) best represents the Maele language. They say there is another dialect (Bakele) spoken in the north-west of Gasia Mabonda chefferie.

H. Napopoyi-ti

The Apopoyi dwell in Bafwasende Territory (7,472) in the extreme north-west corner. Their domain is bounded north-east by River Makeke, south-east by River Nebuku, north-west by River Namubede (tributary of the Longele), and south-west by River Nekboma. Their dialect is close to the Meegye dialect (S. 164).

I. EQUATORIAL BANTOID LANGUAGES

We consider as Bantoid the following languages: (A) Ndungale, Mbani, and Dongoko; (B) Amaalo. We call them Bantoid because they have noun-class systems which, however, do not correspond to Bantu noun-classes and which are indicated by suffixes and not by prefixes. The name 'Equatorial' has been given to facilitate the locating of this group.

A. I. *Ndungale*

The speakers number 2,500, scattered among seven small villages or hamlets 7 to 10 km. north of Lisala (Lisala Territory). Clan traditions do not throw any light on their distant ancestry. They know of no other language connected with their own, but when Mbani texts were read to them they recognized it as a related language. Imbued with a great affection for their language, they have been able to preserve it in all its richness, thereby giving proof of its exuberant vitality (S. 175).

II. *Mbani* (16,600)

The Mbayi (known to the Administration as Bamanga) know that, according to the Rev J. F. Carrington, there is a related group downstream from them on the River Congo. The present group is situated in the Bengamisa area 27 km. north of Stanleyville in Banalia Territory.

They too keep a firm grasp on their mother tongue and oppose all attempts at emigration. Unfortunately they are ravaged by tuberculosis and sleeping sickness. Their two main dialects are:

(*a*) the central dialect of the Bengamisa area (S. 174);
(*b*) the southern dialect of the Kaporata area (S. 176).

Those who live on the borders of the area are now beginning to show foreign influence in their speech. This is the case with the Mbayi of (i) Banalia, on the fringe of Baangba and Baboro country; (ii) Kondololo (where a few are mixed with the Babaali); (iii) Yambuya where they are intermingled with riverine tribes of the River Aruwimi.

III. *Dongoko*

Unlike the speakers of the two preceding languages, the Dongonyo are threatened with extinction. Statistics in 1948 put them at 5,600 strong; by 1949 the figure had fallen to 4,870. There is no doubt about this information; it is based on actual fact. They all live on Obi Kibali, the mountain peak in the south-east corner of Faradje Territory, near the Mangutu of Watsa Territory. There are four dialects named after the chiefs: (*a*) Ndakala; the chief boasts that his is the only chefferie which has retained its independence, and that this is considered to be the purest dialect (S. 172); (*b*) Deso; this chefferie has for some time been under Logo domination and the dialect has been influenced accordingly (S. 173); (*c*) Sirika; the same remarks apply as for (*b*) (S. 173*a*); (*d*) Sirika/Djama diverges more violently than the other dialects, due to the fact that in the past they were subjugated by their southern neighbours the Mangutu (S. 174*c*).

B. AMAALO

Throughout the River Uele area this has the reputation of being the most difficult language of all. There are many bilingual Amaadi, i.e. who speak their own language and also Pazande, but the converse is rarely if ever found. Unfortunately a grave threat of extinction hangs over the Amaadi; in the last remaining pocket where they still speak their own language the mortality rate exceeds by far the number of births. This last refuge is on the right bank of the Uele, Amadi chefferie under the old chief Boso, Poko Territory (4,700) (S. 139; S. 140 Madi; S. 142 Dakwa).

There are also a few Amaadi villages scattered along the right bank of the Uele north-west of Niangara, but admixture with the Azande having taken place, the dialect spoken there is less pure (S. 141 Niangara).

The same group extends south of the Uele between that river and the River Gada. The Matshaga chefferie Okondo I under Chief Napanga is for the most part composed of Amaadi, the remainder being Duga (total population 13,418), but almost all now speak Namangbetu-ti. We were told of about fifty Amaadi in Kumba-Wanda *sous-chefferie*, to the south of Dungu, mixed with Mamvu, Bangba, and Amangbetu. We were also informed of a group of Amaadi (called Ogo) living south of the River Uele in Poko Territory among the Abarambo of Batenado sector. They are said to have retained their language. The Survey found it impossible to visit them as the information was received too late for any action to be taken.

4. PYGMY GROUPS

THE survey did not aim to study Pygmy languages as this would have demanded entirely different methods of travel and of investigation from those used. However, we could not resist making tentative inquiries along our route when a Pygmy group was encountered. The results are not claimed to be anything more than provisional indications which may in some cases point the way to more detailed researches to be undertaken later. We encountered the following Pygmy groups, while following our itinerary:

A. EFE-SPEAKING

Group	Locality	Territory	
1-2	Lolwa	R. Epulu	(P. 2, P. 10)
3-4	Oitshia	Beni	(P. 3, P. 5)
5	Epulu	R. Epulu	(P. 7)
6	Arambi	R. Epulu	(P. 8)
7	Mungbwalu	Bunia	(P. 11)
8	Avakubi (Bafwa Miti)	Bafwasende	(P. 21)

B. IBUTI-SPEAKING

Group	Locality	Territory	
9–11	Lolwa	R. Epulu	(P. 1, P. 9, P. 28)
12	Oitshia	Beni	(P. 4)
13	Epulu	R. Epulu	(P. 6)
14	Bafwabaka	Wamba	(P. 14)

KAANGU-SPEAKING (i.e. a mixture of Ibuti and Indaaka)

15	Babeyru	Wamba	(P. 18)
16–17	Bafwa Miti, Avakubi	Bafwasende	(P. 19, P. 20)
18–20	On the Bafwesende–Bomili road	Bafwasende	(P. 22, P. 23, P. 24)

IBUTI + IMBO-SPEAKING

21	Maboma	Wamba	(P. 13)

C. AKA-SPEAKING

22	Niakpu-Kasanga	Poko	(P. 15)
23	Medje	Isiro-Paulis	(P. 16)
24	Babeyru	Wamba	(P. 17)
25	Panga	Bafwasende	(P. 25)

D. MAMVU-SPEAKING

26	Ingi	Watsa	(P. 12)

E. LIMBINGA-SPEAKING

27	Libenge	Libenge	(P. 26)
28	Mawuya	Libenge	(P. 27)

INDEX TO PART II

Simplified Stem	Ethnic Name Plural	Ethnic Name Singular	Linguistic Name	Page
Abulu	Aabulu	Naabulu	Naabulu-ti	85, 110, *111*
Aka	Aka	Aka	—	*110*, 115
Alur	Aluur	Jaluur	Dho Aluur	90, 94
Amadi	Amaadi	Amaadibo	Amaalo	100, 102, 111, 113, 114
Amba	Baamba	Muamba	Kuamba	*84*, 88
Amengi	Amengi	Amengi	Amengi	94, *96*
Amiangba	Aamiangba	Amiangba	Paamiangba	93, 100, *102*, 111, 114
Angada	Angada	Angada	—	101
Angba	Baangba	Maangba	Leangba	72, 78, *80*, 113
Apagibeti	Apagibeti	Apagibeti	Apagibeti	*78*, 79, 103
Apindi	Apindi	Apindi	Apindi	73
Avare	Avare	Avare	Avare-tu	94
Avokaya	Avokaya	Avokaya	Avokaya-ti	*92*, 93
Badi	Mabadi	—	—	74, 111
Baidumba	Babaidumba	Mubaidumba	—	83
Baka	Baka	Baka	Baka	65, 75, *91*, 100
Bakpa	Bakpa	Bakpa	Bakpa	109
Bale	Bale	Bale	Bale-dha	88, 90, 94, 97, *98*
Balese	Balese	Balese	Balese	97
Baletse	Baletse	Baletse	—	97
Bali	Babaali	Mbaali	Libaali	*75*, 113
Bali/Duwa	Babaali	Mobaali	Dibaali	70
Balia	Babalia	—	—	79
Bamwe	(ba) Bamwe	(o) Bamwe	(ma) Bamwe	70, 73
Banda	—	—	—	99, 103, *104–6*, 107
Bandia	Abandia	Bandia	Bandia	79, 81, 100, *101*, 105
Banga	Babanga	—	—	74
Bangba	Bangba	Bangba	Li-Bangba	74, 93, 95, 96, 102, 108, *109*, 111, 114
Bango	Babango	Bobango	Ebango	76, 77
Bangu-bangu	Babangu-bangu	Mubangu-bangu	Kibangu-bangu	90
Banza	Mabanza	—	—	70
Baonde	Baonde	Baonde	—	72
Barambo	Abarambo	Barambo	Barambo	93, 99, *101*, 111, 114
Bari	Bari	Bari	Bari-tile	92, *93*, 95, 108, 111, 112
Bati	Babaati	Embaati	Libaati	78, 79
Beka	Babeka	—	—	83
Beke	Babeeke	Mbeeke	Ibeeke	85
Bembe	—	—	Ebeembe	89
Bembe	Mabembe	—	—	70
Bendia	Bobendia	Mobendia	Lebendia	80
Bendja	Babendja	Mobendja	Lebendja	78, *80*
Benge	Babenge	Mobenge	Libenge	78, *79*, 101, 103
Bila/Forest	Babila	Mbila	Kibila	82, *83*, 84, 85
Bili	Babili	Mbili	Ibili	82, *83*
Bindja	Babindja	Mubindja	Ibindja	77
Binza	Babinza	Mubinza	Libinza	76, *77*, 79
Bira/Plain	Babira	Mbira	Kibira	82, *84*, 97
Bita	Bobita	Mbita	Libita	80
Biti	Mabiti	—	—	75
Bito	Ababito	Omubito	Ekibito	87
Bobala	Bobala	Bobala	—	73
Bodjinga	Bodjinga	—	—	70
Bodo	—	—	—	75
Bogoro	Babogoro	Mabogoro	Kogoro	65, 75

INDEX TO PART II

Simplified	Plural	Ethnic Name Singular	Linguistic Name	Page
Bogulu	Babogulu	—	Egulu	*78*, 103
Boguru	—	—	—	75, *91*
Boloki	(ba) Boloki	(wa) Boloki	(mwa) Boloki	70
Bolondo	Bolondo	Bolondo	—	70
Bolongo	Bolongo	Bolongo	—	73
Bomane	Bomane	Bomane	—	72
Bombi	Babombi	Mubombi	Libombi	84
Bombi	Babombi	Mbombi	Kibombi	83
Bomboli	(ba) Bomboli	(wa) Bomboli	—	69
Bombongo	(ba) Bombongo	(wa) Bombongo	(mwa) Bombongo	69
Bongambo	(ba) Bongambo	(a) Bongambo	(ma) Bongambo	76
Bongono	Bobongono	Mobongono	Libongono	79
Boro	Baboro	Mboro	Leboro	72, *80*, 113
Boshwa	Boshwa	Boshwa	—	73
Budja	(wa) Budja	(u) Budja	Ebudja	76, 77
Budjaba	(ba) Budjaba	(wa) Budjaba	Budjaba	69, *74*
Budu	Babudu	Mubudu	Ebudu	75, *84*, 85, 95, 111
Buku	—	—	Ebuku	74
Bugbuma	Babugbuma	Bugbuma	Ebugbuma	*78*, 103
Bugombe	Badugombe	Mbugombe	Ebugombe	82, 83
Bukur	Babukur	—	—	75
Buraka	Buraka	Buraka	Buraka	110
Buti	Babuti	Mbuti	Ibuti	*82*, 115
Buyu	Babuyu	Mubuyu	Kibuyu	90
Bvanuma	Bobvanuma	Mubvanuma	Libvanuma	84
Bwa	Bobwa	Imbwa	Libwa	*78–80*
Bwa	Bobwa	Imbwae	Libwali	72, 78, *80*, 100
Bwela	Bweela	Bweela	—	73
Diko	(ba) Diko	(wa) Diko	(mwa) Diko	76
Diyo	Adiyo	Diyo	—	81, 101
Djandu	Djandu	Djandu	Lidjandu	73
Dji	—	—	Dji-dha	98
Djinga	Bodjinga	—	—	70
Djo	—	—	Djo-dha	98
Djoo	—	—	Djoo-dha	98
Doko	Dooko	Dooko	—	73
Dombi	Badoombi	Mudoombi	Kidoombi	83
Dongbale	Bodongbale	Modongbale	Ledongbale	80
Dongo	Dongonyo	Dongogo	Dongoko	94, *113*
Duga	(see Amiangba)			
Dumbi	Waduumbi	Muduumbi	Eduumbi	71
Dyobo	Dyobo	Dyobo	—	73
Efe	Efe	Efe	Efe	94, 97, 114
Enya	Baenya	Mweenya	Tsheenya	72, 90
Fadjulu	—	—	—	91
Fuma	(ba) Fuma	(wa) Fuma	—	71, 82
Furu	Gbaya	Gbaya	Gbaya	91, 106, 107
Gala	Bogala	—	—	81
Ganga	Boganga	—	—	79
Ganzulu	Boganzulu	Moganzulu	Liganzulu	79
Gbali	Bogbali	Mogbali	Ligbali	79
Gbanziri	Gbanziri	Gbanziri	Gbanziri	110
Gbasa	Bogbaasa	Mogbaasa	Ligbaasa	79
Gbase	Bagbaase	Mogbaase	Ligbaase	79
Gbati	Bagbati	Gbati	Gbatiri	*74*, 95
Gbaya/Furu	Gbaya	Gbaya	Gbaya	91, 106, 107
Gbaya/Ngbaka				106
Gbe	Bagbe	Mogbe	Ligbe	79
Gbele	Bagbele	Mogbele	—	75
Gbendere	Gbendere	Gbendere	Gbendere	109
Gbugo	Agbugo	Gbugo	Gbugo	104, *105*
Gbuta	Bagbuta	Mogbuta	Egbuta	78
Gendja	Bagendja	Mugendja	Ligendja	77, 78
Gendza	Bagendza	Mugendza	Ligendza	77
Gendza/Dibaali	—	—	Ligendza	78
Gengele	Bagengele	Mogengele	Kegengele	90

INDEX TO PART II

Simplified Stem	Ethnic Name Plural	Ethnic Name Singular	Linguistic Name	Page
Genza	Bagenza	Mogenza	Legenza	80
Gezon	—	—	—	78
Go	—	—	Go-dha	90, *98*
Gobu	Agobu	Gobu	Gobu	92, 104, 105
Gomba	Gomba	Gomba	—	73
Gongeya	Bogongeya	—	—	79, *80*
Hambo	Avahambo	Omuhambo	Ekihambo	88
Hanga	Bahango	Mohanga	Lehanga	80
Havu	Avahaavu	Omuhaavu	Ekihaavu	88
Hianzi	Bahianzi	Muhianzi	Kihianzi	84
Hima	Ayahima	Omuhima	Oruhima	*86*, 90, 98
Hira	Avahira	Omuhira	Ekihira	87
Hokohoko	Bahokohoko	—	—	83
Homa	Bahoma	—	—	74
Homba	Avahomba	Omuhomba	Ekihomba	87
Hororo	Avahororo	Omuhororo	Etshihororo	86
Humu	—	—	Kihumu	84
Hunde	Bahunde	Muhunde	Kihunde	85, 88, *89*
Hutu	Bahutu	Muhutu	Kihutu	87
Hwindja	Avahwindja	Omuhwindja	Amahwindja	89
Iboko	Iboko	Iboko	Iboko	70
Ilombo	Ilombo	Ilombo	—	78
Ilongo	Ilongo	Ilongo	—	72
Isanza	Wanisanza	Munisanza	Ekisanza	88
Kaiku	Bakaiku	Ngaiku	Ikaiku	82, *83*
Kakwa	Kakwa	Kakwa	Kakwa	91
Kaliko	Kaliko	Kaliko	Kaliko-ti	92, *93*
Kango	Bakango	Mukango	Likango	*80*, 81, 100, 101
				102, *108*, 112
Kangu	—	—	Kaangu	115
Kanu	Vakaanu	Mukaanu	Kikaanu	89
Kapu	Bokapu	Nkapu	Likapu	80
Kari	Bakari	Akari	Likarili	74, 101
Kazibati	Akazibati	Kazibati	Kazibati	104
Ke	—	—	Ke-dha	98
Kebo	Okebo	Kebo	Kebo	94
Kele	Bokele	Mukele	Likele	72
Kete	Bokete	Nkete	Lekete	80
Kiba	Bokiba	Nkiba	Likiba	80
Kiga	Abakiga	Omukiga	Igikiga	87
Kipa	Bokipa	Nkipa	Likipa	80
Kira	Avakira	Omukira	Ekikira	87
Kondjo	Bakondjo	—	—	88
Kpala	Kpala	Kpala	Kpala	69, 105, *109*
Kredj	Kredj	—	—	65, 91
Kula	Bokula	Mokula	—	70
Kumbule	Avakumbule	Omukumbule	Ekikumbule	*87*, 89
Kumu	Bakuumu	Nkuume	Kikuumu	82, *83*
Kunda	—	—	—	72, *75*, 103
Kutu	Bokutu	—	—	73
Kutu	Kutu	—	—	74
Kwanza	Bakwaanza	—	—	83
Labibi	—	—	—	79
Langba	Alangba	Langba	Langba	104, *105*
Langbase	—	—	—	104, *105*
Ledji	Baleedji	Muleedji	Eleedji	83
Lega	Avalega	Omulega	Ekilega	88
Lega	Baleega	Muleega	Kileega	89
Lende	Bolende	—	—	79
Lendu	(see Bale and Ndru)			
Lengola	Balengola	Mulengola	Kilengola	82, *84*
Lese	—	—	—	94, 95, 96, 97
Libinza	(ba) Libinza	(wa) Libinza	Libinza	70, 71
Libobi	Liboobi	—	—	73
Likaw	(see Diko and Bongambo)			
Likila	(ba) Likila	(wa) Likila		70

INDEX TO PART II

Simplified Stem	Ethnic Name Plural	Ethnic Name Singular	Linguistic Name	Page
Liko	Baliko	Muliko	Liliko	75, 76, *111*
Likolo	—	—	—	81
Likombe	Likombe	Likombe	—	72
Lileko	(ba) Lileko	(wa) Lileko	—	71
Lima	Balima	Molima	Lelima	80
Lindja	Avalindja	Omulindja	Amalindja	89
Lingunda	Lingunda	—	—	74
Lisi	Balisi	Enlisi	Lelisi	79
Lituka	Lituuka	—	—	73
Liutwa	—	—	—	81
Lobala	(ba) Lobala	(wa) Lobala	(mwa) Lobala	69, 74
Lobo	Balobo	Mulobo	—	70
Logo	Logo	Logo	Logo-ti	91, 92, 114
Loi	Baloi	Moloi	—	70
Lokele	(ba) Lokele	(wa) Lokele	(lya) Lokele	*71*, 81
Lombi	Odyalombi	Nodyalombi	Odyalombi-tu	83, 110, *111*
Lomboki	Alombooki	Lombooki	—	81
Longe-longe	Avalonge-longe	Omulonge-longe	—	89
Longwa	Bolongwa	—	—	80
Lugbara	Lugbara	Lugbara	Lugbara	92, *93*, 94
Luombila	Baluombila	Muluombila	—	81
Mabale	(ba) Mabaale	(wa) Mabaale	(la) Mabaale	69, 71
Mabendi	Mabendi	Mabendi	Mabendi	84, 94, 97
Mabisanga	Mabisanga	Mabisanga	—	102, *111*
Maele	Amaele	Namaele	Namaele-ti	110, *112*
Maidjiru	Maidjiru	Maidjiru	—	96
Maidjuwu	Amaidjuwu	Maidjuwu	—	112
Makere	Amakere	Namakere	Namakere-ti	79, 110, *112*
Malele	(see Maele)			
Mambisa	Mambisa	Mambisa	—	90, 98
Mamvu	Mamvu	Mamvu	Mamvu	74, 84, 94, 95, 97, 100, 108, 111, 112, 114, 115
Mangbele	—	—	—	74, 108, *112*
Mangbetu	Amangbetu	Namangbetu	Namangbetu-ti	74, 75, 93, 94, 95, 102, 108, 110, *111*, 114
Mangbutu	(see Mangutu)			
Mangutu	Mangutu	Mangutu	Mangutu	84, 94, 95, 96, 97, 108, 113, 114
Mate	Avamate	Omumate	Ekimate	87
Mayogo	Mayogo	Mayogo	—	95, 96, 100, 102, *108*, 109, 111, 112
Mba	Mbayi	Mbagi	Mbani	72, 113
Mbandja	Ambandja	Mbandja	Mbandja	77, 91, 103, 104, 105, 107, 109, 110
Mbanga	Bombanga	—	—	77
Mbati	Mbaati	Mbaati	—	99, 102, *103*, 104
Mbati-Ngombe	Mbaati	Mbaati	—	76, 105
Mbele	Bombele	—	—	73
Mbenga	Bombenga	—	Limbenga	73
Mbesa	Bombesa	Mombesa	Umbesa	72
Mbinga	Bambinga	Mombinga	Limbinga	69, 115
Mbinga	—	—	Mbinga	70
Mbiya	Bumbiya	—	—	73
Mbo	Bambo	Umbo	Imbo	85, 115
Mbole	Bambole	Bombole	Lombole	71, *82*
Mboma	Bomboma	—	—	76
Mboso	Mbooso	Mbooso	—	71, 82
Mbudja	—	—	—	77
Mbuti	(see Buti)			
Medje	Ameegye	Nameegye	Nameegye-ti	110, *112*, 113
Mimbo	Mimbo	Mimbo	Mimbo	73
Mituku	Banya Mituku	Munya Mituku	Kinya Mituku	82, *84*

INDEX TO PART II

Simplified Stem	Plural	Ethnic Name Singular	Linguistic Name	Page
Moingi	Moingi	Moingi	—	71
Mongandjo	Mongandjo	Mongandjo	—	72
Mongoba	Amongoba	Mongoba	Mongoba	104
Mongombo	Mongombo	Mongombo	—	73
Mongwandi	—	—	—	*103*, 105
Monia	Moonya	Moonya	—	73
Monjombo	Monjombo	Monjombo	Monjombo	69, 103, 105, *110*
Mono	Amono	Mono	Mono	*104*, 110
Mpesa	Empesa	—	Limpesa	72
Muledre	Muledre	Muledre	—	96
Mumbi	Mumbi	Mumbesu	Mumbesu-nu	94, 98
Mundjinga	—	—	—	73
Mundo	Mundo	Mundo	Mundo	91, *108*
Mundongo	Mundongo	—	—	73
Mvuba	Mvuba	Mvuba	—	97
Mwangi	Bumwangi	—	—	72
Nande	Avanande	Omunande	Ekinande	85, *87*, 88, 89
Ndaka	Bandaaka	Mundaaka	Indaaka	85
Ndanda	(ba) Ndaanda	(wa) Ndaanda	(mwa) Ndaanda	69
Ndeke	Ndeke	Ndeke	—	73
Ndo	Ndo	—	—	94
Ndobo	(ba) Ndobo	(wa) Ndobo	—	70
Ndokoyi	Bondokoyi	—	—	70
Ndolo	(bo) Ndoolo	(mo) Ndoolo	(mo) Ndoolo	70
Ndru	Ndru	Ndru	Ndru-na	98
Nduli	Bunduli	Munduli	Linduli	79
Ndunga	Ndungaye	Ndungagi	Ndungale	113
Ngala	(Bangala)	(Mongala)	Lingala	66, 71
Ngbaga	Ngbaga	Ngbaga	Ngbaga	105, 106, *109*
Ngbaka/Gbaya	Ngbakano	Ngbaka	Ngbaka	103, 105,*106*, 110
Ngbandi	Angbandi	Ngbandi	Ngbandi	76, 78, 91, 101,*103*, 104, 105, 106
Ngbele	Bangbee	Mungbee	Lingbee	74, 79, 112
Ngbelima	Wangbelima	Mungbelima	Lingbelima	71
Ngbinda	Bangbinda	Mungbinda	Bungbinda	75, 100, 101
Ngbundu	Angbundu	Ngbundu	Ngbundu	104, *105*
Ngingita	Bangingita	Mongingita	Lingingita	79
Ngombe	Ngombe	Ngombe	Ngombe	73, 76, 78, 92, 103, 104, 105
Ngombe/Winza	—	—	—	77, *78*
Ngongoli	Bongongoli	Mongongoli	—	70
Ngundji	—	—	Ingundji	72, 73
Nkembe	Bonkembe	Monkembe	Linkembe	70
Nyali	Banyali	Munyali	Linyali	84
Nyambo	—	—	Runyambo	86
Nyanga	Banyanga	Manyanga	Nyangali	74, 95, 112
Nyanga	Vanyanga	Munyanga	Kinyanga	89
Nyango	Nyango	Nyango	Nyango	109
Nyindu	Banyindu	Munyindu	Kinyindu	89
Nyoro	Avanyoro	Omunyoro	Olunyoro	85, 90
Nzakara	Anzakara	Nzakara	Nzakara	*101*, 103
Odjiga	Odjiga	Odjiga	—	92
Odjila	Odjila	Odjila	—	92
Ogambi	—	—	—	93
Olombo	(ba) Olombo	(a) Olombo	(li) Olombo	72, *81*
Onga	Baonga	—	—	72
Pambia	Pambia	—	—	65, *99*, 102
Pandu	Bopandu	Mopandu	Lipandu	79
Patri	—	—	Patri	101
Pi	—	—	Pi-dha	98
Popoi	Apopoyi	Napopoyi	Napopoyi-ti	71, 110, *113*
Popolo	Popolo	Popolo	—	73
Poto	Wapoto	Upoto	Lipoto	70, *72*
Ragwe	Wa(ka)ragwe	Mu(ka)ragwe	Ru(ka)ragwe	86
Rhinyi-rhinyi	Barhinyi-rhinyi	Murhinyi-rhinyi	Kirhinyi-rhinyi	89
Rundi	Abarundi	Umurundi	Ikirundi	85, 86, *87*

Simplified Stem	Ethnic Name Plural	Ethnic Name Singular	Linguistic Name	Page
Rwanda	Abanyarwanda	Umunyarwanda	Ikinyarwanda	85, *86*
Sali	Basali	Musali	Lisali	*79*
Salia	Bosalia	Mosalia	Lesalia	*80*
Sanga	Bosanga	—	—	*73*
Sango	Sango	Sango	Sango	102
Sanwa	Bosanwa	Musanwa	Lisanwa	*80*
Sanzi	—	—	Kisanzi	90
Sele	Sele	Sele	Sele	*101, 107*
Sena	—	—	Lisena	*77*
Shi	Avashi	Omushi	Amashi	88
Shu	Avashu	Omushu	Ekishu	87
Shukali	Avashukaali	Omushukaali	Ekishukaali	88
Soko	Basoko	Musoko	Lisoko	*72*
Songola	Basongola	Mosongola	Kesongola	90
Songora	Avasongoora	Omusongoora	Ekisongoora	85, *88*
Swaga	Avaswaga	Omuswaga	Ekiswaga	87
Talinge	Watalinge	Mutalinge	Kitalinge	*85, 97*
Tangi	Avatangi	Omutangi	Ekitangi	87
Tembo	Batembo	Mutembo	Kitembo	89
Tembo	Motembo	—	Litembo	*73*
Tike	Batike	Mutike	Etike	*83*
Togbo	Atogbo	Togbo	Togbo	*104*, 105, 110
Topoke	(ba) Topoke	(ga) Topoke	Topoke	71, *81*
Toro	—	—	Olutoro	85
Tshiga	—	—	Igitshiga	87
Tshogo	—	—	Itshogo	87
Tumbwe	Batumbwe	Mutumbwe	Etumbwe	89
Tungu	Watungu	Mutungu	Litungu	71
Vulangba	Vulangba	—	—	*77*, 78
Winza	Bawiinza	Muwiinza	Liwiinza	*77*, 79
Winza/Ngombe	—	—	—	77, *78*
Winza/Dibaali	—	—	—	*78*
Yakoma	Ayakoma	Yakoma	—	102
Yakpa	Ayakpa	Yakpa	Yakpa	*104*, 105, 110
Yalihila	(ba) Yalihila	(wa) Yalihila	—	*71*, 82
Yalikanza	(ba) Yalikanza	(wa) Yalikanza	—	*71*, 82
Yalikoka	(ba) Yalikoka	(wa) Yalikoka	—	*71*, 82
Yamanongeri	—	—	—	*72*
Yambumba	Yambumba	Yambumba	—	*72*
Yanga	Boyanga	Moyanga	Liyanga	*79*
Yangonde	Yangonde	Yangonde	—	*72*
Yanongo	Yanongo	—	—	71
Yanzila	—	—	—	*77*
Yaokandja	Yaokandja	—	—	71
Yaolema	Yaolema	—	—	*72*
Yasanga	Yasanga	—	—	*72*, 90
Yawembe	(ba) Yawembe	(wa) Yawembe	—	71
Yeka	Mayeka	—	—	*74*
Yew	Bayew(u)	Muyew(u)	Liyew(u)	78, 79, *80*
Yira	Avayira	Omuyira	Ekiyira	85, 86, *87*
Zande	Azande	Zande	Pazande	*74*, 75, 79, 86, *99–101*, 102, 107, 111, 114
Ziba	Avaziba	Omuziba	Amaziba	89

References in italics are to pages where the language is fully treated.

Part III

FAR EASTERN SECTION

GREAT LAKES TO INDIAN OCEAN

CONTENTS

BANTU LANGUAGES	127
PARTLY BANTU LANGUAGES	138
NON-BANTU LANGUAGES	138

FAR EASTERN SECTION

THE section of the Bantu Line lying between the Great Lakes and the Indian Ocean is perhaps the best known. Besides being the most fully documented from the linguistic point of view, it has been studied tribally by local governments, and tribal maps, based on the layout of the various reserves, have been made.[1] No specific expedition was therefore considered necessary, and the authors' task has been in the first place one of collating and assessing extant published material. Fortunately, however, both authors have at various times conducted individual research in many of the languages along this part of the line, and speakers of some of the languages have been discovered in London. In most instances the authors have thus been able either to contribute direct from their own field notes, or to give a phonetically checked summary of a language compiled from published works.

Further the authors have been greatly assisted by the original researches of colleagues at the School of Oriental and African Studies and elsewhere, notably Professor M. Guthrie, B. W. Andzrejewski, D. H. Ebeling, P. E. Hackett, Mr. and Mrs. A. Harris, G. W. B. Huntingford, A. E. Sharp, W. Whiteley, G. M. Wilson.

It will be noticed that the authors' classification occasionally differs somewhat from that of other writers like Guthrie, Hulstaert, and Van Bulck (even within this work, where the Central and Eastern areas overlap). Such divergencies are the result of the authors' considered opinion in the light of the evidence at present available.

BANTU LANGUAGES

1. VANUMA

Dialect: VANUMA (BVANUMA) (lį-vanumá).

Where spoken: Uganda: in AMBA territory (see p. 138).

This dialect forms part of a Cluster of which the other dialect is NYALI (lį-nyàlì) (see above, p. 84); HUKU is perhaps also related.

VANUMA, though BANTU in grammatical behaviour, appears to contain many non-BANTU Roots. The *VANUMA* are called *BAMBUTUKU* by the Amba.

2. KONZO *Dialect Cluster*

Dialect: KONZO (KONJO) (oṛu-kɔ́nzɔ̀).

Number: 73,745.

Where spoken: Uganda: high up on the slopes of Ruwenzori.

Note: Many *KONZO* have come down from the mountains into the country around Katwe and Muhokya, but there is a tendency for these people to lose their dialect in favour of TOORO.

[1] Atlas of the Tanganyika Territory. Survey Division, Dept. of Land and Mines, Dar-es-Salaam 1942; Tribal map of Eastern Africa, Sheet 1, E.A.F. No. 1549, 1943.

FAR EASTERN SECTION

The *ABANYAISUUBI* (so called by the Tooro) on the hills to the west of Lake Edward, near Mpondwe customs post, are said to be KONZO-speakers.

Other dialects in this Cluster are NANDI (NANDE, also known as YIRA), spoken in the Belgian Congo and KOBI (HUNDE), spoken in a small enclave in Kigezi District.

It will be noted that Van Bulck places KONZO in the YIRA Group of 'Extreme East' Bantu languages; in the latter he includes part of the Inter-lacustrine Group (see above, pp. 85–89).

3. *Inter-lacustrine Language Group*

BWISI-TALINGA. Dialect Cluster.

Where spoken: Uganda: in *AMBA* Territory on the western foothills of Ruwenzori; also in the Belgian Congo, Beni Territoire (see above, pp. 85–86).

Dialects: BWISI (oɾu-ʋwîsì).
TALINGA (**ki-talíŋgà**).

NYORO-TOORO. Dialect Cluster.

Dialect: TOORO (TORO) (**orú-tóórò**).

Where spoken: Uganda: at the southern end of Lake Albert on the eastern flanks of Ruwenzori, extending westwards almost to Mubende.

Number: 162,659.

Note: The triangular area in Buganda between Bunyoro and Butoro Districts is occupied by a mixture of *TOORO*, *NYORO*, and *GANDA*, the speech of all three tribes being used.

TOORO is also spoken by those *KONZO* (see p. 127) who have come down to the plains from Ruwenzori, and by many *BWISI*.

Dialect: NYORO (**orú-nyórò**), also known as GUNGU, KYOPI.

Where spoken: Uganda: mainly in Bunyoro District, between Lakes Albert and Kyoga, south of the Victoria Nile, but extending southwards beyond River Kafu in the no-man's land near Mubende.

Number: 180,610.

GANDA (**olu-gânda**). Language.

Where spoken: Uganda: in Buganda District, north and north-west of Lake Victoria, in an area bounded in the south-west by the lower Kagera River, in the east by the Victoria Nile, in the west by about Long. 21° 20' E. There are also colonies of *GANDA* round most of the government posts: Mbale, Arua, Seroti, Kaberamaido, &c.

Number: 836,091; there are about 5,500 *GANDA* in Tanganyika.

SOGA (olú-sògà). Language or Dialect Cluster?

Where spoken: Uganda: Busoga District, east of the Victoria Nile, south of Lake Kyoga; dialectal variants are spoken in the north and on Buvuma and Bugaya islands.

Number: 426,608.

GWERE (lu-). Language ?

Where spoken: Uganda: in a small area at the eastern end of Lake Kyoga.

Number: 83,223.

KENYI (lu-). Language?

Where spoken: Uganda: near the GWERE area.

SYAN (oru-), also known as Bantu SABEI. Language.

Where spoken: Uganda: Mbale District, in a small area north-west of Mt. Elgon near Bulegenyi.

Number: estimated *c*. 10,000 by Huntingford in 1925.

NYALA (NYARA) (olu-). Language.

Where spoken: Kenya: in a small area on the north-eastern shore of Lake Victoria west of Mjanji.

This language might, however, be related to the speech of the *NYALA*, in the LUHYA Cluster (see p. 130).[1]

Other units in this Group are: SESE, (NYA)NKORE, KIGA (CIGA), KOOKI, HAYA, ZIBA, ZINZA, KARA, KEREBE, JITA, and KWAYA, around Lake Victoria to the west and south; also (NYA)RWANDA and RUNDI.

4. *Language Group?*: GISU

Note: It is not certain whether KISU and BUKUSU are to be considered as separate units, or as dialects of the GISU Cluster.[2] The name *MASABA* is sometimes applied to some of the peoples speaking these dialects.

GISU, GISHU (ulú-gìsù, -gìʃù). Dialect Cluster.

Where spoken: West of Mount Elgon.

Number: Uganda 243,742, Kenya 9,681; these figures possibly include speakers of KISU and BUKUSU.

Dialects: At least three dialects are known to exist: Northern; Central: DADIRI (ulu-dádírì); Southern: BUYA (ulú-vùyà); also perhaps KISU (ulu-).

BUKUSU (ulu-), also known as KITOSH. Language?

Where spoken: Kenya: south of Mount Elgon in the northern corner of the 'Bantu Kavirondo pocket' (see note below).

---

[1] A. Maleche, personal communication.
[2] Considered as dialects by Guthrie (*Classification of the Bantu Languages*, 1948).

FAR EASTERN SECTION

A note on 'Bantu Kavirondo'

This name refers to a pocket of BANTU-speaking peoples (see inset on map) between the *LUO* (sometimes known as 'Nilotic Kavirondo') on the south and the *JOPADHOLA* and speakers of NANDI dialects on the north. BANTU languages spoken in this 'pocket' belong to three different Groups, the LUHYA Group predominating.

5. *Language Group*: LUHYA (LUYIA)

NYULI (**olu-**). Language.

Where spoken: Uganda: in a small area south of Mbale, in Busoga and Mbale Districts.

Number: 56,975.

Note: This is the only unit in the LUHYA Group not spoken in the 'Bantu Kavirondo pocket'.

LUHYA, LUYIA. Dialect Cluster.[1]

Note: Speakers of these dialects have recently adopted the name LUHYA or LUYIA as a general name covering several tribes and their dialects[2] (for distribution, see below).

Number: Kenya 653,774 (this figure probably includes speakers of all those dialects for which no separate figures are given). There are a few thousand *LUHYA* in Uganda.

Dialect: SAAMIA (SAMIA) (**lù-sáàmìà**).

Where spoken: Uganda and Kenya: on the northern shore of Lake Victoria, extending northwards for about 25 miles.

Number: Kenya 43,377, Uganda *c*. 16,000.

Dialect?: GWE (**lú-ġwê**).

Where spoken: In the central part of *SAAMIA* country, Uganda.

Number: *c*. 20,000.

Dialects: XAAYO (KHAYO, TINDI) (**lù-xáàyò**), MARACI (**lù-máràcì**), HANGA (WANGA, KAWANGA) (**lù-háŋgà**).

Where spoken: In the central and western part of the 'Bantu Kavirondo pocket'.

Dialects: TSOOTSO (**lú-tsóòtsò**), KAKELELWA (LEWI) (**lù-kákèlèlwà**), NYALA (KABARASI) (**lù-nyálà**).

Where spoken: In the eastern part of the 'Bantu Kavirondo pocket'.

---

[1] The name means 'fellow-clansmen' and is said to have originated among the *HANGA*. It has been in general use since about 1940.

[2] Vernacular names mainly supplied by A. Maleche (a member of the *IDAXO* tribe) (personal communication).

Dialects: ISUXA (ISUKHA) (lw-ísùxà) and IDAXO (ITOKHO) (lw-ídàxò) (together known as 'Kakamega', 'Kakumega').
Where spoken: In the south-eastern part of the 'Bantu Kavirondo pocket'.

Dialect: TIRIKI (lù-tírìkì).
Where spoken: Between the *IDAXO* and the NANDI-speaking *TERIK*.

Dialects: MARAMA (lù-màràmà) and KISA (lù-ʃísà).
Where spoken: Between the *NYOLE* and *HANGA*.

Dialect: NYOLE (NYORE) (lù-nyóɾè).
Where spoken: West of the *TIRIKI*, north of the *LOGOOLI̥*.

The *TATSONI (TACONI, TADJONI)*, east of the *BUKUSU* area, present a problem. Although recognized as *LUHYA*, they claim to have come from *ZIBA* country;[1] their speech is reported as being totally unintelligible to the *LUHYA*.[2]

6. *Language Group*: GUSII

LOGOOLI̥ (RAGOLI, MARAGOLI) (l-lógòòlị). Language.
Where spoken: Kenya: north of the Kavirondo Gulf, in the southern part of the 'Bantu Kavirondo pocket'.

GUSI̥I̥ (GUSII, KISII, GUZII, KOSOVA). (ekɪ-ġùsịị). Language.
Where spoken: Kenya: in the highlands south of the Kavirondo Gulf to about Lat. 10° S. (including Kisii to the west).
Number: Kenya: 255,108, Tanganyika 3,361.

KURI̥A (KURIA, KURYA, also known as TENDE). (eki-). Language.
Where spoken: Tanganyika: in the extreme north of Musoma District; Kenya: the southern part of South Nyanza District.
Number: Tanganyika 55,636, Kenya 28,873.

NGURIMI (NGOREME, NGRUI̥MI̥, NGRUIMI, NGURUIMI) (ɪkɪ-ŋġʊrɪmɪ). Language.
Where spoken: Tanganyika: between the *KURI̥A* and *NATA*.

According to Whiteley[3] this language is related to the ZANAKI dialects, which belong to this group.

NATA (ɪkɪ-), also known as IKOMA. Language.
Where spoken: Tanganyika: round Ikoma south of River Mara, bounded in the west by Long. 34° 10' E.
Number: 9,487.

Nothing further is known of the *WARE*, who in Johnston's time were living on one

[1] Huntingford, personal communication.   [2] Maleche, personal communication.
[3] Personal communication.

of the islands in the Kavirondo Gulf of Lake Victoria, and whose speech may be related to this Group.

The ZANAKI Dialect Cluster in Tanganyika also belongs to this Group.

7. *Language Group*: SUKUMA

SUKUMA (ki-sṵkṵma) or GWE (ki-). Language.

Where spoken: Tanganyika: south-east of Lake Victoria, in an area bounded by Mwanza, Shinyanga, Lake Eyasi, and about Lat. 2° 20′ S., Long. 35° E.

Number: 888,800.

The other units of this Group are NYAMWEZI̧ (NYAMWESI), SUMBWA, KIMBU, ḄUNGU,[1] also spoken in Tanganyika, but not within the area of this research.

8. *Language Group*: NI̧LYAMBA

NI̧LYAMBA (NILYAMBA, NILAMBA, NIRAMBA, IRAMBA). (kı-) Language.

Where spoken: Tanganyika: in an area bounded by Lakes Eyasi and Kitangiri, River Wembere, and about Lat. 4° 50′ S., Long. 55° E.

Number: 170,697.

RIMI̧ (RIMI, REMI, LIMI̧, also known as NYATURU). (kı-ṱími̧). Language.

Where spoken: Tanganyika: in the southern part of the Singida area on both sides of the Kitangiri–Manyoni railway, extending westwards to River Wembere, eastwards to Lake Balanigida Lelu.

Number: 181,738.

LANGI̧ (LANGI, IRANGI). (kı-laŋgi̧). Language.

Where spoken: Tanganyika: in an enclave in Kondoa District among non-Bantu speakers.

Number: 95,422.

MBUGWE. Language?

Where spoken: Tanganyika: in an enclave among non-Bantu speakers round Lake Manyara, mainly to the east.

Number: 7,436.

9. *Language Group*: GOGO

GOGO (ci-). Language.

Where spoken: Tanganyika: Dodoma District, north of Rivers Njombe and Great Ruaha, roughly between Long. 34° and 36° 40′ E., extending north as far as Lat. 5° 20′ S.

Number: 271,254.

---

[1] Guthrie, *Classification of the Bantu Languages*.

KAGULU (KAGURU, also known as North SAGARA) (ci-). Language.
Where spoken: Tanganyika: north east of Mpwapwa about Lat. 6° 30' S., Long. 37° E.
Number: 58,669.
Note: There are said to be two dialects, which differ slightly;[1] the dialect called MEGI is spoken at Berega Mission.

10. *Language Group*: ZIGULA

NGULU (kí-ŋgùlù). Language.
Where spoken: Tanganyika: in a narrow area about Long. 37° 30' E., Lat. 5°–6° 30' S.
Number: Census figures for '*NGUU*' 65,672.

Other units belonging to this Group are ZIGULA (ZIGUA), DHWELE, ZARAMO, RUGURU, KAMI?, KUTU, VIDUNDA, SAGALA, also spoken in Tanganyika but not within the area of this research.

11. *Language Group*: SHAMBAA (SHAMBALA)

SHAMBAA (SHAMBALA, SCHAMBALA, &c.) (ki-ʃambaa). Language.
Where spoken: Tanganyika: in the Lushoto area north of River Pangani as far as the Kenya border.
Number: 129,466.

ATHU (ASU, also known as PARE) (ci-aθu). Language.
Where spoken: Tanganyika: in the Pare mountains, except the northern tip.
Number: The Census figure for *PARE*: 98,959, probably includes the *GWENO* (see p. 134). There are a few *ATHU* in Kenya.

TUBETA (TAVETA). (ki-tuveta). Language.
Where spoken: Kenya: south-east of Kilimanjaro, about Lat. 3° 30' S., Long. 27° 50' E.
The other unit belonging to this Group is BONDEI, in Tanganyika.

12. *Language Group*: SHAKA (CHAGGA)

KAHE (ki-). Language?
Where spoken: Tanganyika: in the vicinity of Kahe junction south of Kilimanjaro.
Number: 1,801.

SHAKA (CHAGGA, CHAGA, DSCHAGGA, &c.) (kì-ʃàkà). Dialect Cluster.
Where spoken: Tanganyika: on the eastern, southern, and western flanks of Kilimanjaro.
Number: 237,343.

---

[1] Information given to M.A.B. by local informants.

FAR EASTERN SECTION

The dialects of this Cluster may be conveniently grouped as follows:[1]

Dialects of Vunjo administrative division, of which that of Marangu may be taken as typical.

Dialect: MOCI, of old Moshi (**ki-motʃi**).
Dialect: MASHAMI (MACHAME, MACAME) (**kì-màʃàmì**).
Dialect?: known as SHIRA.
Dialects of Rombo administrative division.
Dialect?: RWO (also known as MERU[2]) (**ki-**).

  Note: The *RWO*, on the eastern slopes of Mount Meru, are not administered with the *SHAKA*.

  Number: 25,040.

GWENO (**ki-**). Language.

Where spoken: Tanganyika: on the northern slopes of the Pare mountains.
Number: probably included in *PARE* in the Census (see *ATHU*, p. 133).

RUSHA (ARUSHA).[3] Language.

Where spoken: Tanganyika: in a small area south of Kahe.
Number: included in *MAASAI*.

13. *Language Group*: GIKUYU

GIKUYU (KIKUYU, GEKOYO) (**ɣɪ-ɣɪkúɣʊ**). Language.

Where spoken: Kenya: the Kikuyu highlands between the upper Tana River and the southern slopes of Mount Kenya, the south-western limit being the Nairobi area, the eastern Long. 37° 50′ E.

Number: 1,026,341 (including *THARAKA*—see below).

EMBU (**ki-**). Language.

Where spoken: Kenya: south-east of Mount Kenya, around Embu town.
Number: 203,690.

MERU (**ki-**). Language.

Where spoken: Kenya: north-west of Mount Kenya, roughly as far north as Chandler's Falls on River Uaso Nyiro, and eastwards to the Nyambeni hills.
Number: 324,894.

THARAKA (**kɪ-θaraka**). Language.

Where spoken: Kenya: on the north bank of River Tana just before it reaches the equator, between Long. 37° 50′ and 38° 30′ E.
Number: included in *KIKUYU* in the Census; according to Lambert[4] 16,505.

---

[1] A. E. Sharp, personal communication.
[2] Not to be confused with MERU of Kenya (see under GIKUYU). Guthrie considers RWO as a separate Language.
[3] This is the language of the so-called 'Bantu-speaking *ARUSHA*'; for other *ARUSHA* see under *MAASAI*, p. 141.   [4] Quoted in Middleton, *The Kikuyu and Kamba of Kenya*, 1953.

KAMBA (ki-). Language.

Where spoken: Kenya: south of River Tana from the equator to its source, and thence eastwards to Lake Ambroseli, the Chyulu hills, and Mtito Andrei on the Kenya–Uganda railway.

Number: 611,725.

SONJO (SONYO). Language.

Where spoken: Tanganyika: in an enclave among the *MAASAI* about Lat. 1° 50′ S., Long. 34° 40′ E., i.e. about 25 miles north-west of Lake Natron.

Number: 3,436.

The other unit in this Group is DHAJSO (also known as SENGEJU[1]).

According to Lambert,[2] MERU has affinities with the TAITA Group (see p. 137), and THARAKA stands between the two Groups, as does the speech of the '*CHUKA*' in Meru District (18,480).

14. Language Group: SWAHILI

SWAHILI (ki-). Dialect Cluster.

Where spoken:

(a) On the Kenya and Tanganyika coast and islands from Lamu in the north to Dar-es-Salaam in the south; SWAHILI is spoken as the mother tongue of many coast-dwellers, and is also spoken fluently by those to whom it is not the mother tongue.

Farther north, it is spoken sporadically as far as Mogadishu.

The main dialects in the SWAHILI-speaking area are:

MRIMA (ki-), spoken on the coast, roughly between Vanga and Kilwa.

UNGUJA (ki-), spoken in the central area of Zanzibar Island, especially in Zanzibar city.

TUMBATU (ki-), spoken on Tumbatu Island off the north of Zanzibar Island, on the northern tip of Zanzibar, and at the southern end of Pemba Island.

HADIMU (ki-), spoken at the southern end of Zanzibar Island.

PHEMBA (PEMBA) (ki-), spoken on Pemba Island, except the southern end.

MVITA (ki-), spoken in and around Mombasa.

AMU (ki-), spoken on Lamu Island.

PATE (ki-) and SIU (ki-), spoken on Pate Island.

VUMBA (ki-), spoken on Wasin Island and Jimbo, near Vanga, also on the mainland.[3]

---

[1] According to Lindblom (quoted in Middleton, op. cit.) this is a KAMBA dialect.
[2] Quoted in Middleton, op. cit.
[3] H. E. Lambert, 'The Vumba verb' (*Bull. Inter-territorial Language Committee*, xxiii, 1953).

FAR EASTERN SECTION

BAJUNI (ki-),[1] spoken mainly on islands from Pate in the south to Fuma and Kismayu in the north, also scattered along the coast and islands from Zanzibar to Mogadishu.

The *BAJUNI* are called *GUNYA* by the Swahili. They are also known as *TIKUU (TIKULU, TUKULU)*, probably meaning 'from the big country'.

MBALAZI (ci-), spoken by the *AMARANI* of Brava (Barawa) town.

NGAZIJA (ki-), and NJUANI (ki-), spoken in the Comoro Islands, north-west of Madagascar.

(b) Inland.

(i) Tanganyika. SWAHILI is the language of administration and education throughout the Territory. Standard SWAHILI (based on the UNGUJA dialect), being sponsored by Government, is fairly uniform among people who have any contact with Europeans. Beyond that, however, the language varies with individual speakers.

(ii) Kenya. It is the language of administration, but other languages have also been recognized for use (a) in education, (b) as alternatives in administration. The standard varies enormously, and there are several dialects. These range from pure SWAHILI dialects to various forms of bastard SWAHILI, e.g. dialects known as KI-VITA (war-time, army SWAHILI), KI-SETTLA, KI-SHAMBA, &c., as well as KI-HINDI (as spoken by Indians) and innumerable other Pidgin forms. In certain areas there is resistance to SWAHILI, notably in the GIKUYU (Bantu) and the LUO, MAASAI, NANDI-KIPSIKIS (non-Bantu) areas.

(iii) SWAHILI is understood in a considerable part of Uganda.

(iv) A dialect known as (ki-)NGWANA is used in parts of the Belgian Congo as the language of education and administration.

NYIKA. Dialect Cluster.

The dialects of this Cluster are generally considered as belonging to the same Group as TAITA and POKOMO (see below). There appear, however, to be great divergences between the dialects. GIRYAMA shows such marked affinities with SWAHILI that it is here tentatively placed in the same Group.

GIRYAMA (ki-).

Where spoken: Kenya: a strip of country beginning about 10–15 miles inland, parallel with the coast, about from the Mombasa–Nairobi railway in the south to beyond River Sabaki in the north.

Number: No separate figures available (included in total figure for *NYIKA*).

Other members of this Cluster are KAUMA, CONYI, DURUMA? and RABAI, spoken in Kenya, but not within the area of this research.

---

[1] Information on BAJUNI and MBALAZI from V. L. Grottanelli (personal communication). Note that TIKUU has long been known to be a SWAHILI dialect; Grottanelli confirms the suggestion originally made by Johnston that it is BAJUNI.

15. Language Group: ? TAITA

TAITA (TEITA). Dialect Cluster.

Where spoken: Kenya: west of Voi about Lat. 3° 25′ S., Long. 38° 20′ E.; also in Tanganyika.

Number: Kenya 48,561, Tanganyika 8,330.

Dialect: DAḆIDA (**ki-ďaviďa**), spoken (with local variants) in the northern part of the area, on Dabida massif, also on part of Sagala massif.

Dialect: TERI, also known as SAGALA (SAGALLA) (**ki-**), spoken on part of Sagala massif.

The two dialects differ considerably.

DIGO (**ki-**). Language.

Where spoken: Tanganyika and Kenya: in a coastal area from just south of Mombasa to north of Tanga, and for about 60 miles inland (in this area there is also a small settlement of *DHAISO* north of Tanga).

Number: Tanganyika 32,144, Kenya no figures available.

ṖOKOMO (**ki-ɟokomo**). Dialect Cluster?

Where spoken: Kenya: along the banks of the Tana River, from the equator to the sea (an enclave among non-Bantu speakers).

Number: 16,355.

Although tentatively classed together in one Group, these units show considerable divergencies. According to Guthrie[1] the dialects of the NYIKA Cluster also belong to this Group (but see SWAHILI Group pp. 135–6).

16. BANTU enclaves in the SOMALI and GALLA areas

There are several small settlements of non-*SOMALI* peoples on the Webi Shabelle and Juba rivers; they are said to be fugitive ex-slaves from the south, and to speak a Bantu language or languages.

On River Webi Shabelle:
'Shabelle' (probably a geographical name only);
MAKANE;
'Shidle' (possibly a place-name);
KAWOLE;
there is also said to be a settlement of non-*SOMALI* people inland from the town of Barawa (Brava).

[1] *Classification of the Bantu Languages.*

FAR EASTERN SECTION

On River Juba:

So-called *GABAWEN*, near Lugh Ferrandi;

GOSHA. The name *GOSHA* (forest-dwellers) is used by the Somali to denote a mixed population on the lower Juba, consisting of people from a large number of Bantu-speaking tribes, of whom the majority are *ZIGULA* (Grottanelli estimates them at perhaps 15,000–20,000).[1] Other tribes represented include *MAKUA, YAO, 'NIKA', NYAMWEZI, NYASA, NGINDO* or *NJINDO, SHAMBAA*, &c.

PARTLY BANTU LANGUAGES

A. *Western*

1. *Language Group*: BIRA (*Sub*-BANTU)

AMBA. Dialect Cluster.

Dialect: HYANZĮ (**ki-hyânzį**).

Where spoken: On the Uganda–Belgian Congo border on the slopes of Ruwenzori.

Dialect: AMBA (HAMBA, BULEBULE) (**ku-âmba = kwâmba**).

Where spoken: Uganda: Toro District, north-west of Fort Portal on the western foothills of Ruwenzori.

Number: 26,519.

Dialect: SUWA (**kʊ-súwà**), spoken by a few Pygmies living among the *AMBA*.

Other units of this Group are BIRA and PERI (PERE) in the Belgian Congo.

Note that Van Bulck does not regard the BIRA Group as 'Sub-Bantu' but includes it in his 'Eastern' Bantu languages (see pp. 82–84).

B. *Eastern*

2. *Isolated Unit?* MBUGU (*Bantoid*)

MBUGU (own name uncertain). Language.

Where spoken: Tanganyika: in the western Usambara mountains, among the *SHAMBAA* and *ATHU*, by people who call themselves **ʋa-ma'a**.

Number: No separate figures available.

NON-BANTU LANGUAGES

A. Moru–Mangbetu Languages[2]

Of the languages belonging to this Larger Unit which are spoken on the Bantu Line the majority are spoken entirely in the Belgian Congo (see pp. 92–99).

There are, however, a few scattered speakers in Uganda of:

MVU'BA (**mvʊ́ɓà**). Dialect of the LESE Cluster.

Where spoken: In a few villages in AMBA territory (see above).

---

[1] Personal communication.

[2] This is the name adopted in the forthcoming volume III of the *Handbook of African Languages* for the languages dealt with in Tucker, *Eastern Sudanic Languages*, vol. i, 1940, under 'Moru-Madi'.

DRUNA. (Southern LENDU) (dru-na).
Where spoken: In Butoro, west of Fort Portal, and in West Nile District.
Number: c. 2,500 in Uganda.

B. NILOTIC LANGUAGES

Note: All the Nilotic languages spoken in the area dealt with here belong to the Southern LWO Language Group.

LWO (DHOPALWO, also known as CHOPI). Language.
Where spoken: Uganda: mainly in the south-eastern part of Acholi District and the northern part of Bunyoro District.
Number: estimated by Crazzolara[1] at c. 6,000.

ACOLI (ACHOLI, ACOOLI, also known as GANG) (loġ acóli, dók àcòli). Language.
Where spoken: Uganda: the greater part of Acholi District, extending into Southern Sudan.
Number: 209,161.

LANGO (LADO) (leb laŋo). Language.
Where spoken: Uganda: Lango District and part of Acholi District.
Number: 265,296.

KUMAM. Language. Spoken by *IKOKOLEMU*, who call themselves **laŋo ikokolemu**.
Where spoken: Uganda, mainly in Teso District, but also in Lango District.
Number: 55,900.

The *KUMAM (IKOKOLEMU)* are of Nilo-Hamitic origin, but the language which they now speak is closer to ACOLI than to TESO, although it contains many TESO words.

ADHOLA, usually known as DHOPADHOLA (or BUDAMA) (ɖó p áɖɔ́là). Language.
Where spoken: Uganda: Mbale District, extending into Kenya.
Number: c. 73,000.

LUO of Kenya, also known as DHO LUO (or 'Nilotic Kavirondo') (ɖó luò). Language.
Where spoken: Kenya: Central, Southern, and Northern Nyanza Districts, extending southwards into Tanganyika.
Number: Kenya 725,585, Tanganyika c. 50,000.

The only other Nilotic language spoken on the Bantu Line is ALUR (see above, p. 90), spoken in the Belgian Congo, also in West Nile District of Uganda (80,697);

[1] *The Lwoo*, 1950.

it is also spoken by the *JO NAM* (c. 15,000) between the Nile at Pakwach and the Alur escarpment to the west.

C. Nilo-Hamitic Languages

(*see also* p. 91 for KAKWA and PÖJULU (FADJULU))

1. *Language Group*: Teso

TESO (a-tesò). Language.

Where spoken: Uganda: Teso District; also a small pocket on the Kenya–Uganda border around Tororo (separated from the main body of the tribe by Bantu-speaking *GISU*). These latter *TESO* are known as *ITESYO* (*ETOSSIO*, also as *ELGUMI* or *WAMIA*, or *BAKIDI*, *BAKIDE*).

Number: Uganda 462,644, Kenya 42,288.

Other units in this Group are KARAMOJONG, TURKANA, and TOPOSA.

2. *Language Group*: Nandi

NANDI. Dialect Cluster.

Where spoken: Uganda and Kenya (see details below).

Dialects belonging to this Cluster are spoken by:

SAPINY (*SABEI*) (sàpíny or sàbíny or sàʋíny). In Uganda: Mbale District, on the northern slopes of Mount Elgon.
Number: 24,070.

KONY (*ELGONYI*, 'Elgon *MASAI*) (Ikɔ́ny), on the Kenya–Uganda border south of the *SAPINY*.

POK, also known as *LAGO*, *LAKO*, in Kenya south of the *KONY*, on the southern slopes of Elgon.

These two tribes are included in the Census figure 25,478 under *SABAOT* (possibly a third tribe).

NANDI (na·ndì) Kenya: Nandi District, on the Nandi escarpment and around Kapsabet; some *NANDI* live as squatters on European farms.

Number: The Census figures for 1931, 50,440; and 1948, 116,681 are given without comment.

TERIK, also known as *NYANGORI* (*NYADORI*), adjacent to the south-western corner of the Nandi Land Unit.

KIPSIKIS (*KIPSIGIS*) (kìpsìγí·s), also (erroneously) known as *LUMBWA*: Kenya: Kericho District south of the *NANDI*, separated from them by LUO-speakers.

Number: estimated by Huntingford c. 80,000; Census 1948: 159,692.

NANDI dialects are also spoken by the *OKIEK*, also known as *DOROBO (WA-NDEROBO, TOROBO,* &c.), primitive forest-dwelling hunters living in small scattered settlements in Kenya and Tanganyika, among the *NANDI, MAASAI, GIKUYU*, and various Tanganyika peoples.

Other dialects of this Cluster are spoken by the *KEYO* and *TUKEN* or *KAMASYA*.

TATOGA (TATOG). Language or Dialect Cluster?

Where spoken: Tanganyika: mainly in Mbulu District, round Mount Hanang; also scattered in Musoma and Shinyanga Districts.

Number: c. 64,000.

The *TATOG(A)* consist of several tribes, of which *BARABAIK, BARABAIG* (bárábáík, Sing. barabándâ or baraban) is the largest; it is also the only one of whose speech enough is known for classification. Other tribes are:[1]

GISAMAJENK—largely assimilated to the *IRAQW*: bilingual.
DORORAJEK.
BURADIK.
BAJUT (BAYUTA).
ISEIMAJEK (SIMAJEK, SIMITYEK, also called *WANONEGA).*
RUTAGEINK (ROTAGEINK).
DARAGWAJEK
REIMOJIK
MANGAT'K   almost completely assimilated to neighbouring Bantu-speaking
GHUMBIEK   tribes, but still retaining their own language.
BIANJIT

The other unit in this Group is POKOT (SUK) in Kenya.

3. NGASA

NGASA (Language name not known). Language?

Where spoken: Tanganyika, on the north-eastern slopes of Kilimanjaro among the *SHAKA*.

Number: About 1,000.

NGASA is only known from a short word list collected by H. A. Fosbrooke. The vocabulary shows considerable affinities with MAASAI, but also sufficient divergencies for it to be here provisionally classed as a single unit.

4. MAASAI

MAASAI (MASAI) (εŋkútúk ɔɔ́ l-máásâi). Language.

Where spoken: Kenya: in the Masai Reserve (i.e. Narok and Kajiado Districts) and in Rift Valley Province, Maralal sub-district of Rumuruti District; Tanganyika: Masai and Arusha Districts of Northern Province, and scattered in other districts.

Number: Kenya c. 84,000, Tanganyika c. 103,000.

[1] G. McL. Wilson, 'The Tatoga of Tanganyika' (*Tanganyika Notes*, 1952).

142 FAR EASTERN SECTION

D. Cushitic Languages

1. GALLA (own name in Ethiopia OROMO, **afán ɔrɔmɔ́n**). Dialect Cluster.

Where spoken: Mainly in Ethiopia, but extending into a considerable part of Northern Frontier Province of Kenya, east of Lake Rudolf; also in the lower Tana River region.

Number in Kenya: Estimated at c. 27,000. Total number c. 2,350,000.

Note: GALLA-speaking tribes in Kenya include the *BORAN(A)* (**boorâna**).

2. SOMALI (**af soomááli**). Dialect Cluster.

Where spoken: Mainly in British and French Somaliland, Somalia, and part of Ethiopia, but extending into Kenya (Northern Frontier Province).

Number in Kenya: Estimated at c. 70,000.

Note: SOMALI-speaking tribes in Kenya include the *RENDILE* (*RENDILLE*) south and south-west of Marsabit.

The speech of the *BONI* (*BON*) among the southern *GALLA* east of the Tana River, appears to be mainly SOMALI with many GALLA words, but phonetically differs considerably from the CUSHITIC languages.[1]

E. Iraqw

IRAQW (also known as MBULU). Dialect Cluster?

Where spoken: Tanganyika: mainly in Mbulu District, south and east of Lake Natron.

Number: 100,365; a few thousands outside Mbulu District.

Linguistic material collected by W. Whiteley and M. Guthrie differs sufficiently for it to be assumed that there are at least two dialects.

The speech of the following is related to IRAQW, but how closely it is not possible to determine from available material:

BURUNGI (*MBULUNGE*)
ALAWA or *WASI*
} South of the *LANGI̱*, east of the *SANDAWE*.

GOROWA (*GOROA*) also known as *FIOME* (*FIOMI*), east of the *IRAQW*.

F. Sandawe–Hottentot Languages

SANDAWE (SANDAWI). Language.

Where spoken: Tanganyika: Kondoa District, between the *RIMI̱* in the west and the *BURUNGI* in the east; a few in Arusha District.

Number: 23,366.

The other languages related to the above are the NAMA ('Hottentot'), and NARON dialects of South-west Africa.

---

[1] Grottanelli, personal communication. But see SANYE, p. 143.

G. Bushman–Hadza Languages

HADZA (HADZAPI), also known as KINDIGA, TINDIGA, &c. Language.
Where spoken: Tanganyika: around Lake Eyasi.
Number: A few hundreds.

The other languages related to the above are the South African BUSHMAN languages.

H. Sanye

The speech of the *SANYE*[1] on the Kenya coast opposite Lamu near Mkunumbi appears from the short vocabularies available to be unclassifiable. It contains words which have cognates in GALLA, SOMALI, and SWAHILI, but also some words with clicks. These, however, appear to have no correspondences in SANDAWE or HADZA. The language is fast disappearing in favour of GALLA.

The *SANYE* may be the same as the *ARIANGULU (LANGULO)* and *BONI* in the same area,[2] and are possibly also known as *WATTA* (a name also applied to some small tribes in Ethiopia).

---

[1] See Dammann, 'Einige Notizen über die Sprache der Sanye (Kenya).' (*Z. Eingeb. Spr.* 1950).
[2] Prins, *The coastal tribes of the north-eastern Bantu*, 1952.

INDEX TO PART III

Abanyaisubi, *see* Konzo
Acoli, Acholi, Acooli, 139
Adhola, 139
Alawa, 142
Alur, 139–40
Amarani, *see* Mbalazi
Amba, 138
Amu, 135
Ariangulu, *see* Sanye
Arusha, *see* Rusha
Athu (Asu), 133

Bajuni, 136
Bajut, 141
Bakide, Bakidi, *see* Teso
Bambutuku, *see* Vanuma
Bantu Sabei, *see* Syan
Barabaig, Barabaik, 141
Bayuta, *see* Bajut
Bianjit, 141
Bira, 138
Bon, Boni, 142, 143
Bondei, 133
Boran(a), 142
Budama, *see* Adhola
Bukusu, 129
Bulebule, *see* Amba
Bungu, 132
Buradik, 141
Burungi, 142
Bushman, 143
Buya, 129
Bvanuma, *see* Vanuma
Bwisi, 128

Caga, Chagga, *see* Shaka
Chopi, *see* Dhopaluo
Chuka, 135
Ciga, *see* Kiga
Conyi, 136

Dabida, 137
Dadiri, 129
Daragwajek, 141
Dhajso, 135, 137
Dho Luo, *see* Luo
Dhopadhola, *see* Adhola
Dhopalwo, 139
Digo, 138
Dorobo, 141
Dororajek, 141
Druna, 139
Dschagga, *see* Shaka
Duruma, 136

Elgon Masai, Elgonyi, *see* Kony
Elgumi, *see* Teso

Embu, 134
Etossio, *see* Teso

Fiome, Fiomi, *see* Gorowa

Gabawen, 138
Galla, 142
Ganda, 128
Gang, *see* Acoli
Ghumbiek, 141
Gikuyu, Gekoyo, 134
Giryama, 136
Gisamajenk, 141
Gisu, 129
Gogo, 132
Gorowa, Goroa, 142
Gosha, 138
Gungu, *see* Nyoro
Gunya, *see* Bajuni
Gusjj, Gusii, Guzii, 131
Gwe¹, 130
Gwe², *see* Sukuma
Gweno, 134
Gwere, 129

Hadimu, 135
Hadza, Hadzapi, 143
Hamba, *see* Amba
Hanga, 130
Haya, 129
Hindi, 136
Hottentot, 142
Huku, 127
Hunde, *see* Kobj
Hyanzj, 138

Idaxo, 131
Ikokolemu, *see* Kumam
Ikoma, *see* Nata
Iramba, *see* Njlyamba
Irangi, *see* Langj
Iraqw, 142
Iseimajek, 141
Isuxa, Isukha, 131
Itesyo, *see* Teso
Itokho, *see* Idaxo

Jita, 129
Jo nam, 140

Kabarasi, *see* Nyala²
Kagulu, Kaguru, 133
Kahe, 133
Kakelelwa, 130
Kamasya, *see* Tuken
Kamba, 135
Kami, 133
Kara, 129
Karamojong, 140

Kauma, 136
Kawanga, *see* Hanga
Kawole, 137
Kenyi, 129
Kerebe, 129
Keyo, 141
Khayo, *see* Xaayo
Kiga, 129
Kikuyu, *see* Gikuyu
Kimbu, 132
Kindiga, *see* Hadza
Kipsikis, Kipsigis, 140
Kisa, 131
Kisii, *see* Gusjj
Kisu, 129
Kitosh, *see* Bukusu
Kobj, 128
Kony, 140
Konzo, Konjo, 127–8
Kooki, 129
Kosova, *see* Gusjj
Kumam, 139
Kurja, Kuria, Kurya, 131
Kutu, 133
Kwaya, 129
Kyopi, *see* Nyoro

Lago, Lako, *see* Pok
Langj, Langi, 132
Lango, Lano, 139
Langulo, *see* Sanye
Lendu, 139
Lese, 136
Lewi, *see* Kakelelwa
Limj, *see* Rimj
Logoolj, 131
Luhya, 130–1
Lumbwa, *see* Kipsikis
Luo, 139
Luyia, *see* Luhya
Lwo, *see* Dhopalwo

Maasai, 141
Macame, Machame, *see* Mashami
Makane, 137
Makua, 138
Mangat'k, 141
Maraci, 130
Maragoli, *see* Logoolj
Marama, 131
Masaba, *see* Gisu
Masai, *see* Maasai
Mashami, 134
Mbalazi, 135
Mbugu, 138
Mbugwe, 132
Mbulu, *see* Iraqw

Mbulunge, see Burungi
Megi, 133
Meru¹, see Rwo
Meru², 134, 135
Moci, 134
Mrima, 135
Mvita, 135
Mvu'ba, 138

Nama, 142
Nandi¹, Nande, 128
Nandi², 140–1
Naron, 142
Nata, 131
Nderobo, see Dorobo
Ngasa, 141
Ngazija, 136
Nghwele, 133
Ngindo, 138
Ngulu, Nguu, 133
Ngurimi, Ngoreme, Ngrujmj, Ngruimi, Nguruimi, 131
Ngwana, 136
'Nika', 138
Njlyamba, Nilamba, Nilyamba, Niramba, 132
Njindo, see Ngindo
Njuani, 136
Nyala¹, Nyara, 129
Nyala², 130
Nyali, 127
Nyamwezj, Nyamwezi, 132, 138
(Nya)Nkore, 129
Nyangori, Nyaŋori, see Terik
(Nya)Ruanda, 129
Nyasa, 138
Nyaturu, see Rimj
Nyika, 136
Nyole, Nyore, 131
Nyoro, 128
Nyuli, 130

Okiek, 141
Oromo, see Galla

Pare, see Athu
Pate, 135
Pemba, see Phemba
Peri, Pere, 138

Phemba, 135
Pok, 140
Pokomo, 137
Pokot, 141

Rabai, 136
Ragoli, see Logoolj
Reimojik, 141
Rendile, Rendille, 142
Rimj, Remi, Rimi, 132
Rotageink, see Rutageink
Ruguru, 133
Rundi, 129
Rusha, 134
Rutageink, 141
Rwo, 134

Saamia, 130
Sabaot, 140
Sabei, see Sapiny
Sagala¹, 133
Sagala², Sagalla, 137
Sagara, see Kagulu
Samia, see Saamia
Sandawe, Sandawi, 142
Sanye, 143
Sapiny, 140
Schambala, see Shambaa
Sebei, Bantu, see Syan
Sengeju, see Dhajso
Sese, 129
Settla, 136
'Shabelle', 137
Shamba, 136
Shaka, 133–4
Shambaa, Shambala, 133, 138
'Shidle', 137
Shira, 134
Simajek, Simityek, see Iseimajek
Siu, 135
Soga, 129
Somali, 142
Sonjo, Sonyo, 135
Suk, see Pokot
Sukuma, 132
Sumbwa, 132
Suwa, 138
Swahili, 135–6
Syan, 129

Taconi, Tadjoni, see Tatsoni
Taita, 137
Talinga, 128
Tatoga, Tatog, 141
Tatsoni, 131
Taveta, see Tubeta
Teita, see Taita
Tende, see Kurja
Teri, 137
Terik, 140
Teso, 140
Tharaka, 134, 135
Tikuu, Tikulu, 136
Tindi, see Xaayo
Tindiga, see Hadza
Tiriki, 131
Tooro, 128
Toposa, 140
Torobo, see Dorobo
Tsootso, 130
Tubeta, 133
Tuken, 141
Tukulu, see Tikuu
Tumbatu, 135
Turkana, 140

Unguja, 135, 136

Vanuma, 127
Vidunda, 133
Vita, 136
Vumba, 135

Wamia, see Teso
Wanderobo, see Dorobo
Wanga, see Hanga
Wanonega, see Iseimajek
Ware, 131
Wasi, see Alawa
Watta, see Sanye

Yao, 138
Yira, see Nandi¹

Zanaki, 131, 132
Zaramo, 133
Ziba, 129
Zigula, Zigua, 133, 138
Zinza, 129

For Product Safety Concerns and Information please contact our EU representative GPSR@taylorandfrancis.com
Taylor & Francis Verlag GmbH, Kaufingerstraße 24, 80331 München, Germany

www.ingramcontent.com/pod-product-compliance
Lightning Source LLC
Chambersburg PA
CBHW052130300426
44116CB00010B/1840